Covenant &
Constitutionalism

The Covenant Tradition in Politics
Daniel J. Elazar

Covenant &
Constitutionalism

The Great Frontier and the
Matrix of Federal Democracy

Daniel J. Elazar

**The Covenant Tradition in Politics
Volume III**

Transaction Publishers
New Brunswick (U.S.A.) and London (U.K.)

Copyright © 1998 by Transaction Publishers, New Brunswick, New Jersey
08903.

Preparation of this book for publication was made possible through the Milken
Library of Jewish Public Affairs of the Jerusalem Center of Public Affairs,
funded by the Milken Family Foundation.

This book is printed on acid-free paper that meets the American National
Standard for Permanence of Paper for Printed Library Materials.

Library of Congress Catalog Number: 96-52654
ISBN: 1-56000-235-2
Printed in the United States of America

Library of Congress Cataloging-in-Publication Data

Elazar, Daniel Judah.
    Covenant and constitutionalism : the great frontier and the matrix of fed-
eral democracy / Daniel J. Elazar.
        p. cm. — (The convenant tradition in politics ; v. 3)
    Includes bibliographical references and index.
    ISBN 1-56000-235-2 (alk. paper)
    1. United States—Politics and government. 2. Constitutional history—
United States. 3. Covenants—Political aspects—United States—History.
I. Title. II. Series: Elazar, Daniel Judah. Covenant tradition in politics ;
v. 3.
BL65.P7E43   1995 vol. 3
320.437—dc21   96-52654
                                                            CIP

For David and Ruth Elazar, my dear brother and sister-in-law, who carry on the tradition and work of the Elazar family with love through their special talents and competences. May we continue our partnership for many years.

"Prepare your heart to seek the law of the land and to live by it."

—John Wayne from the movie *Chisholm*

Contents

Preface

I

To the two great idea complexes of the covenantal political tradition, covenant and commonwealth, the modern epoch added a third, constitutionalism in its modern meaning. Constitutionalism became both operational and decisive in the course of the modern epoch. The ancient biblical idea of covenant had, in due course, given birth to the late medieval Protestant pursuit of commonwealth in a polity constructed on the proper covenantal principles. These principles subsequently were transformed into the foundations of modern civil society that was given its best political form through constitutionalism.

Clearly, the reconstruction of the ideas of medieval constitutionalism along new lines and through new forms of constitutional government was a critical step made possible by the political ideas derived from the covenantal tradition. The emergence of constitutionalism is the jewel in the crown of the new science of politics of the modern epoch. From it came the emergence of *civil society* as moderns understood it, comprised of governmental, public voluntary (nongovernmental), and private parts, each with its own legitimacy; *modern republicanism* and democracy, with its "republican remedies for republican diseases" in place of the premodern mix of monarchic, aristocratic, and popular institutions to provide balance; and *federalism*, with its combination of self-rule and shared rule involving the separation of arenas and powers. All were rooted in earlier ideas of covenant and the covenanted commonwealth. The way in which those ideas were transformed by modernity is the subject of this book.

II

Once again, I wish to express my deepest thanks to the Earhart Foundation of Ann Arbor, Michigan, its president, David Kennedy, its secretary and director of program, Dr. Antony T. Sullivan, and its former president, Richard Ware, for the very tangible encouragement and assistance they have provided me over the years of this effort, and the understanding that accompanied it. I owe a great debt of gratitude to Liberty Fund of Indianapolis, Indiana for affording me the opportunity to explore many of the themes and issues treated in this volume with colleagues and friends over nearly twenty years. Deepest thanks, too, to the institutions with which I have been associated and their staffs, who have been enormously helpful: the Center for the Study of Federalism at Temple University in Philadelphia, Pennsylvania; the Jerusalem Center for Public Affairs in Jerusalem, Israel; the Department of Political Studies at Bar-Ilan University in Ramat Gan, Israel. All three have also provided support for this project: the Jerusalem Center through the Milken Library of Public Affairs, and the Bar-Ilan Department of Political Studies through the Senator Norman M. Paterson Chair in Intergovernmental Relations. They have my deepest gratitude. Thanks also to the Milken Family Foundation for their support of the publication of this book through the Jerusalem Center.

I would like to especially thank Mark Ami-El, publications coordinator of the Jerusalem Center for his vital role in bringing this book to publication, and Deborah Gerber and my other research assistants in both the Philadelphia and Jerusalem centers for their contribution to its final preparation. The final stages of the research for this volume benefitted from a sabbitical at Harvard University in 1993–1994, and its Widener Library, one of the major repositories of European and American covenantal materials in the world.

A project of the magnitude of this one requires considerable support from many sources, but no support is more extensive or more critical than that provided by one's own family. My wife Harriet and my children were everything that one could possibly expect in this connection and even more, making it possible for me to live and work in a way most conducive to beginning this undertaking, staying with it, and finally bringing it to a proper conclusion. My love for them is inexpressible as is my gratitude.

D.J.E.
Philadelphia, PA
(in the shadow of Independence Hall)
October 1996

Introduction

The New World Experience

What we can learn from history is that great transformations rest on the combination of great ideas, great movements, and great actions, and occur when all three come together. Thus at the very beginning of the history of covenant there was the great idea of biblical covenantal monotheism whereby humans were envisaged as entering into morally grounded pacts with God out of which came, *inter alia*, the covenant with Noah binding all of humanity and that with the people Israel formed through the Exodus from Egypt and the Sinai experience. In the sixteenth century Protestant Reformation, a new theology of covenant gave rise to Reformed Protestantism and the theo-political transformation that followed in countries such as Switzerland, the Netherlands, Scotland, and England.

What the combination of covenant theology, religious reformation, and local or national political transformation did for the sixteenth century, a revolution in political philosophy, a series of more or less radical movements culminating in the British Isles and British North America as Whiggism, which culminated in the Glorious Revolution of 1688–89, and the formation of the American colonies across the Atlantic on a Reformed Protestant base during that same period, did the same for the seventeenth century. In the eighteenth century the great wave of ideas derived from the Enlightenment helped bring about the two great revolutions of the modern epoch, the American and the French, and the invention of both Federalist and Jacobin democracy, modern constitutionalism, the United States of America and modern democratic republicanism on both sides of the ocean.

* * *

Here we must remind ourselves of the three forms from which all polities are derived and through which all are organized: *hierarchical, organic, or covenantal*—as *The Federalist* put it in *Federalist #1*: force,

1

accident, or reflection and choice. Polities in the hierarchical model are generally founded by conquest in some form, either external or internal (palace revolt, coup d'etat), and are organized as power pyramids more or less in the manner of military formations. The ruler or rulers sit at the apex of the pyramid commanding those below, who are organized into "levels" of authority and power, each level subordinate to the one above it. In hierarchies, administration take precedence over politics. Politics takes the form of court politics, i.e., the struggle for the ear and favor of the ruler. All of this is rarely constitutionalized, but if it is in some form, the constitution consists of a charter granted by the ruler to those subordinate to him. An army is the apotheosis of this kind of political organization.

Polities founded and organized on the organic model seemingly grow "naturally," and as they develop, the more powerful or otherwise talented leaders form a political elite at the polity's center that rule over the vast majority in the polity who are relegated to the peripheries. Thus the model of the organic polity is that of two concentric circles, center and periphery, with those at the center ruling those in the periphery, even if the latter have a role in selecting who is in the center. Power, if not both power and authority, is concentrated in the center, and those in the center determine the connections between center and periphery. In the organic model, politics come first but they are the politics of the club. Administration flows from those politics and, indeed, the heads of the administration also have to be members of the club. The constitution, insofar as there is one, is the traditional body of accepted rules regarding the workings of the club and the administration that is dependent on it. The apotheosis of this model is Westminster-style parliamentarism with the parliament sovereign and dominated by those who have been able to enter the club; the administration is also led by club members but subordinate to parliament.

The covenantal model functions on an entirely different basis, characterized schematically by a matrix, a group of equal cells framed by common institutions. Its founding comes about because equal individuals or individual entities join together through a covenant or political compact as equals to unite and establish common governing institutions without sacrificing their respective integrities. For the matrix model, the constitution is preeminent since it embodies the agreement that joins the entities or individuals together and establishes agreed-upon rules of the game which all have to observe. The politics that flows from that constitution

TABLE 1
Models of Foundings/Regimes

	Conquest	Organic	Covenant
Founding:	Force	Accident	Reflection and Choice
Model:	Pyramid	Circle	Matrix
Structure of Authority:	Hierarchy	Center-Periphery	Frame and cells
Mechanisms of Governance (in rank order):	Administration-Top down bureaucracy	Politics-club-oligarchy	Constitution-written
	Politics-court	Administration-Center outward	Politics-open with factions
	Constitution-charter	Constitution-tradition	Administration-divided
Apotheosis:	Army	Westminster system	Federal system
Excess:	Totalitarian dictatorship	Jacobin state	Anarchy

is a politics of equals based on negotiation and bargaining and designed to be as open as possible, where all the actors will know what is happening. Administration is dependent upon the constitution for its authority and politics for its powers. This system is not hierarchical, even if hierarchies are sometimes organized within it. Nor does it have a single center. Rather it is based upon multiple centers, each constitutionally protected. Its apotheosis is a federal system in which the constituent units are represented in the framing government and also preserve their own existence, authority, and powers in those areas which are not delegated to the framing institutions.

While hierarchical and organic polities can merge because they are on the same continuum, federal polities are located on an entirely different continuum. Table 1 portrays and contrasts the three models. The struggle between or synthesis of the three has continued throughout history. It took some new turns in the modern epoch.

The New World Experience

In the last third of the fifteenth century, in the period between the failure of the councillor movement in the Catholic Church and the inauguration of the Reformation by Martin Luther in 1517, the Europeans discovered the New World. While Columbus is the official "discoverer," his voyages were part of a larger movement involving scientists and navigators, Spanish, Portuguese, Italian and Jewish; the first inventing the instruments to make it possible and the second conducting the voyages of discovery in the Western Hemisphere, around Africa, and across the Indian Ocean or into the Pacific.

Those explorations launched what Walter Prescott Webb, the Texas historian, described 450 years later as "the great frontier" whereby Europe embarked on an expansion that made Europeans and their descendants the rulers of the world for 500 years. That great frontier was seen by most of those involved in it as a great opportunity for beginning again. It launched a movement of migration and colonization unprecedented in the history of mankind until then. It transformed people of high and low station, empires, societies, economies, and technologies in unprecedented ways, but as both Catholics and Calvinists—the two main religious groupings among the settlers discovered, the discovery of new worlds did not eliminate "the old Adam."

The human beings who discovered and settled the new worlds brought with them their old habits and standards, good and bad, enlightened and benighted, gentle and cruel, whether by nature or by culture. The Europeans soon proved to be far more aggressive than the natives wherever they settled, even though in many cases the natives could manifest cruelty even beyond what was accepted by the Europeans. Five hundred years later it is very difficult to issue score cards balancing civilization and barbarism for the parties involved. We have long since given up European triumphalism and a monochromatic Euro-centered history of the discovery, conquest, and settlement of those new worlds. The pictures we draw today are drawn in subtler hues. There are swirls, zigzags, and broken lines making the tapestry more complex. Still, as a general rule, we can draw some conclusions with which to begin our exploration of the covenant tradition in the new worlds.

First, the New World was indeed a beginning again, but the beginning from the first was as flawed as life in the Old World and had to be transformed by human will, that even when it seemed to be, beginning again was not simply a matter of letting nature take its course. Second, for that human will to be thrust in a moral direction, humans had to covenant and compact with one another to specify that the liberty they sought in the New World would be federal liberty—the freedom to make and keep one's covenants under God and to live according to their terms and not merely natural liberty—the freedom to do what one pleases limited only by nature or one's neighbor—and to require that this be the standard for all. Third, the spell, one probably should say the romantic spell, of the New World environment led many—in the new world and the old alike—to believe that the return to the natural would enable humans to eliminate the corruptions of civilization a la Europe. Indeed, even realists saw the future design of progress in the implementation of natural law and natural right, stripped of the encumbrances of a corrupt or corrupted civilization and society.

These ideas were no more than romanticism unless concrete ways and means were developed to achieve these dreams. Those ways and means were developed through constitutionalism, a modern reinterpretation of the covenantal tradition that gave it flesh and blood and enabled it to become the instrument of liberty, equality, justice, and democracy that it did. Thus, for all of its flawed beginnings and flawed history, where Europeans were able to implant the covenantal tradition, the New World did indeed offer an opportunity, if not an entirely unambiguous one, for beginning again. Where that tradition was not or could not be implanted, the barbarisms and abominations of the Old World were doomed to be repeated.

This, then, is our story in this volume—how certain parts of the New World were settled by those who brought the covenant tradition with them, how that tradition was reinforced by the settlers' New World experiences in founding new societies, and, with all of the flaws in that experience, how those settlers pioneered the development of modern democracy or, more appropriately, modern democratic republicanism, or, still more accurately, modern federal democratic republicanism, using "federal" not only in its later governmental sense of federalism but in its original political sense of covenantal. It is the story of the human pacts of modernity, made "under God" rather than with the Supreme Being, to establish ordered liberty under the law involving the combination of self-rule and shared rule that made modern democracy possible.

We begin with the New World experience because it actually preceded the Old World philosophizing about it. While Hobbes, Spinoza, Locke, and their contemporaries were the ones who formulated the modern expressions of covenantalism through their ideas of the political compact and civil society and as such have become generally recognized as the founders of the new or modern science of politics based upon modern ideas of natural right rooted in human psychology rather than moral principle, in fact the people who came to the New World, especially the Puritans among them, had begun building institutions based upon neo-covenantal models a generation earlier and, by the time that the great seventeenth century political philosophers began their work, were already well along toward modifying those institutions in light of both New World and modern conditions, so that what were intended to be Puritan commonwealths in the New World, and indeed were established in that manner, were within two generations transformed into something else, that something else which the political philosophers in the Old World named "civil society," but which, even more than in the Old World, retained its covenantal roots. Indeed, one might say that the apotheosis of the modern experience in the United States was based upon the synthesis of and tension between biblical covenantalism as filtered through Reformed Protestantism and modern ideas of political compact and civil society.

In many respects the modern epoch brought with it a secularization of the covenant tradition as the aspirations to achieve a covenantal commonwealth gave way to the aspiration to achieve a civil society. Indeed, as the modern epoch progresses, the covenantal commonwealth even began to be forgotten in the pursuit of civil society as liberal democracy. This not only suited the modern temper but the modern environment, one that was far more legitimately heterogeneous than earlier environments.

Because of the major, if not dominant, role of Reformed Protestantism in establishing the United States and the other New World polities derived from similar roots, the original covenantalism of the Bible reached the New World primarily through the Reformed Protestant, usually Calvinist, filter. There it was transformed into a set of operational principles, institutions, and practices. What had been primarily an ideological expression of a grand theory became a fundament of culture, a shaper of institutions, and a major influence on political and other behavior. In the process it was modified by modernity, a modification that ultimately was to have consequences far beyond those intended at the beginning of the modern epoch. Nevertheless, the covenantal foundations remain and manifest themselves in those polities even in unexpected ways in every generation.

Covenant, Compact, Contract

A covenant is a morally-informed agreement or pact based upon voluntary consent and mutual oaths or promises, witnessed by the relevant higher authority, between peoples or parties having independent though not necessarily equal status, that provides for joint action or obligation to achieve defined ends (limited or comprehensive) under conditions of mutual respect which protect the individual integrities of all the parties to it. Every covenant involves consenting, promising and agreeing. Most are meant to be of unlimited duration, if not perpetual. Covenants can bind any number of partners for a variety of purposes, but in their essence they are political in that their bonds are used principally to establish bodies political and social.

Covenant is tied in an ambiguous relationship to two related terms, compact and contract. On the one hand, both compacts and contracts are derived from covenant, and sometimes the terms are even used interchangeably. On the other hand, there are very real differences between the three which need clarification.

Both *covenants* and their derivative, *compacts*, differ from *contracts* in that the first two are constitutional or public and the last private in character. As such, covenantal or compactual obligations are broadly reciprocal. Those bound by one or the other are obligated to respond to one another beyond the letter of the law rather than to limit their obligations to the narrowest contractual requirements. Hence, covenants and compacts are inherently designed to be flexible in certain respects as well as firm in others. As expressions of private law, contracts tend to be interpreted as narrowly as possible so as to limit the obligation of the contracting parties to what is explicitly mandated by the contract itself.

A covenant differs from a compact in that its morally binding dimension takes precedence over its legal dimension. In its heart of hearts, a covenant is an agreement in which a transcendent moral force, traditionally God, is a party, usually a direct party, to or guarantor of a particular relationship; whereas, when the term compact is used, a moral force is only indirectly involved. A compact, based as it is on mutual pledges rather than the guarantees of a higher authority, rests more heavily on a legal though still ethical grounding for its politics. In other words, compact is a secular phenomenon. This is historically verifiable by examining the shift in terminology that took place in the seventeenth and eighteenth centuries. While those who saw the hand of God in political affairs in the United States continued to use the term covenant, those who sought a secular grounding for politics turned to the term compact. While the distinction is not always used with strict clarity, it does appear consistently. The issue was further complicated by Rousseau and his followers who talked about the social contract, a highly secularized concept which, even when applied for public purposes, never develops the same level of moral obligation as either covenant or compact.

Covenant is also related to constitutionalism. Normally, a covenant precedes a constitution and establishes the people or polity which then proceeds to adopt a constitution of government for itself. Thus, a constitution involves the implementation of a prior covenant—an effectuation or translation of a prior covenant into an actual frame or structure of government. The constitution may include a restatement or reaffirmation of the original covenant, as does the Massachusetts Constitution of 1780, but that is optional.

Although perhaps more difficult than tracing covenantal ideas expressed in political thought, covenant as ideology is more easily identifiable since ideology is a very public form of theory. Covenant-as-culture persists even when it is not necessarily recognized as such, while covenantal ideology had its ups and downs in the modern epoch. It was strong in the mid-seventeenth century in the British Isles, the Low Countries and in the American colonies; again at the time of the American Revolution; and periodically thereafter in covenant-based civil societies, but never again during the modern epoch did it achieve the same status.

One of the tests of the presence of the covenantal dimension is to be found in the institutions that developed within the covenantal matrix, particularly in matters of their institutional governance and culture. These, indeed, can be identified throughout the epoch. Even if the larger environment is less covenantal, institutions remain carriers, at least until some massive change comes to transform them. Thus the behavior of people functioning within those institutions, particularly their political behavior, is a clear manifestation of covenant where it exists. Less easy to identify than institutions, nevertheless political behavior can be studied sufficiently well in most cases.

Covenant entered the modern epoch as a manifestation of Reformed Protestantism and in every respect it was tied to the rise and fall of Puritanism and the residues Puritanism left in certain parts of the world. Reformed Protestant had two principal sources: one was in Huldreich Zwingli, Heinrich Bullinger and their colleagues and disciples in Zurich and the Rhineland, principally in the German-speaking territories of Switzerland and western Germany. The other was the product of John Calvin and his associates and students in Geneva. Calvin came on the scene after Zwingli had been killed and Calvin's doctrines rapidly became the most influential in the Reformed Protestant world.

These influences affected the Huguenots in France, the Netherlanders, the Scots, and the English Puritans as well as the Puritans in British North America. In matters theological, Calvinism was the stronger influence, but in matters political the influence of Zwingli and Bullinger was the greater. While every nation influenced by Reformed Protestantism developed its own synthesis of the two, the most influential synthesis in the world was that formed by the English Puritans. In no small measure, this was because of the power of first England and then its successor, Britain, as the greatest power in the world from the beginning of the eighteenth century until nearly the end of the modern epoch, with influence that stretched far beyond its tight little island. That influence was further increased by the fact that the Puritans fought, and in the short term won, a civil war in England itself which not only brought them to power in their own country, but enabled them to conquer Scotland and Ireland. Even prior to that, they settled a good part of British North America and the deep Southern Hemisphere as well.

Religious-based covenantal thinking undoubtedly reached its most sophisticated level of development under Reformed Protestantism and most particularly Puritanism, finding major expression on the European continent, in the British Isles, and in New England where it had lasting impact on subsequent generations, even after the Puritan commonwealths had passed from history, to be replaced by modern, secularized civil societies. Only at major historical intervals has a movement had as much impact as Reformed Protestantism has had on the history of the world.

Nevertheless, the kind of integral society that was required to maintain Reformed Protestantism came under great assault in the seventeenth century. It ultimately was brought down in favor of a far more heterogeneous world view, in part because the demands of Puritanism, and Reformed Protestantism in general, on individuals were too high. For better or for worse, most people did not want to live Puritan lives, seeing Puritanism as far too serious, demanding, and unsatisfying. Moreover, those who saw Puritanism as an appropriate way of life often could not personally sustain its demands and hence were perceived by others to be hypocrites.

Thus we had a paradox. On one hand, Reformed Protestantism developed very important and compelling theories, ideologies, and cultures supporting liberty and equality, two of the principal political aspirations of the modern epoch, but the Reformed way to achieve them required institutions insufficiently broad or free and behavior of an impossibly high standard to be realized by the vast majority of people. It remained for the new science of politics and its developers and exponents, who began with a very secular, if equally pessimistic, approach to human nature (the development of which Reformed Protestantism actually facilitated) to provide not only a bridge but a more satisfying framework for political theory and practice, both of which drew on covenant ideas in new ways.

The climax of the modern drive for civil society actually came when the two principles of commonwealth and civil society came together and were intertwined in the birth of the United States of America, both as an independent polity and as a constitutional regime. The generation that achieved the Declaration of Independence, fought the Revolutionary War, and established the United States under its new constitution was led by two groups: one coming out of the older religious tradition, primarily the covenantal tradition of Reformed Protestantism who saw the imperatives of their tradition leading in the direction of a federal democratic republic under God, and the second group who came out of the Enlightenment, influenced primarily by the Scottish Enlightenment which was part of the covenantal tradition one step removed, who sought a federal democratic republic in North America as the way to actualize civil society. The great achievement of the Americans in their revolutionary era was that the moderates from both camps found a common language and a common program upon which to agree, while the extremists in both camps were pushed aside, thereby enabling the United States to be born as a synthesis of the two conceptions of humanity, society, and polity, thereby enhancing the strengths and moderating the weaknesses of each.

Covenantal and Hierarchical Models

The modern epoch witnessed a major conflict between covenantal and hierarchical models of polity. Indeed, modern European statism was based upon the hierarchical model or, as it was democratized, its transformation into a center-periphery model. Thus, as parliaments acquired power from kings, they modified the monarchic pyramids in such a way as to establish parliamentary centers of power while the rest of the polity remained on the periphery, at most selecting who would be in the parliamentary "club." Moreover, as kings become weaker those committees of parliament originally chosen to advise the monarch became cabinets or governments. Either way, the models resembled military formations or exclusive clubs rather than open societies.

The hierarchical models were generally founded in conquest, either internal or external, and organized as power pyramids with the ruler or rulers at the apex of the pyramid and commanding those below who were organized into levels of authority and power, each level subordinate to the one above it. Administration took precedence over politics and the latter existed primarily in the form of court politics, i.e., the struggle for the ear of the ruler. If these hierarchies had to be constitutionalized, they were constitutionalized by the ruler granting a charter to the subjects. Indeed, this had been the formal pattern of medieval constitutionalism and medieval regimes generally. It was made even more draconian in the early modern epoch as the hierarchies more fully took military form.

Where modified by a center-periphery model, the political elite was able to take control of the country's center, essentially by forming a club. Indeed, their politics, which precede both administration and the constitution, was and is the politics of a club. Their administration is tied to that politics and its heads also had to be members of the club. A constitution, for them, tends to be a traditional body of rules. Westminster-style parliamentarism is the apotheosis of this model, with the politically sovereign parliament as the club of clubs.

In contrast to both of these models, associated with modern statism is the covenantal model associated with modern federalism. Although developed in concept and theory even earlier, its complete modern theoretical development and successful practical application came in the United States at the end of the eighteenth century. The covenantal model consists of a matrix of equal cells framed by common institutions. The matrix is founded by individuals or individual entities who join together as equals through a covenant or political compact establishing their common governing institutions without sacrificing their respective integrities and retaining a fair measure of their independence. Because of the very nature of the model, the constitution is preeminent since it embodies the agreement that specifies the linkages and establishes agreed-upon rules of the game for all.

The politics that flows from that constitution is a politics designed for people of equal status based upon negotiation and bargaining among them which is designed to be as open as possible. Administration is dependent upon the constitution for its authority and the politics of equals for its powers. The system is not hierarchical even if small hierarchies may form within it for reasons of efficiency. Also, it is multi-centered. No single center can come into existence because the multiplicity of centers is constitutionally protected. In its most complete form it is a federal system with a separation of powers, in which the common institutions have only those powers delegated to it by the constituent entities.

The Federalist, the finest modern theoretical formulation for this model, describes these three forms of polity as, respectively, produced by force, accident, or reflection and choice. Indeed, the first Federalist paper makes the point that all regimes prior to the United States had to rely upon force and accident and that it has been given to the Americans to be able to construct a regime based on reflection and choice, showing that the American founders were very much aware of the fundamental difference between federal polities and others.

The Europeans who came to the New World did not see themselves as directly influenced by its indigenous inhabitants whom they came to know as "Indians," and who are now referred to as "Native Americans." Those Native Americans, however, contributed more to successful European settlement in North America than the Europeans perceived at the time, not only in new products—potatoes, corn, chocolate, tobacco, and many others—but also in new techniques of confronting what for Europeans was a new world. Without making too much of it, in many cases they also were organized on a federal basis with tribal confederacies and leagues from coast to coast. The most prominent of those leagues was the League of the Iroquois, the precursor to the Iroquois Confederacy. It had as its proximate founder an

Onondaga named Hiawatha, and an expatriate Huron (the Iroquois' principal enemies) known as "Peacemaker." The sacred story of how they did so is one of the three great elements of Iroquois cosmology (the others are the creation myth and the Code of Handsome Lake which founded a new religion for the Iroquois at the end of the eighteenth century based upon a synthesis of traditional Iroquois beliefs and attempts to harmonize the new realities of the times). The Constitution of the Five Nations includes both mythic and historical elements. The League was held together by the condolence ceremony that reasserted and then disposed of the collective grief of the members when a death occurred. The entirely native-originated League of the Iroquois was replaced in the seventeenth century by the Iroquois Confederacy which already was influenced by contact with the Europeans.[1]

The Creek Confederacy in the south central part of North America was another example. North of it was the Illinois Confederacy between the Great Lakes and the Mississippi. Other leagues and confederacies linked tribes in various other parts of the country. With the exception of the Iroquois Confederacy which had a certain influence on Benjamin Franklin and those of his compatriots who sought broader union for the British colonies in North America, these indigenous American arrangements essentially stand as testimony to the federal qualities of the country rather than as examples for the white men.

To describe certain peoples or civil societies or cultures as covenantal is only to suggest that their dominant ideologies and modal personalities are covenantal. These may encompass a majority of the population or a key minority in key positions that shape the cultures, peoples, or civil societies. We know that most historical movements are generated and achieve whatever they achieve through such key minorities. In that sense it can be said that most people at all times and in all places are the same, desiring only to achieve pleasure and avoid pain in small, conventional ways, but they do not set the tone. It is the key minorities that do, and if they are covenantal, then the societies become covenantal.

On the other hand, this does not mean that covenantal attributes are not to penetrate deeply into the culture where they exist, and are not found among people who would not have the slightest awareness that they had them. If all peoples have hierarchical, organic and covenantal leanings, in covenantal cultures and polities, those are the elements that the key minorities have featured and fostered in one way or another.

Note

1. Dean R. Snow, *Hiawatha: Constitution-Maker* New York Notes; A.C. Parker, "The Constitution of the Five Nations," in Parker, *On the Iroquois*, edited by W.A. Fenton (Syracuse: Syracuse University Press, 1968), and E. Tooker, "The League of the Iroquois: Its History, Politics, and Ritual," in *Handbook of North American Indians*, vol. 15, edited by B.G. Trigger (Washington, D.C.: Smithsonian Institution, 1978), pp. 418–441.

Part I

The United States:
An Almost Covenanted Polity

1

Covenant and the American Founding

On his way to Washington to take the oath of office as president of the United States of America, at a time when the U.S. itself seemed destined for dissolution, Abraham Lincoln pointedly stopped in Philadelphia to visit Independence Hall. Standing before that historic landmark on February 21, 1861, Lincoln emphasized to his audience that he had come "to listen to those breathings rising within the consecrated walls where the Constitution of the United States, and I will add, the Declaration of Independence was originally framed." Lincoln continued:

> I have never asked anything that does not breathe from those walls. All my political warfare has been in favor of the teachings coming forth from that sacred hall. May my right hand forget its cunning and my tongue cleave to the roof of my mouth, if ever I prove false to those teachings.[1]

America's Covenantal Vocation

Lincoln's paraphrase of the fifth and sixth verses of Psalm 137 is one of many manifestations of his view of the American experience as being parallel to that of biblical Israel. If Americans were not *the* chosen people, they were at least, in his eyes, an "almost chosen people."

The content and every cadence of Lincoln's remarks at Independence Hall and on similar occasions suggest that he shared the sense of an American vocation similar to that described by Governor John Winthrop, the foremost among the American Puritan founders.[2] In his *Modell of Christian Charity* delivered aboard the *Arrabella* on the Atlantic Ocean in 1630, Winthrop summarized the enterprise upon which the first Puritan emigrants from England had embarked in the New World: "We are entered into Covenant with him for this work, we have taken out a Commission."

In January 1965, Winthrop's statement found an echo in President Lyndon B. Johnson's inaugural address:

> They came here—the exile and the stranger, brave but frightened—to find a place where a man could be his own man. They made a covenant with this land. Conceived in justice, written in liberty, bound in union, it was meant one day to inspire the hopes of all mankind; and it binds us still. If we keep its terms, we shall flourish.
>
> The American covenant called on us to help show the way for the liberation of man. And that is today our goal. Thus, if as a nation there is much outside our control, as a people no stranger is outside our hope.[3]

Thus, almost 3,000 years after the covenant at Sinai, when the Israelites ratified their exodus from pharaonic bondage and signified their consent to Moses with amens, the Pilgrims, who saw themselves as new Israelites embarked on a venture into their own "hideous and desolate wilderness," likewise consented to a covenant with their signatures and amens.[4] In doing so, the Pilgrims introduced into North America a major stream of thought derived from the biblical idea of covenant. While often more latent than manifest since the days of the Puritans, and partially submerged within other streams and eddies of American thought and culture—especially secular constitutionalism—covenant ideas not only formed a significant part of the foundation of the United States, but have continued to influence American life in various ways.

As Henry Steele Commager has observed:

> All through the colonial era Americans went from compact to compact—the Fundamental Laws of Connecticut of 1639, the 'Solemn Compact' at Portsmouth of 1638, and its successor the Charter of the Providence Plantations of 1647, the Pennsylvania Charter of Privileges of 1701 (not quite so clear a case, to be sure), and thereafter a score of compacts and agreements on one frontier after another."[5] As Richard Niebuhr observed some years ago: "one of the great common patterns that guided men in the period when American democracy was formed...was the pattern of the covenant or of federal society.[6]

Thus, from their earliest beginnings, the people and polities comprising the United States have bound themselves together through covenants to erect their New World order, deliberately following biblical precedents. The covenant concluded on the Mayflower on November 11, 1620, remains the first hallowed document of the American constitutional tradition:

> In the name of God, Amen. We whose names are under-writen, the loyall subjects of our dread soveraigne Lord, King James, by the grace of God, of Great Britaine,

Franc, and Ireland king, defender of the faith, etc., haveing undertaken, for the glorie of God, and advancemente of the Christian faith, and honour of our king and countrie, a voyage to plant the first colonie in the Northerne parts of Virginia, doe by these presents solemnly and mutualy in the presence of God, and one of another, *covenant* and combine our selves togeather into a civill body politick, for our better ordering and preservation and furtherance of the ends aforesaid; and by vertue hearof to enacte, constitutions, and offices, from time to time, as shall be thought most meete and convenient for the generall good of the colonie, unto which we promise all due submission and obedience. In witnes wherof we have hereunder subscribed our names at Cap Codd the 11. of November, in the year of the raigne of our soveraigne lord, King James, of England, France, and Ireland the eighteenth, and of Scotland the fiftie fourth. Ano: Dom. 1620.[7]

A classic covenant, it explicitly created a community and the basis for its subsequent constitutional development. With more pride than accuracy, John Quincy Adams once referred to that Mayflower Compact as "perhaps the only instance in human history of that positive, original social compact which speculative philosophers have imagined as the only legitimate source of government."[8]

In fact, there were many such covenants at the time of the settlement of British North America. His point is an important one, however. The Mayflower Compact occurred at least thirty years before the speculative philosophers of Europe imagined it. By the time that Hobbes and Locke formulated their compactual theories, there were already many compactual civil societies in the New World.

The American people have developed two major covenantal celebrations that persist into the postmodern epoch, albeit with their covenantal messages considerably diminished and confined to the ritual or the pro forma. They are Thanksgiving and Independence Day. The first commemorates the first founding in the colonial period before independence.

Although the idea of thanksgiving was used by subsequent generations of Americans for other kinds of commemorations as well, the Thanksgiving that survives and has become the premier American national holiday is the November Thanksgiving attributed to the Pilgrims. It is the premier national holiday because of what it combines and what it excludes. It combines both religious and patriotic sentiments in proper proportion. It is exclusively American and celebrates not only the American civil religion but the religious character of the American people, yet it is not identified with any specific religion or religious denomination. Hence it is open to full participation on the part of all Americans, which none of the denominational holidays or holy days are or can be without being denatured. Thanksgiving is not strictly religious just as it is certainly not strictly civil, but each generation can develop its own combination of the two. For many generations the religious motif was dominant. The civil motif gained in importance in the latter part of the nineteenth century and on into the twentieth but the public motif remained mainly religious.

As those original motifs were modified, both the religious and civil motifs became more a matter of private observance through families and churches while the public celebration came to identify with the motifs of twentieth-century America, of those of the American dream rather than the American vision, with commercial Thanksgiving Day parades to open the Christmas buying season and professional football contests to provide entertainment and capitalize on people being free from work on that day. In this sense Thanksgiving, with all the changes involved, continues to speak to the American people even in its new emphasis on their dream rather than their vision.

For the patriots of Samuel Adams's "solemn league and covenant" against British oppression; for the framers of the constitutional compact of 1787; for Jefferson, who referred to the young republic in his first inaugural address as a "chosen country"; for Lincoln, who often characterized the American union as "a regular marriage"; for Johnson; and for millions of ordinary Americans, the concept of covenant has been reflected in real experiences from Jamestown to the present whereby individuals and families have come together to establish governing arrangements by compact.

The Puritans: Covenant Comes to the New World

Perry Miller, the great scholar of American Puritanism summed up the earliest foundations of American political theory in this way:

> To the [Puritans] the basic idea was the covenant...primarily a grandiose theological conception, it became also a theory of society.... In the Puritan formulation it held that a body politic could be constituted only out of the consent of the governed, yet also out of an agreement not to terms of the people's own divising but only to the pre-stated terms of God's eternal law of justice.

The great revival of the covenant tradition in sixteenth- and seventeenth-century Europe was connected with the economic, social, and political transformations taking place on that continent at that time. The

rise of early modern capitalism and republicanism led to a breakdown of
the medieval connections between persons, communities, and places.
People became more detached, even alienated, from their surroundings
as they had to leave the places of their birth to search for work and had to
find new places as individuals without the protections and supports of
community. These socially naked individuals sought to continue their
connections with communities through the religious ideas embodied in
the covenant theology and their political manifestations.[9]

The covenant tradition was linked with the development of psycho-
logical individualism as people began to conceive of themselves apart
from their classes, communities, and families, as a means of both recognizing and modifying that individualism. John Peacock describes the
change in this way:

> The individual as he was emerging in the sixteenth and seventeenth centuries was
> beginning to imagine himself, not as an organ of the social body, nor as a person-
> ality in the psychological sense—an organization integratable with other indi-
> viduals into family, occupation, class, church, government, etc., yet by nature
> sufferable from these institutions as never before, since they were all becoming
> more and more separate from each other.... Medieval man, by contrast, had pic-
> tured himself less as an individual than as an organ of the body politic—whether
> a limb or a head, depended on his class position. Organic imagery abounded in
> medieval public records, and in secular and religious literature. The body politic
> was thought to be God's ordinary Providence for society: He had ordained for each
> nation an organic life, integrated in all its parts, destined to thrive for its natural
> life like any organism, and destined to die like one.... Three organic principles
> constituted the medieval body politic ideal: (1) organic hierarchy among the body's
> superior and inferior organs; (2) organic involuntarism ("one part set against the
> head...tends to the dissolution of the whole"—quotation from Henry Ferne, a
> royalist pamphleteer during the English Civil War); (3) organic cyclicism (nations
> "have their youth, their strength and after a while their delineation"—cited from
> Stephen Marshall).[10]

While the Puritans often used the organic imagery of the time, in fact
their ideas and behavior were designed to undermine organicism and were
contrary to it.[11]

The covenant idea provided the Puritans with a way out. History was
no longer viewed as cyclical as organic thought demanded, but, like biblical history, as teleological; that is to say, with a beginning and an end as
prescribed in the Bible, though, because of man's fall, requiring God's
intervention to bring it to its appropriate end. The result was an ambiguous language of discourse and, since language is man's "program," am-

biguous thought on the matter in certain quarters that led to the idea of an elected nation, originally applied to England by the Puritans and later to New England by its Puritan settlers. Peacock describes the transformation in this way: "In the early modern body politic, organic reciprocity replaced organic hierarchy."[12]

Covenant identity is "federal identity"; that is to say, one's identity is defined through the reciprocal relationship. It is no longer defined organically by birth which fixes the individual's place in the community, but by agreement and the assumption of certain obligations in return for certain liberties. Thus John Winthrop could try to balance personal and federal identity among the passengers on the *Arrabella* in his famous sermon to them. As Peacock concludes, "'A Model of Christian Charity' is one of the first steps in an American evolution from covenant to constitution."[13]

A major problem in this new situation was how to reconcile commerce and charity. The idea of charity or, as it was often known, Christian charity, was a Christian modification of the biblical concept of *tzedakah* (derived from the Hebrew word *tzedek* or justice). As for Judaism, it was and is one of the fundaments of proper life in this world. Most pronouncedly, this was true with regard to Reformed Protestantism. Yet the new economics, based on commerce and a blending of commerce and individualism, was not necessarily conducive to charity, so the two had to be reconciled. This has been, indeed, a major problem for Americans since the very founding of the first English colonies on North American shores. American political culture itself is rooted in the two bases of marketplace and commonwealth as a result.

The Puritans confronted the problem head on. John Winthrop, the first governor of Massachusetts Bay Colony addressed it aboard the Arabella on the voyage over and suggested the reconciliation of the two through the Puritan's covenant with God.[14] He specified the articles of that covenant as a practical guide to that reconciliation. In true covenantal style, Winthrop's discussion emphasized the obligations on the rich to help the poor, not the virtues of the poor or any rights of theirs to that help. A proper Christian thus was obligated to reconcile charity and commerce and to provide his share of Christian charity for those less fortunate than he, no matter whether the recipients were deserving or not.

Covenant, then, was designed to mediate between self-interest and conscience, material means and transcendental ends, and personal and collective destinies in the commonwealth. Winthrop's title for his lecture, "A Model of Christian Charity," suggests how he intended to address those tasks. It was in this address that he spoke of the New Englanders as being "a city upon a hill" with "the eyes of all people...upon us," and that the Puritans "shall find that the God of Israel is among us."[15] All of this contingent upon maintaining the articles of the covenant and providing Christian charity so as to approach, if not achieve, saintly conduct. The body politic, indeed, could only stand if it were properly informed religiously since by itself it was too weak a reed. Indeed, the synthesis between the religious spirit in its demands and the necessities of civil life is the key to Winthrop's thought.

Covenant used in this way undermined feudal hierarchy. The new body politic under special Divine providence did not involve superiors and inferiors in an army-like chain of command, but mutual consent among "the members of this body one towards another" who served "out of love [and] sympathy,"[16] a concept akin to the biblical *hesed* (freely translatable as loving covenant obligation).

Winthrop's theory of affections was the cement that linked his ideas of sacrifice, commerce, and equality within the body politic. Note his definition:

> [I]t is not possible that love should be bred or upheld without hopes of requital.... Love is always under reward, it never gives but it always receives with advantage.... Among the members of the same body, love and affection are reciprocal in a most equal and sweet kind of commerce.... regard of the pleasure and content that the exercise of love carries with it as we may see in the natural body...labor...is accompanied with such pleasure and content as far exceeds the pains it takes: so is it in all the labor of love, among Christians, the party loving, reaps love again as what was showed before, which the soul covets more than all the wealth in the world...for to love and live beloved is the soul's paradise, both here and in Heaven.[17]

In this way Winthrop replaced hierarchy with reciprocity, theologically reordering feudal reciprocity federally, that is, through covenant.

Edmond Morgan sums up the meaning of this transformation:

> The transition from medieval to modern times, as has often been suggested, was marked by a transformation in which one's relationship to another ceased to depend so much on the estate or station in life occupied by each and came to be based more on whatever covenant, that is, contractor agreement might exist between them. Whether this change owed anything to religious ideas or whether certain religious ideas were themselves the product of the change can never be known, but it is clear that many sixteenth and seventeenth century Protestants, and especially Puritans thought about their relationship with God as though it were based on covenant."[18]

Morgan was writing with the skepticism of the twentieth-century historian. Nevertheless, he properly connects covenant and contract. Sir Henry Maine had earlier set forth the fundamental theory that the transition from the medieval to the modern epoch was a shift from status to contract.[19]

In the last analysis, Maine is right, but it is important to recall the difference between covenant and contract. For those concerned with more than material relationships, neither status nor contract is enough. There must be the bridge of covenant in between. Preceeding Lincoln, Winthrop referred to covenant as a marriage, that is to say, what one might call a sacramental contract freely entered into, yet binding, requiring the highest religious obligation together with the most worldly pursuit of happiness.[20]

How do moderns enter into covenant and know that it is a covenant that they have entered into? Winthrop tells us: "The Lord hath given us leave to draw our own articles.... Now if the Lord shall please to hear us, and bring us in peace to the place we desire, then hath He ratified this covenant."[21]

Thus the first political principles systematically enunciated in America were extensions and adaptations of the Puritans' federal theology which saw all society as an outgrowth of the basic biblical covenants between God and His people.[22] Winthrop referred to the good commonwealth as one committed to "federal liberty," or the freedom to freely hearken to the law of the covenant. The Puritans sought to place all relationships between people on a covenantal basis. Their congregations were covenant-formed partnerships of "saints" that came into existence only when potential members covenanted among each other, and survived only so long as the covenantal act remained valid (potentially but not necessarily forever).

Similarly, civil government among the Puritans was instituted by civil covenant among the residents (or potential residents) of virtually every town in most of the New England provinces.[23] The Mayflower Compact (originally known as the Plymouth Combination) was the first of these covenantal acts. Subsequently, the same mode of town formation was extended to virtually every settlement created in New England and to many created in the other colonies as well. Connecticut and Rhode Island, for example, were formed by their towns covenanting together. John Clarke and his Narragansett associates expressed the basic idea in their Plantation Agreement:

It is agreed by this Present Assembly thus Incorporate, and by this Present Act declared, that the Forme of Government Established in Providence Plantations is Democraticall; that is to say, a Government held by ye Free and Voluntarie Consent of all, or the greater Parte of the Free Inhabitants.[24]

The ability of all to enter into the covenant meant that all were, ipso facto, equal in the most crucial manner, that is, in the ability to bind themselves to proper standards of life.

The New England town was the highest embodiment of the Winthropian covenanted community. Based on the voluntary commitment of its residents to the congregational covenant as a basis for civil citizenship, it was illegal to live more than half a mile from the meeting house and biblical laws were applied in many areas of personal behavior. It was the severity of some of those laws plus the limitations on normal life that contributed to the westward migration of many of the children of those towns because however much the Puritan model drew on earlier times, New England was a modern colony with modern aspirations of individual self-fulfillment and success.

As Winthrop and his colleagues such as Thomas Hooker, the Mathers and John Cotton reveal in their works, the Puritans who settled in New England combined a fundamental conservatism with an unhesitating radicalism in a way that was to become as paradigmatic for Americans as other aspects of their approach to life. That combination was no doubt directly related to their covenantal ideology, which saw humans as bound to God through predestination, yet through that binding free to live according to the constitution He provided for their salvation. To implement that constitution required a revolt against the existing society, but the goals of that revolt were to restore prelapsarian (before Adam's fall) harmony to the world. The Puritans came to the New World to build a new society, but never lost sight of human weakness in trying to do so.

The synthesis did not always hold together. Those who leaned more to the radical side, such as Roger Williams and Ann Dickinson, almost immediately broke away. Williams established his own covenantal commonwealth of Rhode Island and Providence Plantations that was as firmly grounded in covenant in matters civil and political as Massachusetts, only it was so grounded in order to guarantee openness in matters religious, something that the Puritans believed was impossible for the attainment of salvation.

Others occasionally allowed the conservative dimensions of Puritanism to overwhelm them; namely the Salem witch trials in which the continued Puritan emphasis on the deviltry in human souls got out of hand as a result of popular mischief. But for the most part the synthesis held, spinning off different versions. Thomas Hooker, for example, moved his congregation from Massachusetts to found Connecticut in 1636 to develop a more egalitarian Puritan commonwealth, but one no less faithful in combining conservative and radical dimensions. Here his supporters wrote the first full American constitution, The Fundamental Orders of Connecticut, and adopted the Mosaic law as the basis of Connecticut law, by reference.

Puritan federalism expressed itself philosophically and socially through the concept of "federal liberty" which John Winthrop articulated in his Address to the General Court in 1645. For Winthrop and the other Puritans, federal liberty stood in contradistinction to natural liberty. John Winthrop, one of the founders of Massachusetts, enunciated his famous doctrine of federal liberty in 1645:

> There is a two-fold liberty, natural (I mean as our nature is now corrupt) and civil or federal. The first is common to man with beasts and other creatures. By this, man, as he stands in relation to man simply, hath liberty to do what he lists; it is a liberty to evil as well as to good. This liberty is incompatible and inconsistent with authority and cannot endure the least restraint of the most just authority. The exercise and maintaining of this liberty makes men grow more evil and in time to be worse than brute beasts: *omnes sumus licentia deteriores*. This is that great enemy of truth and peace, that wild best, which all of the ordinances of God are bent against, to restrain and subdue it. The other kind of liberty I call civil or federal; it may also be termed moral, in reference to the covenant between God and man, in the moral law, and the politic covenants and constitutions between men themselves. This liberty is the proper end and object of authority and cannot subsist without it; and it is a liberty to that only which is good, just and honest. This liberty you are to stand for, with the hazard (not only of your goods, but) of your lives if need be.

> Whatsoever crosses this is not authority but a distemper thereof. This liberty is maintained and exercised in a way of subjection to authority; it is of the same kind of liberty where with Christ hath made us free. The women's own choice makes such a man her husband; yet, being so chosen, he is her lord, and she is to be subject to him, yet in a way of liberty, not of bondage; and a true wife accounts her subjection her honor and freedom and would not think her condition safe and free but within her subjection to her husband's authority. Such is the liberty of the church under the authority of Christ, her king and husband; his yoke is so easy and sweet to her as a bride's ornament; and if through forwardness or wantonness, etc., she shake it off at any time, she is at no rest in her spirit, until she takes it up again; and whether her lord smiles upon her and embraceth her in his arms, or

whether he frowns, or rebukes, or smites her, she apprehends a sweetness of his love and all, and is refreshed, supported, and instructed by every such dispensation of his authority over her. On the other side, ye know who they are that complain of this yoke and say, let us break their bands, etc.; we will not have this man to rule over us. Even so, bretheren, it will be between you and your magistrates. If you want to stand for your natural corrupt liberties, and will do what is good in your own eyes, we will not endure the least weight of authority, but will murmur and oppose, and be always striving to shake off that yoke; but if you will be satisfied to enjoy such civil and lawful liberties, such as Christ allowes you, then will you quietly and cheerfully submit unto that authority which is set over you, in all the administrations of it, for your good.[25]

James Wilson was to restate Winthrop's point in connection with the proposed Federal Constitution of 1787:

In considering...the system before us, it is necessary to mention another kind of liberty...*federal liberty*. When a single government is instituted, the individuals of which it is composed, surrender to it a part of their natural independence.... When a confederate republic is instituted, the communities, of which it is composed, surrender to it a part of their political independence.... The states should resign to the national government, that part, and that part, only, of their political liberty, which, placed in that government, will produce more good to the whole, than if it had remained in the several states. While they resign this part of their political liberty, they retain the free and generous exercise of all their other faculties, as states, so far as it is compatible with the welfare of the general and superintending confederacy.[26]

In truth, others who came to America were attracted by the openness of a wild land and sought natural liberty. Natural liberty means that everyone is free to do what he or she pleases provided it is perceived as not hurting anyone else. In colloquial American, it is "doin' what comes naturally" rather than being bound by any human social or political restrictions. In American mythology, in general, frontiersmen who went beyond the limits of civilization, most especially mountain men, were best able to fulfill this desire for natural liberty while, just as federal liberty is a Puritan idea whose roots go back to the Bible, natural liberty as moderns and postmoderns understand it philosophically is Rousseauian but has far earlier roots. This has been a continuing tension in American society.

Donald Lutz comments that federal liberty rests upon a combination of virtue and trust, and a tension between individualism and communitarianism. Although the combination originally relied upon religion, it has been transformed into a civil concept.

Puritan covenantalism touched every sphere of life. Even the militia, which at first glance seems to be merely a continuation of medieval organizational patterns, was covenanted and became both an instrument and a manifestation of Puritan covenantalism.[27]

From the first, the Puritan settlers of New England had to organize their defense, particularly against the Indians. They did so in the English way, not by standing armies but through the train band militias, at times organized and trained by a handful of veteran soldiers who were paid for the task. In this respect they continued the ancient tradition of the role of the militia in covenanted polities as the means for individuals to express a major part of their obligations to the community as legitimizing their rights of citizenship.

Unlike the English militias which were confined to certain middle and upper classes, the New England militia train bands democratically accepted just about everybody from the first. Moreover, in the spirit of Puritan covenantalism, the train band was based on voluntary consent. The train bands were covenanted organizations by design, one aspect of which was the selection of their own officers. This power evolved over a period of years but it came to be because it fit into the general pattern of civil and ecclesiastical elections in the colony. One qualified as a militia participant by taking the oath of fidelity which was viewed as the basic act of consenting. By 1652 the Massachusetts legislature declared that "all Scotsmen, Negers, and Indians having with or servants to the English" would be enrolled, thereby further expanding the militia's openness and the military franchise. There were even controversies over elections and who had been elected.

By the 1650s locals who were not Puritans could in many places outvote those who were in the militia and the legislature began to be concerned by what for them was an excess of democracy. From 1656 on, the legislature tried to limit the franchise to real members of the Puritan community until in 1668 the Massachusetts General Court abolished local train band elections altogether and left only the right of the freemen to select a major general, the colony's highest ranking officer, ostensibly to abide by the rules imposed by Charles II after the restoration of the monarchy in England.

In terms of political organization, the high point of Puritan federalism was in the New England Confederation, which in the end was destroyed by the British as a threat to the empire. Organized originally by the four New England colonies of Plymouth, Massachusetts Bay, Rhode Island, and Connecticut for defensive purposes, it followed the style of confederacies of communities in which the real locus of power and commitment remained in the constituting units, but it soon showed signs of going beyond a mere military alliance.[28]

Although the New England Puritans remained the most eloquent articulators of the covenant idea, they were not the only ones to bring it to America. The Scotch-Irish of the mountains and piedmont from Pennsylvania to Georgia; the Dutch of New York; the Scottish Presbyterians; and to a lesser extent, the Quakers and German Sectarians of Pennsylvania and the Middle States; and the Huguenots of South Carolina were all nurtured in churches constructed on the covenant principle. The first ministers of the Gospel in Virginia—the colony usually cited as the antithesis of New England—were also Puritans.[29] Indeed, the tradition became so widespread that by 1776 over half of the new nation's church congregations were based on covenant principles.

Initially, the basic covenants of town and congregation united individuals and families. Parallel to those covenants there developed the network of voluntary associations—commercial, social, church, and civic—which represent the nongovernmental aspects of a civil society founded on the principles of free contract. From the first, networks of communities were united as colonies, then states. Ultimately, the network of states was linked in a federal union, always paralleled by a similar network of associations.

Covenants and Other Bonds

The American federal system is very much an outgrowth of both the theological and philosophic streams of covenantal thought and the political experiences of the emergent American people that converged about covenant by the late seventeenth century. If covenant ideas were first brought to the New World in an organized fashion by the Pilgrims and Puritans who settled New England, another set of covenant-related ideas entered America through the teachings of the new political science, especially those of Harrington, Locke, Montesquieu, and the Scottish Enlightenment. That is why federalism in the United States is more than a political device for dividing and sharing power among the state and federal governments but, rather, the *form* of the American polity in the eighteenth-century sense of the term, that is to say, the principle that *informs* every aspect of the polity.[30]

As the form of the American polity, federalism has its roots not only in the political dimension of American society, but in the economic, social, and religious dimensions as well. As we have seen, the political and religious dimensions are closely linked. Significantly, the economic roots of American federalism also have a compactual base. They can be traced back to the early trading companies that sponsored British and Dutch settlement in North America and to the system of governance encountered by those settlers on the voyage over.[31]

The trading companies, each with its royal monopoly, were organized on a shareholding basis, so that both ownership and control was spread among the shareholders. In some cases, the shareholders remained in Europe and tried to hold the actual settlers within their grasp on the basis of their control of the company. Invariably, this failed for political reasons. In a few cases, the settlers or some significant portion of them were themselves shareholders and, as such, combined political and economic control. In either case, the pattern of shareholding led to a corporate structure that was at least quasi-federal in character.

In the very earliest days the line between the political and economic aspects of the charters establishing the colonies was not at all clear. As the companies lost their monopolies, charters turned more in the direction of political constitutions, pure and simple, thereby reinforcing the theopolitical covenantal dimension where it was present or providing a complementary, compactual alternative where it was not.

Even the voyage over contributed to the covenantal experience of the colonists. The governance of ships had a contractual character that at least involved federal principles to the extent that every member of a ship's crew was in some respects a partner in the voyage. By signing the ship's articles, a crew member was entitled to an appropriate share of the profits of the voyage while at the same time formally submitting himself to the governance of the captain and the ship's officers. Since every ship that ventured forth on the ocean was, in effect, leaving civil society for a state of nature, every voyage had to be based upon a prior compact among all participants that would determine the political arrangements that would prevail for that voyage and the distribution of the economic benefits that would result.

Two centuries later, this system resurfaced in slightly different form in the organization of the wagon trains that crossed America's western plains. They also left civil society—this time for a land voyage through the state of nature. Their members also had to compact with one another to provide for their internal governance during the long trek westward. Echoing their earlier seaborne predecessors, they did so by compacting to establish a (temporary) political order.

These religious, political, and economic elements combined to socialize Americans into a kind of federalistic individualism. That is to say, not the anarchic individualism of Latin countries, but an individualism that recognized the subtle bonds of partnership linking individuals even as they preserve their respective integrities. William James was later to write about the federal character of these subtle bonds in his prescription for a pluralistic universe.[32] Indeed, American pluralism is based upon the tacit recognition of those bonds. Even though in the twentieth century the term pluralism has replaced all others in describing them, their federal character remains of utmost importance. At its best, American society becomes a web of individual and communal partnerships in which people link with one another to accomplish common purposes or to create a common environment without falling into collectivism or allowing individualism to degenerate into anarchy. These links usually manifest themselves in the web of associations that we associate with modern society but that are particularly characteristic of covenanted societies such as that of the United States.[33]

In a covenanted society the state itself is hardly more than an association, writ large and endowed with exceptional powers but still an association with limited means and ends. Were Americans to adopt a common salutation for some farfetched reason, like "comrade" in the Soviet Union or "citizen" in the days of the French Revolution, in all likelihood the American salutation would be "pardner," the greeting of the archetypal American folk figure, the cowboy, who embodies this combination of individualism and involvement in organized society and who expresses the character of that involvement through the term "pardner."

The American Colonial Experiments
with Covenants and Constitutions

As noted above, many of the early settlers in British North America explicitly used covenants to found their communities and polities. Covenants were particularly useful in the founding of towns and congregations, often involving the same people, especially in New England, less so in the other colonies except where Reformed Protestants settled.

Since the United States was "founded from the ground up," in the words of Donald Lutz, this is enormously significant.[34] In a certain way this was a continuation of late medieval Old World Reform and Protestant theory practice, albeit with a radically new turn, since opportunities presented themselves in the New World to turn theory into practice that had not existed in the Old due to the settlers' having had to establish new settlements where none (or at least none recognized by Europeans) had previously existed. The European settlers saw themselves as beginning from a political tabula rasa, the state of nature, as they phrased it, and hence were able not only to start anew but to design their institutions and constitutions from the very beginning according to their beliefs.

That kind of constitutional design could work as long as those beliefs squared with the necessities of living in the New World. Frederick Jackson Turner has emphasized the degree to which those necessities also differed from those the settlers knew in Europe and hence served to radically shake up the new societies they founded, basing success and prosperity of whatever kind on the ability to cope with the new situations; in other words, on merit rather than on a previously ascribed status.[35]

The combination of covenantal ideology and practical necessity was most felicitous in terms of the development of modern democratic republicanism. Covenants among equals, who established or reaffirmed their equality through achievement in a relatively harsh environment, led to communities and polities whose democratic orientation was built in from the first and was reaffirmed by critical subsequent experience.

The British settlers' use of covenants did not stop there. Having no indigenous traditions to draw on and having the necessity to constitute new civil governments for their new territories, the settlers were propelled from covenants to constitutions. Thus they were the first people at the eve of the modern epoch or after its beginning to develop constitutions of government of their own, based upon civil principles or, in many cases, on the half-civil, half-religious covenants they had established for themselves as their initial means of self-organization.

As scholar after scholar has shown in research in this century, the development of modern constitutions of government by the Puritans did not rest upon the work of John Locke, his predecessors, or his successors among political philosophers and could not have, because they preceeded Locke by as much as two generations, certainly half a century.[36] Indeed, as Perry Miller has demonstrated quite convincingly, Puritan political thought explaining, elaborating, and justifying the Puritan system of government with its covenants and constitutions also preceded Locke by at least a generation. Its first exponents were contemporaries of Hobbes and Harrington, but the content of their thought was indigenous and original, derived from the same biblical, Puritan, and European sources that influenced the great political philosophers, and which they transformed in a quasi-Puritan way, similar to the way that the latter revolutionized classical political thought. Thus both in practice and in theory American covenantalism and constitutionalism were unique, independent inventions, based upon new and independent experience. At the same time, they drew upon an old, classic, and hallowed tradition dating back to the Bible.

If Perry Miller was the leading discoverer of this tradition in America, Donald Lutz is the leading collector and interpreter in our time of the documents of this political foundation.[37] Lutz identifies the two stages of the covenantal founding of society, the founding of a people and then the founding of a governing arrangement for them. As he points out, in indigenous American developments these were in place before Locke, who conventionally is given credit for the idea of that two-fold founding, was even born. By paying careful attention to the language used as a guide to uncovering what Lutz, following Voegelin, describes as the symbols and the myths that form the founding story of the American people, we can see even more clearly how covenantalism led to constitutionalism in colonial America and the United States.

A mere listing of the documents to which Lutz refers is impressive. One is provided in table 1.1.

Lutz brings documents from eleven of the thirteen states, all except Georgia, which was not founded until 1732, and North Carolina, whose only seventeenth century document was also that of South Carolina and which Lutz brings. The oldest is "Articles, Laws and Orders, Divine Politic and Martial for the Colony in Virginia" established between May 1610 and June 1611, that is to say, assembled and approved by different persons on those two dates, and the last, "The Act to Ascertain the Manner and Form of Electing Members to Represent the Inhabitants of this Province in the Commons House of Assembly of South Carolina" in 1721.

Lutz also presents a set of principles which he derived from his analysis of these foundation documents. They are as follows:

1. The use of the covenant form for political foundation is derived from the use of covenants for the foundation of religious communities.

TABLE 1.1
Colonial American Founding Documents

Document Number and Short Name	Type of Document	Foundation Elements	Who is Acting
1 Articles, Laws (1610–1611)	I&J	3	executive
2 Laws enacted (1619)	I&J	3	legislature
3 Agreement (1620)	A,D,G&H	1,2,3,&4	people
4 Laws and Orders (1624)	J	3&4	legislature
5 Plymouth Oath (1625)	C	1&3	people
6 Salem Covenant (1629)	A	1&3	people
7 Agreement (1629)	A,D&G	1&2	people
8 Watertown Covenant (1630)	A&G	1&3	people
9 Mass. election (1631)	G&J	4	people
10 Oath of a Freeman (1631)	C	1&3	people
11 Mass. Agreement (1632)	G	4	people
12 Cambridge Agreement (1632)	D&G	4	people
13 Dorchester Agreement (1633)	D&G	4	people
14 Cambridge Agreement (1634)	G&J	4	people
15 Mass. Agreement (1634)	G&J	4	legislature
16 Oath of a Freeman (1634)	C	1&3	people
17 Salem Oath (1634)	C	1&3	people
18 Watertown Agreement (1634)	B	4	people
19 Enlarged Salem Covenant (1636)	A&F	1&3	people
20 Plymouth Agreement of 1636	D,G&H	2	special body
21 Pilgrim Code of Law (1636)	B,D&J	3&4	special body
22 Dedham Covenant (636)	D&G	1,3&4	people
23 Providence Agreement (1637)	G	2	people
24 Orders (1638)	J	3&4	legislature
25 Act for Establishing the House (1638)	B&D	4	leg. & people
26 Government of Pocasset (1638)	A&D	1,2&3	people
27 Plantation Covenant at Quinnipiack (1638)	A&D	3	people
28 An Act for Church Liberties (1638)	J&G	3	prop. & people
29 Act for Swearing Allegance (1638)	A,C&J	3	legislature
30 An Act What Persons (1638)	B&J	4	legislature
31 Act for the Liberties (1638)	J	3	legislature
32 Fundamental Orders of Conn. (1639)	A,D&I	2&4	people

TABLE 1.1 (continued)
Colonial American Founding Documents

Document Number and Short Name	Type of Document	Foundation Elements	Who is Acting
33 Newport Agreement (1639)	D&G	1,2&4	people
34 Government of Portsmouth (1639)	B&D	2&4	people
35 Guilford Covenant (1639)	A&D	1&3	people
36 Structure of Town Governments (1639)	H	4	legislature
37 Fundamental Articles of New Haven (1639)	A,D&I	2,3&4	people
38 Agreement of Settlers (1639)	A,D,G&H	1,2&3	people
39 Plantation Covenant (1640)	G&H	3&4	people
40 Connecticut Oath of Fidelity (1640)	C	1&3	people
41 Mass. Body of Liberties (1641)	D,I&J	3&4	legislature
42 Piscataqua Combination (1641)	D&H	1,3&4	people
43 Government of R.I. (1642)	D&G	2&4	legislature
44 Capital Laws of Conn. (1642)	J	3	legislature
45 Government of Guilford (1643)	D&G	1,2,3&4	people
46 New Haven Fundamentals (1643)	D,G&I	1,2,3&4	people
47 New England Confederation (1643)	D,G&H	2,3&4	legislature
48 Mass. Bicameral Ordinance (1644)	J	4	legislature
49 Mass. Ordinance on the Legislature (1644)	J	4	legislature
50 Majority Vote of Deputies (1645)	J	4	legislature
51 Warwick Agreement (1647)	D&G	2&3	people
52 Acts and Orders (1647)	D,I&J	2,3&4	people
53 Laws and Liberties (1647)	F,I&J	3&4	legislature
54 Mass. Ordinance (1648)	J	4	legislature
55 Charter of Providence (1649)	J&L	2&4	legislature
56 Maryland Toleration Act (1649)	J	3	legislature
57 Towns of Wells (1649)	D&H	2&4	legislature
58 Connecticut Code of Laws (1650)	F&J	3	legislature
59 Cambridge Agreement (1652)	G	3&4	people
60 Puritan Laws and Liberties (1658)	F&J	2,3&4	legislature
61 An Act of General Court (1661)	J	3&4	legislature
** Charter of Conn. (1662)	B&L	1,2,3&4	king&leg.
** Charter of R.I. (1663)	B&L	1,2,3&4	king&leg.
** Concessions and Agreement of N.J (1664)	D&G	1,2,3&4	leg.&props.

TABLE 1.1 (continued)
Colonial American Founding Documents

Document Number and Short Name	Type of Document	Foundation Elements	Who is Acting
** Concessions and Agreement (1665)	B,D&L	1,2&4	leg.&props.
62 Letter from Governor (1665)	J	3&4	governor
63 General Assembly of R.I.(1666)	J	4	legislature
64 Preface to General Laws (1672)	F&J	3	legislature
** Concessions of W N.J. (1677)	D,G&I	3&4	people&props.
65 Laws and Liberties of N.H. (1680)	F,I&J	3&4	legislature
66 Fundamentals of W N.J. (1681)	D,G&I	3&4	people&props
67 Concessions to PA. (1681)	D,E&J	3	people&props
68 Laws&Liberties of N.H. (1682)	F,I&J	3&4	legislature
69 Frame of Gov. of PA. (1682)	B,I,J&L	4	proprietor
70 Act for Freedom (1682)	G&J	3	prop.&leg.
** Frame of Gov. of PA. (1683)	B&J	4	prop.&leg.
** Laws on Personal Freedom (1683)	J	3	legislature
** Fundamental Constitutions (1683)	B,D,I&L	2,3&4	proprietors
71 Charter of Liberties (1683)			
72 Articles of Agreement (1686)	I&J	3&4	gov.&leg.
** Admonition for Reformation (1689)	F,G&J	3	gov.&leg.
** Frame of Gov. of PA. (1696)	F,I&J	4	governor
73 Division of Conn. (1698)	J	4	legislature
** Charter of Privileges (1701)	F,G&L	3&4	prop.&leg.
74 Act to Ascertain (1721)	J	4	gov.&leg.

Code for Types of Documents (with respect to form):

A - religious	H - combination
B - civil covenant	I - fundamentals
C - oath	J - ordinance
D - compact	K - patent
E - contract	L - charter
F - organic act	M - constitution
G - agreement	

Code for Foundation elements:

1 - creation of a people
2 - creation of a government
3 - provision of a self-definition
4 - creation or description of a specific form of government or set of political institutions

Source: Donald Lutz, *Documents of Political Foundation Written by Colonial Americans* (Philadelphia: ISHI Press, 1986).

2. The political covenant evolved rather quickly into the compact form.

3. The use of the compact form for documents of political foundation was a fundamental step in the development of popular sovereignty.

4. The secular "agreement" was a variant of the compact form.

5. The covenant and compact forms were used in such a way that they could contain any or all of the foundation elements.

6. With few exceptions, when the covenant or compact forms are used it is the people who are acting.

7. When the legislature acts it usually uses the ordinance form, of which the "fundamentals" form is a variant.

8. With few exceptions, the ordinance form is used primarily so as to include only the last two foundation elements.

9. The formal oath, when used by itself, contained the first and third foundation elements, and when embedded in a longer document such as a constitution, it contained only the third element.

10. Although present mainly in embryonic form at the beginning, the fourth foundation element becomes prominent in later documents.

11. While this fourth foundation element was prominent in the early state constitutions, the other three elements were often present also so that these documents in effect were using the compact form.

12. The third foundation element evolved into a form we now call a bill of rights.

13. In 53 instances the third and fourth elements are separated, i.e., one is found in a document without the other. In 28 instances they are found together in the same document. Thus, colonists were twice as likely to separate these two elements as combine them.

14. Number 13 led to some confusion as to whether state constitutions should include bills of rights. Some combined the third and fourth elements in the body of the document, many separated the two elements into two sections, calling only that section containing the fourth element the "constitution," and some did not contain a bill of rights at all.

15. The colonists were willing to let the legislatures speak for them in matters of foundation, except when forming themselves into a people and founding a government. The exception to the latter is found in those documents founding a federation of existing towns.

16. Number 15 leads to the natural expectation that legislatures could write state constitutions, although when these documents were in the compact form, and thus contained all four foundation elements, the expectation was that the people should also approve them. When the first two elements were not present, such popular ratification was not expected.[38]

As we can see from this list, American constitutionalism fits exactly into the covenantal mold and indeed represents the successful adaptation of that mold to modernity. In part this is because, as Lutz also points out, the American constitutional tradition is comprised of a weaving together of two strands, one initially composed of charters issued by the colonizing governments to their settlers in North America, which provided frames of governmental organization but that either required complementary local documents to be drafted by the colonists themselves or provided great room for the colonists to develop their own constitutional expressions within these charters. These charters were in general secular documents, and did not claim to have other than the most nominal religious basis if that. Some were charters of trading companies.

The other strand involved documents drafted and ratified by the colonists themselves—the covenants, combinations, compacts, and constitutions prepared on the ground, as it were, either within frameworks provided by the colonizing charters or even independent of them. These often were highly religious in their bases, although designed for civil purposes. Lutz attributes the basic form of the colonists' founding documents to the Bible, which was omnipresent in all of the colonies, not only New England. He suggests that what is common to these documents is that the operative word is "agreed," and that the agreement is made by everyone in the community, although drafted by representatives. It establishes a people set off from other people and it establishes a government for making the collective decisions required by the community with its form, institutions, and principles.

Moreover, the people is "a religious people who need leaders to keep them close to God" and a common moral code. The influence of the Protestant Reformation and, in particular, Reformed Protestantism is evident here. It should be recalled that the first of these American founding documents came either at the same time as or earlier than the parallel documents in England and Scotland that have been well noted in the history books. These civil documents grew out of and paralleled the many church covenants that established congregations of believers at the time and that did not serve civil purposes.

Both civil and church covenants emphasized such operative words as "bind" and "promise" in addition to "agree" and "covenant." As Lutz explains,

> In almost every significant detail the church covenants written in early colonial America resemble Jewish covenants, with one important exception—they do not

establish a specific form of government. When colonists found themselves in the position of having to create a government, therein to flesh out a government granted in the charter, they tended simply to add this element to the church covenant form and thereby completely recover the foundation elements in Jewish covenants. They did not do so consciously, perhaps, but the radical Protestant return to biblical sources for ordering their lives led to their becoming, to a far greater extent than they realized, precisely what they saw themselves as metaphorically—a modern version of the Jewish people.[39]

The Plymouth Combination (it was not known as the Mayflower Compact until 1793, when it was renamed in the language of the American Revolution) was the first such political covenant. In the document itself, it uses the terms "covenant and combine" (not compact). It is justly revered for what it is, the founding document of New England and much of American civil society, but it also represents the first step in the modern transformation of covenant into compact. In itself it can be viewed as both, especially when we understand that "combine" was the term generally associated with the compact form. Since not all who signed the document were identified Reformed Protestants, covenanting had to be supplemented by combining to bind them all. This, indeed, was the modern problem and project, combining active believers and others into civil bodies politic. This combination of covenant and compact was later to be featured in the Massachusetts Constitution of 1780, the classic American state constitution, still in effect in Massachusetts and probably the oldest continuing written constitution of government of the modern world.

The first true constitution written by Americans that included a detailed description of governmental institutions and their operating principles came to be known as the Pilgrim Code of Law, written by the people of Plymouth Colony in 1636. It was adopted along with the Plymouth Agreement, enacted by the colony the same day and inserted as a preface to the Code of Law, giving it all four foundation elements that Lutz has identified. While the compact dimension was given more emphasis in this document than the covenant dimension, both were still intertwined.

Lutz indicates that the oldest pure compact in American political history that is also complete as a foundation document is the Piscataqua Combination adopted in 1641. Nevertheless, the combination of the two forms persisted. Only occasionally were the colonists willing to put their trust entirely in popular sovereignty. Most of the time they wanted God to be at least a witness to their founding documents. Thus the colonial Americans wrote founding documents that were constitutional and that evolved into constitutions, but they did not use the term "constitution" (although they did periodically use the term "constitute"). These were combinations, agreements, fundamentals, frames, covenants, or the like. Lutz provides definitions of all the terms used and where and how they were used.[40]

The documents themselves indicate the order of progression of terminological development. By the time of the American Revolution the term "constitution" had become the accepted one. The term grew directly out of the covenantal tradition and covenantal language to become one of the great political transformations of the modern epoch and one of the foundations of the modern project.

The American polities began as commonwealths. Four of the American states—Massachusetts, Pennsylvania, Virginia, and Kentucky—officially still are. Three of those are among the original thirteen. Not only that; each is the mother state of its section—in the case of Virginia and Massachusetts, historically as well as constitutionally, and in the case of Pennsylvania, constitutionally only, while Kentucky broke off from its mother commonwealth, Virginia, to become the first western state admitted to the new American union after the adoption of the Constitution of 1787.

Most American states were either founded as civil societies or transformed from embryonic commonwealths to civil societies (as were the four whose names still reflect the old usage). That transformation is marked by their constitutional documents, which can be used as tracers to identify these developments. Thus the American colonies-cum-states culminating in the United States of America made a priceless contribution to the development of modern government and civil society. This contribution was an outgrowth of the covenantal tradition in both of its strands. Even where American political philosophers drew upon noncovenantal sources, they did so either to give a different and more secular justification of covenantal ideas or to buttress a basically covenantal approach at certain points, not from outside of that covenantal framework. Indeed, those they drew upon most frequently, the English political philosophers of the seventeenth century and the political philosophers of the Scottish Enlightenment of the eighteenth, themselves came from covenantal traditions and used those traditions either directly or indirectly in the development of their political philosophies.

This was a new sense of what constituted a constitution. The ancients also knew about constitutions but they saw them as more comprehensive, not simply or predominantly covenants, bills of rights, and frames of government, but involving specified moral foundations and socioeconomic distributions of power as well. The ancient constitutions paid great attention to the family and to inheritance from one generation to the next as the principal foundations of their constitutions. We see strong echoes of that in the early seventeenth century documents before the North American colonists stepped out onto the new road of modern constitutionalism.

At the time of the American Revolution, constitutional treatment of such matters was generally reduced to a kind of irreducible minimum that was deemed to be indispensable for the public order. Thus, early in the Revolution, those American states that inherited them abolished primogeniture and entail in a bid to prevent the formation of a landed aristocracy in their states. Indeed, government continues to provide regulations for family living but changes them by statute as the people change their beliefs as to what is socially desirable, rather than vesting these regulations in the constitution itself.

In other words, as the distinction between public and private grew sharper in the modern world, personal and family matters were relegated to the private sphere and hence were removed from public constitutions. While this change was actually recognizable in the colonial documents, it became fully grounded in first the American and then the modern constitutional system only after the American Revolution. This was a radical change but it was nonetheless within the covenantal tradition, although we can argue about what it did to the essence of the original tradition.

The Covenant Idea and Liberty: A Summary Statement

The covenant principle has also served the cause of individual and social liberty. In its most basic meaning the right to contract implies the freedom of all the contracting parties. This is one reason why the Puritans, even though aspects of their regime in Massachusetts would be considered repressive by contemporary democratic standards, can be regarded as the fathers of American liberty. Their application of the daring biblical idea that people are free enough to make pacts with God became one of the bases for all people's claims to liberty in relation to one another.

Following the Hebrew Scriptures (which they knew as the Old Testament), the Puritan's federal theology held that God voluntarily limited Himself by endowing humans with sufficient freedom to be linked with

Him through a covenant. The terms of God's covenant were clear. People were free to live according to those terms, but could expect punishments if they did not, just as they could expect rewards if they did.[41] What is important is that the freedom to act was endowed them by their Creator, and once that freedom was in their hands, the Puritans could and did argue that people need not be subject to any of their fellows, except by their own consent. Leader, Hobbes, Locke, Spinoza, and others of the same philosophic persuasion embraced this theme and redirected it into more secular channels.

Parallel to the theological and philosophic dimensions is the sociopolitical aspect of the covenantal founding of new societies. A principal, although not necessarily universal characteristic of new settlement is that it tends to promote equality.[42] People come together in a new place, away from the established civil order and must organize their own political life. The natural inclination is for them to do so on the basis of equality because of the equal risks involved. Moreover, they can only do so through some contractual means whereby each agrees to accept the jurisdiction of the whole, and is only likely to do so if each preserves those liberties deemed essential and acquires some share in the common decision-making processes. The further removed a new settlement is from older political orders, whether physically or in other ways, the more likely it is that this will be the model for its founding. Where previously existing political authority can be effectively extended over new territories, and older constitutional arrangements enforced, there is less room for the application of this model, although even in such cases the very fact of new settlement tends to bring some of its elements into play. Where the old order cannot be effectively extended, or where it actively encourages a contractual founding in the new territory, the model is more likely to be implemented in its fullness.

The cases of Switzerland and Sicily illustrate this point. The territories of what is today Switzerland were for many generations wildlands at the peripheries of the various royal, imperial, and feudal domains of Europe. People seeking to be free of autocratic rule fled to those wildlands where they organized themselves into civil communities with a minimum of outside interference. Hence theirs were communities of equals. When the Hapsburg emperors sought to impose their rule on those communities, the Swiss fought back, organizing to do so by applying the same federal principles to the confederation of communities that they had to earlier unions of families.[43]

In nineteenth-century Sicily, on the other hand, the settlement of the interior of the island took place at the initiative of local gentry who mobilized their peasants to establish plantations to empty land under the laws of the island. The founder-leaders of these efforts remained the leaders by predetermined right, with their tenants linked to them by contract. The lot of the latter was improved by virtue of those contracts which advanced their status but they were not equal partners in the new communities.[44]

Thus, the covenant idea has been important for the growth of democratic government. It presupposes the independence and worth of each individual and the truth that each person possesses certain inalienable rights, because only free people with rights can enter into agreements with one another. It also presupposes the necessity for government and the need to organize civil society on principles that assure the maintenance of those rights and the exercise of power in a cooperative or partnerlike way.

On the other hand, covenantal liberty is not simply the right to do as one pleases, within broad boundaries. Contractual liberty could be just that but covenantal liberty emphasizes the liberty to pursue the moral purposes for which the covenant was made. This latter kind of liberty requires that moral distinctions be drawn and that human actions be judged according to the terms of the covenant. This does not preclude changes in social norms but the principles of judgment remain constant. Consequently, covenantal societies, founded as they are on covenantal choice, tend to emphasize constitutional design and choice as a continuing process.

Notes

1. Abraham Lincoln, *Collected Works,* ed. Roy P. Basler (New Brunswick, NJ: Rutgers University Press, 1953–1955), vol. IV, p. 239.
2. John Winthrop, "A Modell of Christian Charity," *The American Puritans,* ed. Perry Miller (Garden City, NY: Doubleday, 1956).
3. Lyndon Baines Johnson, *A Time for Action* (New York: Pocket Books, 1964.
4. On the Pilgrims, see Francis Dillon, *A Place for Habitation: the Pilgrim Fathers and their Quest* (London: Hutchinson, 1973), and John Abbot Goodwin, *The Pilgrim Republic* (Boston: Houghton, Mifflin, 1895).
5. Henry Steele Commager, *The Empire of Reason: How Europe Imagined and America Realized the Enlightenment* (Garden City, NY: Doubleday, 1978).
6. Richard Niebuhr, "The Idea of Covenant and American Democracy," *Church History* 23 (June, 1954), p. 129.
7. Donald Lutz, *Documents of Political Foundation Written by Colonial Americans* (Philadelphia, PA: ISHI Press, 1986).
8. John Quincy Adams *The Writings of John Quincy Adams, 1767–1848* (New York: Greenwood Press, 1968).

9. John Peacock, *Covenant, Body Politic and the Great Migration* (Philadelphia, PA: Center for the Study of Federalism, 1980), deals with this very directly in connection with the founding of the Massachusetts Bay Colony.

10. Peacock, ibid., pp. 4–5.

11. Michael Walzer, *The Revolution of the Saints: A Study of the Origins of Radical Politics* (Cambridge, MA: Harvard University Press, 1965), p. 176.

12. John Peacock, *Covenant in John Winthrop's "A Model of Christian Charity."* Paper presented to the Covenant Workshop of the Center for the Study of Federalism, Temple University, Philadelphia, February 1980, p. 1.

13. Peacock, ibid., p. 16.

14. John Winthrop, "A Modell of Christian Charity."

15. Winthrop Papers, (Boston: Massachusetts Historical Society, 1929–1944), vol. 2, pp. 294–95.

16. Ibid., pp. 289–90.

17. Ibid., p. 291.

18. Edmond S. Morgan, *Puritan Political Ideas, 1558–1794* (New York: Bobbs-Merrill, 1965), p. xx.

19. Henry Maine, *Ancient Law* (London: Dent, 1965).

20. Peacock, "Covenant in John Winthrop's 'A Model,' p. 31- which?

21. Winthrop Papers, p. 294.

22. On Puritan ideas, see Donald Lutz, *From Covenant to Constitution in American Political Thought* (Philadelphia: Center for the Study of Federalism, Temple University, 1980) and Perry Miller, *Orthodoxy in Massachusetts, 1630–1650* (New York: Harper and Row, 1970); Donald Lutz and Charles Hyneman, eds. *American Political Writing During the Founding Era 1760–1805* (Indianapolis, IN: Liberty Press, 1983).

23. On Puritan government, see Ralph Barton Perry, *Puritanism and Democracy* (New York: Vanguard Press, 1944); Virginia Anderson, *New England's Generation* (Cambridge: Cambridge University Press, 1993).

24. Lutz, *Documents.*

25. Lutz, *Documents.*

26. *The Records of the Federal Convention of 1787,* vol. 3, ed. Max Farrand (New Haven, CT: Yale University Press, 1963).

27. E.H. Vreen, "English Origins and New World Development: The Case of the Covenanted Militia in Seventeenth Century Massachusetts," *Past and Present*, no. 27 (1972):74–96.

28. Henry M. Ward, *The United Colonies of New England 1643–90* (New York: Vintage Press, 1961).

29. Lutz, *Documents.*

30. See Daniel J. Elazar, *The American Constitutional Tradition* (Lincoln: University of Nebraska Press, 1988).

31. Andrew McLaughlin, *The Foundations of American Constitutionalism* (Greenwich, CT: Fawcett Publications, 1961).

32. William James, *A Pluralistic Universe* (London: Longmans Green and Co., 1909); Harry Levinson, "William James and the Federal Republican Principle," *Federalism as Grand Design, Publius,* vol. 9, no. 4 (Fall 1979).

33. Robert MacIver, *The Web of Government* (New York: The Free Press, 1966); Corrine Gelb, *Hidden Hierarchies* (New York: Harper and Row, 1966).

34. Donald Lutz, *The Origins of American Constitutionalism* (Baton Rouge: Louisiana State University Press, 1988).

35. Frederick Jackson Turner, "The Significance of the Frontier in American History," *The Frontier in American History* (New York: Henry Holt and Co., 1953).
36. Perry Miller, *Errand into the Wilderness* (New York: Harper and Row, 1956).
37. Donald S. Lutz, ed. *Documents of Political Foundation Written by Colonial Americans from Covenant to Constitution* (Philadelphia: Institute for the Study of Human Issues, 1986); Donald S. Lutz, "From Covenant to Constitution," in *Covenant, Polity, and Constitutionalism*, Daniel J. Elazar and John Kincaid, eds. (Lanham MD: Center for the Study of Federalism and University Press of America, 1986); and Donald S. Lutz and Jack D. Warden, *A Covenanted People: The Religious Tradition and the Origins of American Constitutionalism* (Providence: The John Carter Brown Library, 1987). Through these two works Lutz explores the connections between covenant and constitution in the American historical experience.
38. Lutz, Documents, pp. 23–24.
39. Ibid., pp. 9–21.
40. Lutz, *From Covenant to Constitution*.
41. Sacvan Bercovitch, *The American Jeremiad* (Madison: University of Wisconsin Press, 1978).
42. The classic exposition of this thesis is that of Frederick Jackson Turner in *The Frontier in American History*.
43. Benjamin R. Barber, *The Death of Communal Liberty* (Princeton, NJ: Princeton University Press, 1974).
44. Fillipo Sabetti, *Political Authority in a Sicilian Village* (New Brunswick, NJ: Rutgers University Press, 1984).

2

The Revolution and the
Declaration of Independence

The Revolutionary era required a new round of covenanting as the colonies reconstituted themselves as independent civil societies. Invariably they followed the customary patterns, albeit in the new secularized forms of declarations of rights and of (or in) constitutions. Thus, according to the Virginia Bill of Rights (1776):

> All men are by nature equally free and independent, and have certain inherent rights, of which, when they enter into a state of society, they cannot by any compact deprive or divest their posterity, namely, the enjoyment of life and liberty, with the means of property, and pursuing and obtaining happiness and safety.

The Vermont Declaration of Independence of 1777 holds that:

> We...the inhabitants [of the New Hampshire Grants] are at present without law or government, and may be truly said to be in a state of nature; consequently, a right remains to the people of said Grants to form a government best suited to secure their property, well being and happiness.

All followed the dictum from Leviticus inscribed on the Liberty Bell, rung for the reading of the Declaration of Independence: "Proclaim liberty throughout the land and to all the inhabitants thereof."

These Revolutionary era documents reflect the influence of the new political science that had become prominent by this time. They also reflect the increasing secularization of covenant that had begun to occur after 1690 along with the Puritan decline in Europe and America. By 1776, the word *covenant* had been largely, though not entirely, superseded in political affairs by the words *compact* and *constitution*. It was during this period, for example, that the Plymouth Combination became known as the Mayflower Compact.[1]

As the original Christian and communitarian solidarity associated with the idea of covenant (i.e., both kinship and consent) became more elusive in the face of growing populations, new generations, and rising manufacturing, the old Puritan communities dissolved into more commercial and contractual ones. Consequently, in a movement paralleled in the new political science, there tended to be a greater division of secular and religious affairs, with the formal language of covenant being more confined to the religious sector and the secularized language of constitutionalism becoming more prominent in public sector affairs. In short, the emphasis shifted from communitarianism toward individualism—a movement capped by the disestablishment of state churches in all but the most religiously covenantal states during the immediate revolutionary era. The shift was not complete, of course, and tensions between these conceptions of civil society have persisted throughout American history.

Some of these tensions are also reflected in the Declaration of Independence, the founding covenant of the American people, bound by a shared moral vision as well as common interests. The Declaration of Independence is the most thorough and concise statement of the underlying political and social philosophy of the American people.[2] Whatever Jefferson's and Congress's indebtedness to Locke, which is a subject of much debate, the concept and intention of the Declaration is more covenantal than compactual in the American context. As Jefferson remarked nearly fifty years later: "Neither aiming at originality of principles or sentiments nor yet copied from any particular and previous writing, it was intended to be an expression of the American Mind."[3]

Abraham Lincoln—perhaps the most important political thinker Americans have produced as well as the archetypal American hero—repeatedly affirmed that all of his political principles were drawn from the Declaration which, for him, was at one and the same time a noble accomplishment, a great promise, and a demanding set of goals.[4]

The Declaration stands where it does within the American political tradition because it is the covenant that transformed the disparate colonists into an organized people, the American people. With all the many worthwhile words that have been written or spoken about the Declaration, this has not been made as explicit as it should be. Early orators who spoke in praise of the Declaration, living as they did within a recognized covenant tradition, needed only to treat the covenantal character of the document through use of the appropriately resonating phrases. Even Lincoln, who already had to call attention to the centrality of the Declaration as a cornerstone of American political principles, could benefit from those shared resonances.[5]

Today the resonances are lost on many Americans because the awareness of the covenantal tradition has been lost. Yet the tradition itself persists in more ways than is often recognized. Thus a recovery of the Declaration of Independence as covenant is important for restoring that awareness.

As in England earlier but with its own twist, the operative political ideas of American society by the Revolution had moved from Puritan to Whig. The term itself is from Whiggamore, an appellation for the Scottish covenanters. Whiggism did not have an active theological base but was simply a set of political doctrines derived from the covenantal tradition and first given expression in the English Glorious Revolution of 1688–89, which brought together a synthesis of the English political tradition and the revolutionary politics of Civil War Puritanism. Because of its close relationship to Puritan political ideas, Whiggism became the dominant political doctrine of England and later Britain for 100 years. Initially, the basic party political conflict there was between court and country Whigs, not between Whigs and Tories.

In British North America, Whiggism also developed, American style, and can be seen to have been the dominant set of political ideas at the time of the American Revolution, anchored in the search for a republicanism of virtue rather than simply a republicanism of interest. The Tories, monarchists and loyalists to Britain, generally were expelled from the new United States during the Revolutionary War to become, inter alia, the founders of English Canada. At the end of the war when an opposition to Whiggism emerged, it was a republican opposition in the form of the Federalists, who were to propose a republicanism based on a recognition of interests rather than anchored in a search for civic virtue.

While the Declaration of Independence can be seen as transcending that embryonic division, it can also be seen as an American Whig document, emphasizing republican virtue, just as the revolutionary era state constitutions were Whiggish while the federal Constitution of 1787 focused on harnessing interests to safeguard republican government. There is little resemblance between the Declaration and the Hobbesian compact. While many of the fundamental principles and basic ideas of Hobbes in regard to human nature and natural right are present, the Declaration is prudent but not pessimistic about the possibilities of human self-government, hence it rejects the idea of the absolute sovereign of a leviathan state required by the Hobbesian compact. At the same time, the Declaration is more comprehensive than the Lockean compact and even drops the word "property," which is so essential to Locke's system, in favor of "the pursuit of happiness." Since the Declaration is the statement of a people that has already emerged from the state of nature, it does not use that starting point. In that sense, it is presented as a revision of an earlier compact and appeals to the Laws of Nature and of nature's god.[6]

The Declaration shares many of the characteristics of the classic biblical covenant at Sinai.[7] Central to this similarity is that the Declaration established the Americans as an organized people bound by a shared moral vision as well as common interests. The sense of an American identity, which had been emerging during the previous generation, was formalized and declared to the world much like the Sinai covenant had formally established the people of Israel, whose sense of shared identity and common destiny had emerged earlier but was concretized during the Exodus. Thus, the opening paragraph of the Declaration asserts that Americans are no longer transplanted Englishmen, but a separate people entitled, like all peoples, to political independence. There is, then, a separation of one people from another and a flight from tyranny. The Americans, moreover, are held to be a single people made up of individuals bound in partnership in a common enterprise.

Also like the Decalogue, the centerpiece of the Sinai covenant, the Declaration is not a constitution. It does not establish a particular form of government. That is left open to subsequent constitutional action on the part of the people announced by the Declaration.

Instead, the Declaration sets forth the fundamental principles that define the character of the American people, their basic purposes, and the nature of good government for such a people. Perhaps this is why Abraham Lincoln appealed so often to the Declaration during the Civil War. The Constitution had already been torn asunder by a bloody war between the states that threatened to destroy the American people as well. While constitutional matters could be dealt with in due time, there was the more fundamental promise of peoplehood contained in the Declaration of Independence that had to be reaffirmed and renewed throughout the land. This promise has the character of being perpetual and irrevocable. As Lincoln said in several of his addresses, one part of the people cannot divorce the other part. Lincoln argued that the American people cannot separate unless they go away from each other, not while they remain neighbors, occupying adjacent territories.

While the Declaration does not formally have the force of law in the American system, it is part of the higher law background of the United States Constitution and serves as the standard against which particular constitutions are to be judged by Americans. As such, like a biblical covenant, the Declaration invokes God as both a witness and guarantor. This sets it apart from a simple compact. Richard Niebuhr's description of this dimension as understood by early Americans seems to capture the essential thrust of the Declaration.

> Covenant meant that political society was neither purely natural nor merely contractual, based on common interest. Covenant was the binding together in one body politic of persons who assumed through unlimited promise responsibility to and for each other and for the common laws, under God. It was government of the people, for the people and by the people but always under God, and it was not natural birth into natural society that made one a complete member of the people but always the moral act of taking upon oneself, through promise, the responsibilities of a citizenship that bound itself in the very act of exercising its freedom. For in the covenant conception the essence of freedom does not lie in the liberty of choice among goods, but in the ability to commit oneself for the future to a cause and in the terrible liberty of being able to become a breaker of the promise, a traitor to the cause.[8]

There is an additional reason why the Declaration of Independence, on its surface a secular document with a modern name, that has long been seen as primarily "Lockean," needs to be understood as a covenant, and that lies in the circumstances of the American Revolution. The difference lies in a connection generally ignored by professional historians until the historical writing of the past thirty years, namely, the connection between the American Revolution and the Great Awakening, the great religious revival that took place in the American colonies between approximately 1730 and 1750. The first great American revival was led by Jonathan Edwards, the last great Puritan divine, who also may be considered the greatest American philosopher of the colonial period as well as a compelling religious leader.

Edwards in the Great Awakening was instrumental in detaching Americans from all parts of their country from religious loyalties in England and giving them a new sense of Americanness in that most fundamental of all concerns. More than that, Edwards was concerned with harmonizing the Puritan religion that he inherited with the new ideas of modernity. Edwards was a son of Connecticut, a state always on the cutting edge of American religious and political thought. He was educated there at Yale University. He served as the minister of a Presbyterian church in New York and then as assistant to his grandfather in a Congregational church in Northampton, Massachusetts. Just before he died he was appointed president of the College of New Jersey, now Princeton, a school under Presbyterian auspices.

Just as Edwards was a Puritan among Puritans, so, too, he foreshadowed the later alliance between the Congregationalists and Presbyterians in the effort to conquer the rest of the country outside of New England, which reached its apogee early in the nineteenth century. While recognized in the public eye as the preeminent revivalist, indeed, the reputed inventor of revivalism in America, he was a systematic theologian and philosopher whose revivalism was grounded in a very clear sense of what was both Christian and human, and their relationship. In recent years it has been argued that the itinerant preaching and sermonizing that came out of the Great Awakening laid the basis for intercolonial communication, the roots of the Revolution, and a common American intellectual understanding of the world around them.[9]

Thus religious reform preceded political reform and paved the way for it. Nor was this surprising. In the earlier cases discussed in this series the same has been true, going back at least to the time of Abraham. This was the case with the Israelite exodus from Egypt, with the seventh century BCE Josianic reform when King Josiah of Judah restored the Book of Deuteronomy to the active Israelite canon and then led (and was killed in) an abortive revolt for political independence against the Assyrians. So, too, did the Protestant Reformation lead from a religious to political reforms in the sixteenth and seventeenth centuries, culminating in the English Civil War. The eighteenth-century American Revolution continued in that tradition.

Since earliest times, covenants have followed a formula that has been passed down from generation to generation and epoch to epoch essentially unchanged. This form has been described by students of ancient Near Eastern history as containing the following elements:[10]

1. A preamble indicating the parties to the covenant;
2. A prologue, historical or ideological, establishing the setting or grounding of the covenant;

3. The operative section of the covenant, as stipulations, or what is agreed;
4. Provisions for public reading (proclamation) and deposit of the text for safekeeping;
5. The divine witness to the covenant; and
6. The advantages of performance (blessings) and sanctions for nonperformance (curses).

The Declaration substantially follows the classical covenant formulary. First, there is a statement of who is doing the covenanting, namely, "the Representatives of the United States of America, in General Congress assembled," July 4, 1776. Second, there is a prologue and historical section detailing the prior relationships of England and the American colonies. These establish the setting for the Declaration and give reasons for its preparation. Third, there is a set of stipulations and obligations containing the basic agreements of the American people. These begin as a statement of self-evident truths. Fourth, there is a provision for its public proclamation to mankind (copies were to be sent to Parliament and distributed throughout the newly independent states). While, of course, there are no provisions for depositing the Declaration in a temple, it was eventually enshrined in the nation's capital and even earlier elevated to a hallowed position. During the nineteenth century, moreover, the Declaration was given annual public readings on the Fourth of July in many communities, events that had echoes of covenant renewal ceremonies which often are a feature of covenantal communities. Fifth, there is an invocation of a Divine witness, namely, "the Supreme Judge of the world" and "Divine Providence." Sixth, there are indirect statements of blessings and curses. The blessings for performance are national independence and individual life, liberty, and pursuit of happiness. The curses for nonperformance are tyranny, oppression, and even death.

What follows is an explication of the Declaration as a covenant, including an examination of the meaning of its terms and phrases in light of its covenantal purpose. It is instructive not only as an explication of the founding principles of the United States but as a statement of the fundamental principles of modern political political thought.

1. The preamble, or statement of who is doing the covenanting:

In congress, July 4, 1776, by the Representatives of the United States of America, in General Congress assembled.

1. The heading of the Declaration affirms the democratic manner in which the covenant was made by announcing that the document is the product of a "congress" or coming together of "representatives" of the people living in the thirteen former colonies. In American parlance, the word "congress" refers to an assembly of delegates. The fact that this congress is composed of delegates representing the people not only of the individual states but of the now-United States is the source and basis of their authority to act in this case. Indeed, a major element in the covenant is the identification of who is doing the covenanting, that the representatives were assembled as "Representatives of the United States," already acting in the name of the new nation as a whole.

2. The heading also contains one of the first uses of the term, "the United States of America." It affirms that the thirteen states declared their independence as a united body, but one united on a federal basis of a still unspecified kind. This is significant for the future argument over the true character of the federal union. The parties to this covenant, then, are the people of the United States of America assembled from and by their states.

2. A prologue to establish the setting or grounding of the covenant:

> *When in the Course of human events, it becomes necessary for one people to dissolve the political bands which have connected them with another, and to assume among the powers of the earth, the separate and equal station to which the Laws of Nature and of Nature's God entitle them.*

By emphasizing its connection with the course of history and the laws of nature, the Declaration claims to speak about matters of universal import, not simply the parochial issue of the independence of one (then still) small and distant people. This has been the American claim from the first, that its covenant and history have universal meaning, within the select company of world-shaping covenants and covenant peoples.

1. The writing style of Jefferson's day differed from that of today and capitalization of words often was used for emphasis. The capitalization of "Course" may imply a sense that history is progressive, that it moves along a course toward human betterment. This view of history was especially strong in the eighteenth century, and had its roots in the biblical concept of time. Many ancient societies viewed time, and hence history, as being (a) cyclical—as involving an eternal return to beginnings—and

(b) largely outside of human control—in the hands of the fates. The Bible views history as being (a) generally progressive under God, having a beginning (creation) and an end (the messianic era and the end of days), and (b) subject to significant human control in the partnership with God established by the covenant between them.

Indeed, the very idea of "revolution" depends upon the belief that people can improve their lot by making their own history. By the eighteenth century, this view of history had become secularized and closely associated with the modern idea of "progress"—the belief that the growth of science and knowledge, along with the spread of education, would foster the rational enlightenment and moral excellence necessary to create and maintain good societies but it also remained rooted in Biblical religion, its original source. Both combined to influence the Americans in their revolution.

2. In this opening paragraph, Congress declares that the Americans are no longer transplanted Englishmen (or Britons), but a separate *people* entitled, like all peoples, to political independence if they so choose. The idea that mankind is divided into "peoples," who are not simply congeries of individuals who happen to inhabit particular segments of the globe, is the basis for nationalism, organic or covenantal. The idea of nationalism goes back at least 3,200 years when the first nation-states—Israel, Ammon, Moab and Edom—emerged on the world scene, but it became dominant in shaping political life only in the modern epoch, beginning in the seventeenth century.

While the American founders prided themselves on their commitment to individual choice and claimed that people have a natural right to choose or consent to their national identity, rather than simply remaining bound to the nation of their birth, it is obvious from this passage that they saw the human race as being naturally and appropriately divided into "peoples" who were the building blocks of the international order, such as it was, and who thereby had rights as peoples, including what was a century and a half later defined by Woodrow Wilson as the right of self-determination. The covenant or compact was the vehicle for choosing and consenting to be a people and, hence, an important element in achieving self-determination.

3. The Declaration declares that Americans are a *single* "people" (see also *Federalist*, no. 2). A people is referred to in the Declaration as "they" or "them." At the time, this was the common grammatical usage in connection with plural nouns, but it went out of style in the United

States at about the end of the nineteenth century (It remains the norm in Great Britain to this day.) The present-day substitution of "it" for "they" represents a loss of nuance in the sense that a "people" is now reified, made to seem as if "it" were a monolithic whole having a life apart from the human beings who compose it. The form "they" conveys a clear sense of a people as a compound of many unique individuals and groups. In this sense, the plural usage is federal or covenantal in character, reflecting the establishment of unity through union, a compound, rather than through amalgamation.

4. According to the Declaration, "peoples" and "nations" are equal under the laws of Nature and God, but with the implicit caveat that, in fact, they are equal only when they can exercise the "powers" to which they are entitled. The "Laws of Nature," then, extend to peoples and recognize power as natural. Like other natural forces, power must be brought under control to be exercised properly or safely and, especially, to be exercised well—another purpose of covenanting.

5. The use of the dual phrase, "the Laws of Nature and of Nature's God," reflects an attempt to strike a balance between the secular (or what was then called the Deistic) belief in a self-regulated universe operating according to its own laws, and the more traditional religious belief in God as the governor of the universe. In line with the eighteenth century's emphasis on *reason* rather than *faith* or *revelation* as the proper basis of human knowledge, the Declaration appeals to both reason and faith—in that order.

a decent respect to the opinions of mankind requires that they should declare the causes which impel them to the separation.

1. Aside from the tactical utility of proclaiming to the world—enemies and potential allies, alike—that the Americans were serious, this phrase reflects the founders' commitment to the "new political science" as derived *inter alia* from Hobbes, Locke, Harrington, and Montesquieu. This new political science held, among other things, that legitimate political authority achieved at least partial validation through "the opinions of mankind" which, in turn, deserved "decent respect." Such opining is a step removed from consent but falls within the consensual model of political organization and behavior.

2. As used in the Declaration, "opinion" means *opining* or considered thought, not the kind of instant, off-the-cuff reaction gathered in today's

so-called "public opinion" polls. The difference is crucial. Belief in the human capacity for self-government rests to no little extent on the ability of individuals to respond to issues on the basis of careful and considered reflection, not on the basis of heated passions or momentary impulses. In fact, even after forming an opinion, a person can have second thoughts. The ability to have second thoughts is one of the most important of human qualities. (To an extent, the bicameral legislature which became a feature of American politics is a means of institutionalizing the possibility of second thoughts in a polity.) The founders believed that people are, by nature, capable of listening to reason and of formulating rational opinions. Hence, they can be parties to a covenant or, if not parties, witnesses, and their considered opinions deserve a "decent respect." As witnessed, their opinions can be used, to a degree, to validate the actions of other humans.

3. Underlying this idea of opinion is the even deeper belief that through reason and observation people are capable of discovering true knowledge about the proper forms of government and human conduct, and that, therefore, it is possible to make rational distinctions between good and bad, just and unjust governments. It is in this respect that the founders viewed political knowledge as political science.[11]

Present-day positivism holds that such knowledge is impossible because goodness and justice are merely expressions of individual or group "value" preferences which are based not on objective reason, but on subjective passion and self-interest. Therefore, goodness and justice are simply relative "values" that have different but equally valid meanings among different individuals and societies at different times. We can conduct a public opinion poll to learn what people believe is good or bad, but we cannot know what *is* good or bad. According to this view, then, the founders were motivated by their personal preferences about the good which were based not on any real knowledge of the good, but on passion and self-interest. Hence, the Declaration of Independence is little more than a high-sounding rationalization of their selfish interests.

Yet, if all values are relative, then for example it is ultimately impossible to say anything good or bad about slavery or Adolf Hitler. It is only possible to say that one likes or dislikes Hitler in the same way that one likes or dislikes corn flakes for breakfast. To the founders, this view would have cut against the grain of reason and common sense. The choice between democracy and Nazism is not a choice between Cheerios or

Rice Krispies, but a choice between justice or injustice indeed, life or death. Like all proper covenants, the Declaration is a covenant of life, that is to say it is designed to transform mere life into the good life. What follows defines the basis for the good life reflected in the Declaration.

3. Stipulations and operative elements

We hold these truths to be self-evident, that all men are created equal, that they were endowed by their Creator with certain inalienable Rights, that among these are Life, Liberty and the pursuit of Happiness.

Here, in the few succinct words of the Declaration's most famous phrase, the whole foundation of American political life is sketched out. That foundation is rooted in certain fundamental "truths" which are taken to be "self-evident," that is, axiomatic and immediately accessible to reason and common sense in a manner not unlike the way in which phenomena of nature are immediately accessible to sight and touch. The founders held that these self-evident truths are grounded in reason and experience—especially human experience rightly understood—which allow us to say that these truths are more worthy of our attention than others.

1. The problematic phrase "all men are created equal" has been both a keystone of American political life as well as a major bone of contention. The idea of equality has become a potent force in modern life. The Declaration's position rests, in part, on the Judeo-Christian view that all people are equal before God and, in part, on the teachings of the new political science which argued that all people are equal because they share the same basic nature. Equality is basic to covenantal systems because only equals (at least in the sense of equal for certain purposes) are capable of entering into covenants with one another.

Of course, at the time of the writing of the Declaration, certain people such as slaves were not treated as "equals," even though many of the American founders had broad visions of equality. Jefferson had included an attack on slavery in the first draft of the Declaration, but it was removed at the insistence of Southern delegates, who refused to approve the Declaration in that form.[12]

What is important is that the idea of equality is, nevertheless, stated so broadly and forcefully in the opening of the Declaration, thereby placing it at the center of the revolutionary enterprise and forcing Americans to come to terms with it. As such, it not only makes the covenant possible but stands as a goal toward which American political life ought to be moving, as a standard against which the conduct of that political life can be judged, and as a voice of reason or thorn in the side for those who cling to unenlightened opinions about inequality. Hence, since 1776 the concept has undergone considerable expansion, both in terms of incorporating more and more people within its scope, and in terms of emphasizing more and more ways in which people ought to be equal, or at least more equal.

2. Equality stands as the first self-evident truth, thereby suggesting that equality is a necessary, though not sufficient, condition for the preservation of life, liberty, and the pursuit of happiness. It is not sufficient because people can be equal in the way, for example, that slaves and prisoners can be equal to each other. But it is necessary for liberty because without equality some people would be said to have a natural or legitimate authority to rule others in the way that monarchs asserted a natural or God-given right to rule subjects and that slaveowners claimed a natural right to control slaves because of their alleged inferiority. Hence, if all people are equal, then each person has a rightful claim to self-determination and is under no prior natural or divine obligation to obey any other person without first giving his or her consent. Because this is the essence, though not the whole, of liberty as Americans understand it, we can see why "equality" comes first in the Declaration.

3. The second of the great truths is that people have been "endowed by their Creator with certain inalienable Rights." This means that, just as one is born with two lungs and a heart, each person is also born possessing certain natural rights which belong to him or her by virtue of God's creation or nature's endowment. Therefore, these rights can be said to precede government. They are neither granted nor given by government and, most importantly, they cannot be taken away or surrendered. Indeed, it is the equality of possessing inalienable rights which is the justification for treating all people as politically equal in entering into a covenant and establishing a polity. The purpose of government is to guarantee those rights.

A government may, in fact, deny someone the exercise of his or her rights, just as one person may murder another, thereby destroying the right to life. But the Declaration's point about inalienable rights is that no one has any legitimate authority to do so, except under specific circumstances involving the maintenance of security anchored in law, and that no matter how much a person may be enslaved by another, the slave still retains his or her natural rights even while being unable to exercise them. In a sense, the arbitrary denial of a person's exercise of rights is a crime against nature. The firmness with which this idea of rights is held in the United States is reflected in the fact that there is hardly an American who has not, at one time or another, declared, often angrily: "I know my rights."

On the other hand, by entering into civil society, people consent to limit the exercise of their rights, even their inalienable rights, and to empower government to interfere with the exercise of individual rights for the common good. That is why government must be controlled by the governed, because it possesses the authority and power to interfere with the exercise of individual rights.

4. Life, of course, is the basic right. Protecting the right to life is a serious problem, especially in light of the brutal and casual ways in which individuals and governments throughout history have often treated it. For the founders, the purpose of government is to protect and enhance life, not to destroy it. Government does not have an inherent right to take life, although it may be—and usually is—empowered to do so under certain circumstances.

5. According to the Declaration, mere life is not enough. Humans are endowed with an inalienable right to a life of "liberty" or freedom. In a covenantal system, liberty is as necessary as equality since only free people can enter into covenants. Although liberty has been given many definitions, Americans have usually understood the kernel of liberty to include: a) freedom from arbitrary, external controls, restraints, interference and obligations, and b) freedom to exercise maximum control over one's own destiny.

However, this does not mean absolute liberty for everyone to "do his own thing," which would result in mass pandemonium and destruction. Rather, what is meant is a kind of "federal liberty," that is to say, not the liberty to do whatever one pleases but the liberty to act in accordance with the Constitution. Or, as James Wilson defined it:

> [There is a] kind of liberty which...I shall distinguish by the appellation of *federal liberty*.... When a confederate republic is instituted, the communities, of which it is composed, surrender to it a part of their *political* independence.... The states should resign to the national government, that part, and that part only, of their

political liberty, which placed in that government, which produce more good to the whole, than if it had remained in the several states. While they resign this part of their political liberty, they retain the *free and generous exercise* of all their other facilities, as states, so far as it is compatible with the welfare of the general and superintending confederacy. [My emphasis][13]

What Wilson describes as the liberty of the states within the United States can be applied to the liberty of individuals within civil society. Federal liberty is liberty based on covenant. As such it stands in contrast to natural liberty, the anarchic liberty of the jungle and the state of nature whose problematics lead humans into civil society in the first place. This, indeed, was a central distinction for the founders of the United States. Since we are required (or condemned) by nature to live with one another, it is necessary to restrict certain liberties in order to preserve liberty. This is the American or modern answer to the Maimonodean paradox that humans are the most sacred of all creatures yet have the most difficulty living in society.

The intention of the Declaration is to point us always in the direction of liberty by recognizing first, that the construction of good government must begin with the presumption of liberty and proceed from there. Therefore, government restrictions on individual liberty must be justified on rational grounds as being necessary for the greater preservation and enhancement of everyone's liberty. Finally, restrictions on liberty must be within the framework of the political compact and enacted by the people or their representatives.

6. The third inalienable right is "the pursuit of happiness." The meaning of this right for the founders is not entirely clear. Some have suggested that the founders understood this to mean the right of everyone to pursue, within the limits of everyone else's liberty, their own versions of happiness. Others, accepting the definition of freedom implicit in the above, have suggested that the founders believed there to be such a thing as true happiness but that it could only be discovered and attained through free pursuit. Still others see the phrase as applying to political happiness only.

...that to secure these rights, Governments are instituted among Men, deriving their just powers from the consent of the governed,

1. The attitude toward government expressed here is continuously positive. Government is treated as necessary and useful—a positive good designed to secure human rights. It is not just a necessary evil. At the

same time, the potential for evil in governments is recognized in the phrase "just powers," which implies that government, once in existence, can take power unjustly as well. Here, indeed, is the great political problem of humanity. People have inalienable rights on an equal basis, but since they are otherwise unequal in many respects, they can secure their rights only by banding together and creating a proper government based on a mutual agreement, a covenant or compact.

In other words, power is recognized as a reality. The only question is how to organize and harness it for the common good. A government, to function, must be able to exercise power, including the ultimate power of life and death. This leads to the possibility that government will abuse this power. If government does abuse its powers, it is no longer legitimate and can be rejected by the parties to the compact, hence the emphasis on "just powers."

2. The theory that government is instituted by covenant or compact was so widely acknowledged in revolutionary America that it could be presented in the sophisticated form that it is here, as "the consent of the governed." As we have seen, in the United States, governments were constituted and reconstituted through covenants and compacts from the first foundings of settlements in the seventeenth century. For Americans, then, the compact theory is much more than a convenient myth, it is a reflection of real experiences.

Furthermore, by "consent" the Declaration means consent that is both freely given and informed. Consent cannot legitimately be extracted by force. The Declaration also implies that consent is a continuing process. It is not a onetime act of the founders to be simply accepted by their descendants, but involves a continuing process of participation by which citizens constantly give or withhold their consent. This idea of consent, that "the people shall judge," is the heart of democracy. Although it is based, in part, on the idea that "the opinions of mankind" deserve "decent respect," a continuing problem for any democracy is that the people be able to judge well rather than poorly. Hence, the idea of consent also implies responsibility on the part of the citizen to be informed, and of the government to be informative rather than secretive.

That whenever any Form of Government becomes destructive of these ends, it is the Right of the People to alter or to abolish it and to institute new government, laying its foundation on such principles and organizing its power in such form, as to them shall seem most likely to effect their Safety and Happiness.

1. Here is the right to renegotiate the compact—to establish a new constitution—even through revolution. Revolution is not the preferred way, but it is certainly a legitimate way. Who can undertake the renegotiation (or revolution)? The "People" in the sense used at the beginning of the declaration; not dissatisfied individuals or groups (Individuals or groups may secede from particular civil societies by migrating—the way the migrants to America did from the countries of Europe, or, later, the emigrants to the West, many of whom, in essence, seceded from the class-ridden societies of the eastern states.)

Change cannot lead to the abolition of government, only to the replacement of one form (or system) with another (Form as used in the eighteenth century is roughly equivalent to the term *system* as it is used today. Both, in turn, are roughly equivalent to the ancients' use of the term *constitution*). The change can be radical—meaning that it can get to the root of the matter—since it can involve laying the foundation for the new form on new principles as well as organizing the powers of government in new forms.

2. The Declaration does not specify any best form of government. Every people must develop a form of government specifically suited to them. As long as the form chosen provides ways and means to secure the people's safety and allows them to pursue happiness in a manner fitting their needs, it is deemed suitable. The borrowing of one people's constitution by another is rarely, if ever, successful.

3. The measure of a good constitution or form is whether it is likely to provide a particular people with "Safety" and "Happiness." The former has to do with sheer security, the preservation of life and limb, while the latter is a matter of the quality of life. Government can do much to secure the former; it can only provide a proper climate for the latter.

Prudence, indeed, will dictate that Governments long established should not be changed for light and transient causes; and accordingly all experience hath shown, that mankind are more disposed to suffer, while evils are sufferable, than to right themselves by abolishing the forms to which they are accustomed.

Here the Declaration is double-edged. On the one hand, it makes a valid political observation that, as a matter of fact, people are prone to tolerate bad government rather than to act to change things. On the other hand, it suggests that this caution is a good idea for the sake of the peace and happiness of mankind. Note the use of the plural "they" in connection with "mankind."

> *But when a long train of abuses and usurpations, pursuing invariably the same Object, evinces a design to reduce them under absolute Despotism, it is their right, it is their duty, to throw off such Government, and to provide new Guard for their future security.*

Given the general desirability of caution before changing governmental forms, the Declaration then indicates under what conditions revolutions can legitimately be mounted and even must be. A "long train of abuses and usurpations" leading to "absolute Despotism" makes action necessary. That list is a justification of the American revolution in light of the above principles. As the Declaration states,

> In every stage of these Operations We have petitioned for Redress in the most humble terms: Our repeated Petitions have been answered only by repeated injury. A Prince, whose character is thus marked by every act which may define a Tyrant, is unfit to be the ruler of a free people.

> *For have We been wanting in attention to our British brethren. We have warned them from time to time of attempts by their legislature to extend an unwarrantable jurisdiction over us. We have reminded them of the circumstances of our emigration and settlement here. We have appealed to their native justice and magnanimity, and we have conjured them by the ties of our common kindred to disavow these usurpations, which, would inevitably interrupt our connections and correspondence. They too have been deaf to the voice of justice and of consanguinity. We must, therefore, acquiesce in the necessity, which denounces our Separation, and hold them, as we hold the rest of mankind, Enemies in War, in Peace Friends.*

The list of charges should be read for a better understanding of what Americans consider to be the principles and practices of good government rather than for their precise historical accuracy. In that respect, they represent a negative statement of the stipulations of the covenant. As part of the polemical purpose of the Declaration, it was necessary to attribute to the king many acts really initiated by Parliament. Moreover, some of the "grievances" were as much products of the interests of the dominant circles in America as the consequences of English imperial policy. What is important is that the list conveys a sense of what governments should and should not do. Eleven years later, the Constitution of the United States included provisions precisely designed to prevent many of the "abuses" and "usurpations" listed above.

The last paragraph, containing an oblique reference to the attempts by Parliament to legislate for the colonies, goes to the heart of the matter. Note how delicately the relationship between the two separate yet related peoples is portrayed in order to establish clearly the fact of separateness (which is a result of "the circumstances of our emigrant and settlement") as well as "common kindred."

4 and 5. Publication and divine witness:

We, THEREFORE, the REPRESENTATIVES of the UNITED STATES of AMERICA in General Congress, Assembled, appealing to the Supreme Judge of the world for the rectitude of our intentions, do in the Name, and by Authority of the good people of these Colonies are, Absolved from all Allegiance to the British Crown, and that all political connection between them and the State of Great Britain, is and ought to be totally dissolved;

The final paragraph begins by calling upon God to witness this act and its meaning and concludes by indicating the Americans' firm reliance on the protection of Divine Providence. While it does not specify how, Congress explicitly publishes and declares its actions. In fact, Congress provided elsewhere that the Declaration be read publicly in the square behind the Pennsylvania state house (today known respectively as Independence Square and Independence Hall) and throughout the newly independent United States. It concludes with:

6. Blessings and curses:

...and that as Free and Independent States, they have full Power to levy War, conclude Peace, contract Alliances, establish Commerce, and to do all other Acts and Things which Independent States may of right do. And for the support of this declaration, with a firm reliance on the protection of Divine Providence, we mutually pledge to each other our Lives, our Fortunes and our sacred Honor.

The blessings of freedom and independence, presented in some detail represent the advantages of performance while the sanctions are the risk of life and fortune and sacred honor.

The ambiguity of the final paragraph forms the basis for all subsequent arguments as to whether the United States declared their independence as a unit or simply declared together the independence of the separate states. Later interpretations of the character of the compacts creating the Union (which led to the Civil War) depended upon the different understandings of this paragraph. For practical purposes, the Supreme Court of the United States finally ruled in 1936 (*U.S. v. Curtiss-Wright Export Corp.*) that the United States declared its independence as a unit and that the states were from the first instance bound together as a single nation in matters of foreign affairs and defense.

Appropriately enough, the best explanation of this paragraph is that it summarizes a federal act leading to a federal result. What we have here is a tripartite covenant of people, *free and independent states*, and the *United States of America*, witnessed by God. The American people, their Union, and the States were born at the same moment, through the same act—and they were born free.

Once again we must look at the text in context. It was entirely customary for Congress to establish days of "publick humiliation, fasting and prayer" "to implore the Divine interposition."[14] Indeed, this attention of Congress and for that matter the presidency later on has continued, but it has become increasingly ritualistic as the country has grown less religious. This was not the case in the Revolutionary era when it was still believed that such acts might bring about a proper Divine response. These exercises were not merely petitions to place before Divine authority but they were in the tradition of the New England Jeremiads whereby the first step to securing Divine support was an acknowledgement of and repentence for collective sins.[15]

The United States, like very other country, has a sacred history, a mythic account of its origins and the origins of its people that conveys in it through truth and elaboration of truth in symbolic ways the norms and vision of the community and its polity. American sacred history frequently draws the analogy between the founding and settlement of the United States and the history of ancient Israel, striking several common themes: exodus, covenant, wilderness, opposition to corrupt foreign kings, Divine favor, human failure and repentence, and the necessity to cultivate moral virtue to preserve the benefits of Divine grace, particularly those of freedom. These themes were introduced into American history from the very first by the Puritans but they persisted long after Puritanism had given way to other expressions, the Puritan domain had been submerged into a larger and more heterogeneous American one, and Puritanism itself had undergone great transformations.

Perhaps to the surprise of those who in the twentieth century have been schooled in a different Jefferson, this sacred history was given classical formation by Thomas Jefferson a generation later, in 1805, in his second inaugural address:

> I shall need, too, the favor of that Being in whose hands we are, who led our fathers, as Israel of old, from their native land and planted them in a country flowing with all the necessaries and comforts of life; who has covered our infancy with His providence and our riper years with His wisdom and power.[16]

In this sacred history, British kings, particularly King George III, were compared with Pharaoh. Various American leaders, George Washington among them, were compared with Moses, and later Abraham Lincoln to Jesus based on the sacrifice that both made. Jefferson and others described America as "a chosen country," a promised land, and Americans as a people chosen by God with whom he made a covenant. These themes are continued throughout American history and can be traced through the inaugural addresses of American presidents.[17]

Because Americans are in covenant with God, covenantal unfaithfulness can and has led to calamity, a theme which appears in American sacred history as time goes on and the founding generation gives way to later ones. Lincoln perhaps manifested this idea most fully especially in the conclusion of his second inaugural address.[18]

Or take, for example, Lincoln's proclamation of a national fast day in 1863 (one of the several fast days he proclaimed during the war).

> We have been the recipients of the choicest bounties of Heaven. We have been preserved, these many years, in peace and prosperity. We have grown in numbers, wealth and power, as no other nation has ever grown. But we have forgotten God. We have forgotten the gracious hand which preserved us in peace, and multiplied and enriched and strengthened us; and we have vainly imagined, in the deceitfulness of our hearts, that all these blessings were produced by some superior wisdom and virtue of our own. Intoxicated with unbroken success, we have become too self-sufficient to feel the necessity of redeeming and preserving grace, too proud to pray to the God that made us.
>
> It behooves us then, to humble ourselves before the offended Power, to confess our national sins, and to pray for clemency and forgiveness.[19]

Public fasts, days of prayer and repentance were part and parcel of that sacred history through the Civil War. One of the first acts of the Continental Congress after the outbreak of fighting at Lexington and Concord was to proclaim "a day of publick humiliation, fasting, and prayer" to repent their sins and thereby enlist God on their side. This action, proclaimed on June 12, 1775, less than two months after the war began, set aside July 20 to beseech the great governor of the universe (God was no longer to be referred to as king) to intervene to bring redress the Americans' grievances. Perry Miller has claimed that by doing so Congress essentially extended the Puritan covenant that bound New England to the other colonies, making it a national covenant.[20]

Modern historians may treat the proclamation as an act not of faith but of mobilization and propaganda, but an examination of the events surrounding it and the forms of observance of July 20 in Virginia as much as in Massachusetts. (Thomas Jefferson, for example, described that July 20 in the following words, "The effect of the day through the whole colony was like a shock of electricity, arousing every man and placing him erect and solidly on his centre."[21])

Congress could do so because the federal theology was no stranger to the people of the other colonies. A version of it was clearly part of the Westminster Confession of the Presbyterians who dominated in New Jersey and Pennsylvania. Even the phraseology of Anglican sermons included the idea of covenant.[22] Baptists, north and south, from New England to Georgia, founded their congregational polities on church covenants. At least 50 percent of the churches in the American colonies at that time followed the federal theology regardless of their denomination.[23]

Thus, since the proclamation of days of public humiliation and repentence were common in all the colonies and especially in those churches that embraced the federal theology, the colonists, Anglican as well as Puritan, Baptist and Presbyterian, Congregationalist and Dutch Reformed and Huguenot, even had developed rituals for the day.[24] There are extant sermons from every colony and every denomination linking Christian piety and civil liberty through covenant and repentence in the spirit of the federal theology.[25]

Fasts of thanksgiving as well as repentence were proclaimed periodically throughout the war in times of victory and defeat. On December 11, 1783, just after the conclusion of the peace treaty with Great Britain that formally recognized American independence, Congress proclaimed a day of thanksgiving to celebrate the occassion. Preachers of that day fell into two groups, those who simply emphasized that earlier jeremiads had worked, that the people had humbled themselves and had been rewarded by Divine providence, and those who held that while the American people had been temporarily rewarded, that simply meant that they had the further responsibility of perpetuating their reformation.[26]

The bridge from Puritan covenant to civil compact in British North America was well built. The principles were all laid down in the first years of settlement of the British North American colonies, but they were fully intertwined with the religious dimensions and principles of covenant. As the latter lost some of their comprehensive and compelling power, the political principles took root in the soil of the New World and began to grow and flourish independently, retaining the religious framework but less dependent upon a particular religious doctrine other than the religious doctrine of federalism in general. In the eighteenth century prior to the Revolutionary generation, a systematic covenantal political thought emerged primarily in New England and primarily articulated by ministers who attempted to give form to the New England idea of the polity. Foremost among them were John Wise (1652–1725) and Jonathan Mayhew (1720–1766).[27]

The dissenters from all of this were a small minority, mostly Anglicans in the middle colonies. The paucity of their voices and the little attention given to them are revealing. Even these Anglicans couched their message in words that would fit in with the general climate. The major difference was that they exuded a kind of genial optimism and spent less time calling Americans to repent for their sins as a prerequisite for victory over the British. Similarly, the American voices that tended toward deism were generally silent. It took a Thomas Paine from England to preach a deistic message and he soon left the newly independent United States to go to France where he found a more appealing climate until he was imprisoned. While the Americans may have rejected his ideas, they did not imprison him for them, whereas the French revolutionaries, who appreciated his ideas, also saw him as a danger to the revolution and threw him in jail.

The American Revolution and the subsequent constitutions of the new federal republic were prepared and led by a coalition of moderate partisans of the Enlightenment and moderate partisans of the federal theology. The extremists on both sides were excluded from the arena for lack of support.[28] As Robert Licht has pointed out, moderate exponents of each position joined together on the basis of what they shared in common to write the federal Constitution of 1787, pushing extremists in both camps aside—both Thomas Paine who advocated the secularism of the Jacobin state and those who wanted to maintain state-established religion in the new republic. Part of their compromise was that the general government of the United States would be more attuned to the civil society idea while the state governments would develop the commonwealth model.

In linking reason and common sense with the Scriptural message, commentators of the time, particularly the pamphleteers and sermonizers, gave voice to this happy coalition.

The influence of the Bible was not only with regard to the spiritual message of the text, but also led the colonists to repeat and even reemphasize the role of America as the new Israel, following the ancient Jews and their covenant with God, to establish a similar, hopefully purified, federal republic in America within God's covenant.

While political sermons continued throughout the post-Revolutionary period, especially during the response to the writing of the Constitution of 1787, they did not return to a concern with political threats until the French Revolution which to most of the covenantal churches was frightening indeed. This fear became palpable when Jefferson, the architect of American liberalism and a strong supporter of the French Revolution from afar, was elected president. In sum, the American Revolution was preached to the public as a religious revival and that preaching succeeded in striking roots. The Revolution as religious revival was in many ways simply a continuation of the Great Awakening of the 1740s.

This overwhelming sense of national covenant began to dissolve after the government, under the new constitution, began to function. The new political parties soon became part and parcel, indeed, the mobilizing forces of the new political system and party programs and controversies came to dominate the stage in the place of national unity against a foreign foe. Calls for national days of humiliation and fasting became partisan matters and lost the universal pull that they once had.

There was a brief revival of the older spirit during the War of 1812 when President James Madison invoked the older litany, "the transgressions which might justly provoke the manifestations of His Divine displeasure" to unite the American people at the outset of the War of 1812, but that war, too, was in part a partisan matter. The New Englanders were heavily against it, to the point of calling a convention at Hartford to consider the secession of the New England states. There was no secession, but there was no national covenant either.

Subsequent nineteenth-century efforts were strictly partisan. Civil society had triumphed in the United States. The sense of the country as a homogeneous commonwealth ceased to exist as an effective force. While

Americans continued to be patriotic, many would say even inordinately so, and to believe in the American vision and the American way of life (two twentieth-century phrases), it was not the same.

It remained for the Southerners during the Civil War to adopt the jeremiad and the idea of the broken covenant as some tried to explain their movement toward defeat. Preachers elsewhere also continued to preach jeremiads. There were always those who called upon Americans in that spirit, but they were particularist and not universalist. It was not until the late 1960s that the publication of Robert Bellah's *The Broken Covenant* that the theme once again rose, sporadically, onto the national stage.[29]

Religiously, however, the covenantal system had long since been replaced by revivalism; not the revivalism of Jonathan Edwards in the Great Awakening embedded in the federal theology, but a new kind of evangelistic revivalism, highly individualistic, that laid the foundations for the exaggerated American individualism of later generations.

Jefferson's, Lincoln's, and other presidential statements of this nature can be looked upon as merely ritual, although even that, too, tells us much about what Americans saw as essential to their being. But this was not some mandated ritual but the choices of the men involved. Jefferson certainly had established his freethinking credentials sufficiently to play down such sentiments in his public utterances and Lincoln (also reputed to be a freethinker) was not required to proclaim fast days. In the twentieth century, beginning with Woodrow Wilson, this American vision was expanded to include the international arena. This sacred history, national myth or vision of the American people as a chosen people and the American experience as that of a city upon a hill could be and was drawn upon by all parties to justify emancipation or to justify slavery, to justify the Protestant republic or to insist upon religious pluralism, to promote liberal or conservative purposes. This does not mean that it was meaningless but that it set the framework for Americans' continuing dialogue about themselves and the world they live in.[30]

Notes

1. Donald Lutz, *Popular Consent and Popular Control: Whig Political Theory in the Early State Constitutions* (Baton Rouge: Louisiana State University Press, 1980).
2. Martin Diamond, "The Revolution of Sober Expectations," in *The American Revolution: Three Views*, Irving Kristol, ed. (New York: American Brands, Inc., 1975).

3. Carl Becker, *The Declaration of Independence: A Study in the History of Poliitcal Ideas* (New York: Harcourt, Brace, 1922).
4. Harry V. Jaffa, *Equality and Liberty: Theory and Practice in American Politics* (New York: Oxford University Press, 1965).
5. Daniel J. Elazar, "The Constitution, the Union, and the Liberties of the People," *Publius: The Journal of Federalism*, vol. 8, no. 3 (Summer 1978), p. 141–75.
6. Carl Becker, *The Declaration of Independence*; Elazar, *The American Constitutional Tradition*, ch. 4.
7. Neal Riemer, *Covenant and Constitution* (Philadelphia, PA: Center for the Study of Federalism, Temple University, 1980).
8. Richard Niebuhr, "The Idea of Covenant and American Democracy," *Church History* 23 (June 1954), p. 133.
9. See, in particular, William G. McLoughlin, *Revivals, Awakenings and Reform* (Chicago: University of Chicago Press, 1978); Bernard Bailyn, *Ideological Origins of the American Revolution* (Cambridge, MA: Belknap Press of Harvard University, 1967); Gordon Wood, *Creation of the American Republic* (New York: W.W. Norton and Co., 1969); Charles Hyneman and Donald Lutz, eds., *American Political Writing During the Founding Era* (Indianapolis, IN: Liberty Press, 1983); George E. Connor, "Covenants and Kings: Deuteronomy and the American Founding," unpublished manuscript, 1994.
10. Delbert R. Hillers, *Covenant: The History of a Biblical Idea* (Baltimore, MD: Johns Hopkins University Press, 1969).
11. Martin Diamond, "The Federalist's View of Federalism," *Essays on Federalism,* Benson, Diamond et al. ,eds. (Claremont, CA: Institute for Studies in Federalism, Claremont Men's College, 1961).
12. Winston M. Fisk and Herbert Garfinkel, eds., *The Democratic Republic* (Chicago: Rand McNally, 1966).
13. Steven R. Boyd, "Antifederalists and the Acceptance of the Constitution: Pennsylvania, 1787–1792," *Publius*, vol. 9, no. 2 (Spring 1979).
14. Perry Miller, *Nature's Nation* (Cambridge, MA: Belknap Press of Harvard University Press, 1967), p. 90.
15. Sacvan Berkovitch, *The American Jeremiad* (Madison: University of Wisconsin Press, 1978).
16. Thomas Jefferson, "Second Inaugural Address," 4 March 1805.
17. Charles V. Lafontaine, "God and Nation in Selected U.S. Presidential Inaugural Addresses, 1789–1945," Part I, *Journal of Church and State* (Winter 1976), and Part II (Autumn 1976).
18. Lafontaine, Part II, p. 503ff.
19. Abraham Lincoln, "Proclamation Appointing a National Fast Day," 30 March 1863, in Roy P. Basler, ed., *The Collected Works of Abraham Lincoln* (New Brunswick, NJ: Transaction, 1953–1955), Vol. 4, pp. 155–156.
20. Perry Miller, "From the Covenant to the Revival," in James W. Smith and A. Leland Johnson, eds., *The Shaping of American Religion* (Princeton, NJ: Princeton University Press, 1961), pp. 322–68.
21. (Jefferson citation) As cited in B.F. Morris, *Christian Life and Character of the Civil Institutions of the United States* (Philadelphia, 1864), pp. 526–27.
22. Perry Miller, *Errand into the Wilderness* (Cambridge, MA: Harvard University Press, 1956), pp. 119–122.
23. This writer has calculated the figure based on the evidence provided in Edwin Gausted, *Atlas of Religions in the United States*. My estimates were made con-

servatively, counting only those churches whose proclaimed doctrines included the federal theology in some version, or in the case of the Anglican Church, that were located in New England and hence had been formed as Puritan congregations originally. There is every likelihood that this is an underestimate.

24. B.F. Morris, *Christian Life and Character of the Civil Institutions of the United States* (Philadelphia, PA: George W. Childs, 1961), chapter xxii, "Fast and Thanksgiving Days."

25. Ellis Sandoz, ed., *Political Sermons of the American Founding Era* (Indianapolis, IN: Liberty Press, 1991).

26. An example in the first group is a sermon preached in the Third Presbyterian Church on December 11th by George Duffield and published as George Duffield, "A Sermon Preached in the Third Presbyterian Church, Philadelphia, 1784." An example of the second is to be found in a sermon by Ezra Stiles, the president of Yale College and the leading Connecticut Congregationalist, to be found in John Wingate Thornton, *The Pulpit of the American Revolution* (Boston, 1860), p. 403.

27. Perry Miller, ed., *The American Puritans: Their Prose and Poetry* (Garden City, NY: Doubleday Anchor Books, 1956).

28. Robert Licht, "Church-State Relations: End of the American Jewish Consensus?" Paper presented Dec. 13, 1993 at the 25th Annual Conference of the Association for Jewish Studies.

29. Robert Bellah, *The Broken Covenant* (New York: Seabury Press, 1975).

30. For an antebellum Southern version of this sacred history and its creed, see Richard T. Hughes, "A Civic Theology for the South: The Case of Benjamin M. Palmer," *Social Compass*, vol. 30 (1983/1):447–67. Palmer (1818–1902) was a Presbyterian minister and the son of a Presbyterian minister. He was the first moderator of the General Assembly of the Presbyterian Church in the Confederate States of America.

3

Constitutions as Covenants

From Covenant to Constitution

The anchoring of the American covenant in an appropriate constitution occurred over a period of twelve years. The states were the first to write constitutions. The Massachusetts Constitution of 1780—the oldest written constitution in the modern world still in effect today—is as close to being an example as any.[1] Drafted largely by John Adams, it weaves together the elements of covenant, compact, and constitution quite nicely, as reflected in the preamble quoted earlier:

> The body-politic is formed by a voluntary association of individuals: It is a social compact, by which the whole people covenants with each citizen, and each citizen with the whole people, that all shall be governed by certain laws for the common good. It is the duty of the people, therefore, in framing a Constitution of Government, to provide for an equitable mode of making laws, as well as for an impartial interpretation, and a faithful execution of them; that every man may, at all times, find his security in them.

Similar statements, though usually less eloquent, appear in almost all of the fifty state constitutions.[2]

It should not be surprising, therefore, that the Americans established a federal system of government with sovereignty divided and shared between the states and the nationwide government. American federalism is often treated as an anomaly or as a product of unique circumstances. Yet the governmental outcome of the Revolution could have been very different. The states could have separated as independent nations. They could have been united in one unitary whole or in sections by conquest. The Americans could have erected a monarchy. Indeed, given past experiences with the governance of large territories, these were much more likely outcomes than the actual one.

Instead, the Americans, within their states, sent representatives to a convention, ostensibly to improve the Articles of Confederation, and then ended up ratifying, under pacific conditions, a wholly new constitution that employed federal principles to create the first continental republic in world history. Whereas, historically, large territories (as well as most small ones) were invariably ruled by an imperial center, the United States became governed through a system of dispersed democratic majorities coupled with nationwide representation of both individuals and constituent states.[3]

Although it is impossible to determine definitively the influences upon the minds of the framers of the Constitution who invented the unique American federal system, the most overlooked, yet perhaps most important, source of ideas is the covenant tradition that found its first political expression in the federation of tribes of ancient Israel. One of the few political scientists to recognize this possibility was William C. Morey, in the late nineteenth century. Morey saw the sources of American federalism in "the reappearance of democratic and federal institutions in the Puritan colonies."[4] Although he did not mention federal theology, he regarded the federative system of New England as the model of federalism. After all, there were no extant models for the framers of the U.S. Constitution except New England.

Chapter 1 examined New England covenantalism generally and how it translated into constitutionalism. New England settlements were not only founded on covenants, but within half a generation after the founding of the Massachusetts Bay Colony the four New England colonies then in existence—Plymouth, Massachusetts Bay, Rhode Island, and Connecticut—formed the United Colonies of New England, the first and only inter-colonial confederation until the American Revolution. The Articles of Agreement (1643) that the four colonies adopted and upon which their confederation was based, constituted the first fully federal constitution in North America. Although it was much closer to the later Articles of Confederation than to the federal Constitution of 1787, it set the pattern for future events.[5] While the United Colonies of New England survived only for some fifty years and disintegrated after having been undercut by the British colonial regime, it served its primary purpose in bringing peace to New England by eliminating the Indian threat to the white settlement.

A century later, representatives from New England, especially Connecticut and Massachusetts, were particularly influential in regard to issues of federalism in the Constitutional Convention. The basic federal decision of the Convention was the Connecticut compromise, initiated by those delegates accustomed to the New England legislative system in which one house provided for representation of towns. This compromise lies at the heart of the federal system and makes it, in the words of James Madison, a "compound republic," partly national and partly federal (in the earlier sense of confederal).[6] In addition, the most covenantal of the state constitutions, that of Massachusetts, was among the most influential of the state models for the framers.

Supplementing the New England sectional influences were the ethnoreligious conduits of covenant ideas, especially Congregationalism and Presbyterianism, the two largest denominations in 1787. A majority of the delegates to the Convention were affiliated with covenant-based churches, either the aforementioned ones or others such as the Baptists or the Dutch Reformed, while most of the other delegates were no doubt familiar with the covenant idea, given their Protestantism and attention to the Bible as a source of wisdom and literary enjoyment, if not always spiritual inspiration. The English, Scottish, and Dutch backgrounds of many of the delegates may also have accounted for covenantal influences.

The Congregationalists certainly were grounded in covenant ideas, though their propensity for localism and local control made them somewhat hesitant to leap into large-scale arrangements. The Presbyterians, however, were already moving toward full-scale federalism. As Arthur Schlesinger, Sr. noted, "More than either [the Congregationalists or Anglicans] the Presbyterians in their reliance on federalist and representative institutions anticipated the political makeup of the future United States."[7] Indeed, as the first government came into office under the U.S. Constitution in 1789, the Presbyterians held their first nationwide General Assembly. In the Presbyterian system, congregations in a local area formed a presbytery; several presbyteries in a region formed a synod; and then came the General Assembly. As a result, the system of federal democracy established by the U.S. Constitution has often been referred to as Presbyterianism writ large for civil society.

Moreover, James Madison of Virginia, the principal architect of the theory of federal democracy, was an Episcopalian of Scottish ancestry who had studied under and been greatly influenced by the Scottish reverend, Donald Robertson and the prominent scholar-divine John Witherspoon at the Presbyterian-oriented College of New Jersey (now

Princeton). Although he himself did not use the idea of covenant in his writings, he could not have been unfamiliar with the idea or hostile to the civil principles behind it.

Indeed, six of the delegates to the Constitutional Convention had studied under Witherspoon. As a strong supporter of independence and a signer of the Declaration of Independence, Witherspoon's influence was substantial enough that Horace Walpole is alleged to have complained that "There is no use crying about it. Cousin America has run off with a Presbyterian parson, and that is the end of it."[8]

The comment may be fictitious, but the sentiment is not. Institutional structures and cultural traditions that served as carriers of covenant ideas were still strong in 1787, though increasingly in secular forms. The framers, however they saw themselves engaged in a wholly secular enterprise, could not avoid that influence. Charles Hyneman and Donald Lutz examined all the extant writings of the Revolutionary and constitutional periods, from 1765 to 1805, and discovered the overwhelming preeminence of biblical references and ideas. The Bible was so extensively quoted that there are more references to it than to all of the classical and modern European political philosophers combined. Indeed, citations of the Book of Deuteronomy alone exceed any one of the latter. Montesquieu, the most widely cited figure outside of the Bible, is a distant second, with fewer citations than the Book of Deuteronomy alone.[9]

By 1787 the theological stream of covenant ideas and the philosophic stream of compactual ideas had become so intermingled in the concept of constitutionalism that it is difficult to separate their effects. Albeit, given that the federal system established by the framers bears a much greater similarity to the political systems proposed by the federal theologians and implemented in their church polities than to the political systems proposed by Hobbes or Locke, and given that Americans were already covenanting into civil societies well before the speculative philosophers adopted the idea, it is difficult to avoid the conclusion that covenant ideas had, in the final analysis, a more decisive influence than those of the new political science.

Moreover, the systems of the English philosophers could not be directly applied to America because, even in 1787, the country was simply enormous compared to tiny England. While such prominent revolutionary ideas as "natural rights" certainly belong to the Lockean tradition, they were also grounded in the covenant tradition as interpreted and were further adapted to the federal framework of American constitutionalism rather than the monarchical framework of Hobbes or parliamentary framework of Locke. Thus, it is inaccurate to describe America as simply a Lockean nation.[10]

Popular Government and the Federal Solution

For all intents and purposes, federalism as moderns know it (that is, modern federation) is an American invention. As the literature of the constitutional ratification campaign (both federalist and antifederalist) indicates, federalism was designed and developed by the founding fathers to be more than a pragmatic structural compromise devised to make possible the unification of the several states under a single national government. It was also to be more than a geographic division of power for expediency's sake.

Federalism, to its American inventors, represented a new political alternative for solving the problems of governing civil societies, an alternative that was developed from the political theories, institutions, and patterns of behavior which had evolved out of the various applications of the covenant idea to the colonization of the eastern seaboard from the beginning of the seventeenth century onward. The federalism of the founders was designed to provide substantially new means for the development of a viable system of government, a successful system of politics, a reasonable approach to the problems of popular government, and a decent means for securing civil justice and morality. Moreover, its inventors conceived of federalism as a uniquely valuable means for solving the perennial problems of any civil society seeking to transform itself into a good commonwealth, particularly one which is built on the rock of popular government—the problems of balancing human liberty, political authority, and governmental energy so as to create a political system at once strong, lasting, democratic, and just.

The American founders believed that their invention was capable of solving those problems because it was based on valid fundamental principles and was constructed to employ proper, if new, political techniques necessary to at least approximately effectuate those principles. They were convinced of this—and were soon joined in this conviction by the American people as a whole—not because their invention directly solved important substantive questions which they anticipated would confront the

United States. The essence of their solution was the application of the federal principle not only to relations between governments but to the overall political relationships of groups ("factions" in Madison's terminology) and individuals to government.

Their own sources try to justify their stand by telling us why the founders felt as they did. Unfortunately, current myths prevent many from considering those sources on their own terms. For one thing, there are too many who believe American federalism is the product of circumstances alone, that Nature itself (or at least prior experience) dictated that the American Republic be built on the rock of diffused governmental powers so that any discussion of a "federal principle" is an ex post facto attempt to discover a unique or original political invention when common political considerations actually sufficed. Pointing to the vast expanse of land under the American flag even in 1787, the great diversity of peoples gathered together under its protection, the general commitment to popular government prevalent in the land, and the preexistence of the thirteen colonies, many people conclude that formal distribution of power among "central" and "local" governments was inevitable if there was to be any union at all and that the founders of the Republic simply worked out the mechanisms needed to make the status quo politically viable.[11]

This view has become widespread in the twentieth century because it is particularly useful to those who accept two companion views of American federalism current today. One is the notion that the framers of the Constitution were hostile to popular government and used federalism to limit "democracy" by distributing powers undemocratically. This school views subsequent American history as the struggle to establish popular government against the will of the founders' Constitution. Accordingly, they believe that the Constitution's system for the distribution of power becomes increasingly obsolete as the nation becomes more "democratic." The other accepts the premise that the founders were antidemocratic but "excuses" them on the grounds that problems of communication over such a vast and diverse area then required the federal distribution of powers. Their claim is that as problems of fast communications are lessened, this distribution of powers becomes increasingly obsolete.[12]

Superficially, history appears to support the current myths. The implantation of settlements on the American shores under different regimes and charters had led to the emergence of at least thirteen firmly rooted colonies-cum-states by 1776. The new nation did inherit the basis for some type of federal plan and, it might even be said, had no choice in the matter. Recent research has heightened the plausibility of this view by indicating the extent to which the American colonies enjoyed a de facto federal relationship with the English king and Parliament prior to independence.

The existence of states, however, was no guarantee that they could be united under one government. Moreover, there was no guarantee that unification could take any form other than loose confederation so long as the states remained intact as sovereign civil societies, or any form other than consolidation if they did not. In this respect, the factors of size and diversity were in no way determinative. Distribution, as opposed to concentration of power, is not a function of size and diversity per se but a function of republican political inclinations.

Students of comparative government—from the days of Aristotle to our own and including the generation of the founders of the Republic—have been fully aware of the possibilities for centralized government in even the largest and most diverse empires. In Aristotle's day the Persian empire extended for over three thousand miles "from India to Ethiopia" in the words of the Bible, and included over a hundred different nationality and ethnic groups, each located in its own land, yet throughout its two hundred years of existence, it was governed by a despotism which, while maintaining a benevolent attitude toward the maintenance of local customs and civil laws, carefully concentrated as much political power as possible in the hands of the emperor.[13]

Locke, Montesquieu, and the founding fathers were acquainted with the similarly organized Ottoman Empire. They, like our own generation, also encountered one of the greatest centralized despotisms of all time in the form of the Russian Empire. When Cortez was viceroy in Mexico, the Russian Empire under Ivan the Terrible already covered an area larger than the original United States (888,811 square miles in 1789). The Russians began their march eastward in the sixteenth century, and by the time the Puritans were settling New England, they had reached the Pacific. By the year of the Glorious Revolution and the establishment of parliamentary supremacy in England, the Russians had consolidated their centralized rule over some seven million square miles and dozens of nations, peoples, and tribes. An eighteenth-century Russian, if asked about the political consequences of a large domain, would have been likely to say that an expanse of territory is useful in protecting absolutism since the difficulties of internal communication that it creates help prevent popular uprisings on a nationwide scale.

A Frenchman of the same century, if asked the best method of creating a nation out of a number of smaller "sovereignties," would undoubtedly have recalled the history of France and advocated the complete political and administrative subordination of the entities to be absorbed under a central government and the elimination of all vestiges of their local autonomy so as to minimize the possibilities of civil war. Even an eighteenth-century Englishman, aware of the centuries-old problem of absorbing Scotland into Great Britain, would have been likely to approach the problem of national unification in a somewhat similar manner, except that he might have added a touch of decentralization as a palliative to libertarian sentiments. Thinking Americans were aware of all these examples in 1787. It is no accident that *The Federalist* had to concentrate heavily on refuting the argument that a stronger national government would inevitably open the door to centralized despotism.

Closer examination of the situation between 1775 and 1801 provides convincing evidence to the effect that, regardless of the factors present to encourage some form of division of power between national government and the state governments, the development of a federal system stronger than that embodied in the Articles of Confederation was by no means foreordained. What such an examination does reveal is the extent to which the founders of the United States were committed to the idea of popular government and were really involved in a search for the best form of organization—the best constitution—for the republic, one that would secure the liberties of the people while avoiding the weaknesses of past experiments in popular government.

Even here the founders had little precedent to guide them. Not only were there no extant examples of the successful government of a large territory except through a strong centralized government, but there were few small territories governed in a "republican" manner and none offered the example of federalism as Americans later came to know it. The two nations then existing that had come closest to resolving the problems of national unity without governmental centralization were the United Provinces of the Netherlands and the Swiss Confederation, both of which served covenantal societies. Not only were both very small republics indeed, about the size of Massachusetts and New Jersey, but the failure of the former to solve its constitutional problems and its consequent lapse into government by an incompetent executive and an antirepublican oligarchy was well known while the latter was hardly more than a protective association of independent states with little national consciousness. Neither could be an attractive example to the American nation builders, who were committed to both republicanism and the common nationality of all Americans.

In one sense, then, the founding fathers had only two contemporary models to choose from, both of which showed great weakness and promised little for the perpetuation of popular government. They could have attempted to bring the several states together into a single unified but decentralized state on the order of the government of Great Britain, or they could have been satisfied with a loose confederation of sovereign states, united only for purposes of defense and foreign relations which, while barely able to govern adequately even in the areas of its responsibility, would offer minimal opportunities for national despotism.

There were those who advocated the former course, particularly among the younger officers of the Continental Army. At various times, they urged Washington to establish a constitutional dictatorship (which possibly could have led to a political system akin to the kind of totalitarian democracy established by Napoleon in France in the 1790s) or assume the crown as a constitutional monarch (which presumably would have led to a political system akin to the kind of aristocratic oligarchy that existed in eighteenth century England). While Washington effectively subdued most of them on several occasions during the war itself (the most famous of which was his confrontation with them at Newburgh, N.Y.), one of their number, former lieutenant colonel Alexander Hamilton, continued to advocate the latter position as much as he dared right through the Constitutional Convention.

The second course was the one followed during the war as a natural outgrowth of the Continental Congresses assembled from 1765 through 1775. If the founders had been content with a "foreordained" system, one "dictated" by the actual status of the United States in 1776, they would have accepted this alternative and retained the Articles of Confederation, which were adopted to ratify just that kind of confederacy. That system has been most frequently compared to the various Hellenic leagues which united several city-states only insofar as they shared a common purpose—invariably that of defense. Such leagues embraced small despotisms as well as small democracies. They had no role to play in determining the internal regimes of member states and were in no sense protectors of human liberties or popular government.

Among those who advocated this course of action were some of the most notable patriots of the early Revolutionary struggle. Above all, they feared despotism in large governments and distrusted any notion that a national government with energy could by kept republican. Whatever their views as to the potential tyranny of the majority, they were more willing to trust smaller governments with the supervision of the people's liberties on the grounds that they were more accessible to the people. Patrick Henry was the most outspoken of this group. He held his ground to the bitter end, uncompromising in his belief.[14]

As we all know, the founders chose neither alternative but, rather, invented a third alternative of their own. Their alternative was animated by a desire to perfect the union of what they believed to be an already existing nation, to give it the power to act as a government while keeping it republican and democratic. In developing their solution, they transcended the limits of earlier political thought in order to devise a way to protect the people's liberties from every threat.[15]

Their alternative reflected a great step forward in thinking about popular government because, while accepting the same idea of covenant and compact that animated the Articles of Confederation, they refused to accept the simplistic notion that the possibilities for despotism increased in direct proportion to the size of the country to be governed. They were fully convinced by history and personal experience that small governments, in their case the states, could be as despotic as large ones—that the issue was on what principles and along what lines a civil society and its government were structured.

Moreover, the founders were convinced by history and experience that democratic governments could be as tyrannical as autocratic ones if they were based on simple and untrammeled majoritarianism. Pure democracies, in particular, were subject to the sway of passion and hence to the promotion of injustice, and even republics were susceptible if faction was allowed to reign unchecked. As friends of human liberty and popular government, they felt it necessary to create a political system that would protect the people from despotic governments whether they be large or small, democratic or not.

Their solution, federalism—the operationalization of the covenant idea—was designed to deal with all these contingencies by balancing them off against one another so as to create a number of permanent points of tension that would limit the spread of either popular passion or governmental excess, break up or weaken the power of factions, and require broad based majorities to take significant political actions. Locating all sovereignty in the people as a whole while dividing the exercise of sovereign powers among several governments—one general, the others regional—was, to the founders, a means of checking the despotic tendencies, majoritarian or other, in both the larger and the smaller governments, while preserving the principle of popular government. The interdependence of the national and state governments was to ensure their ability to check one another while still enabling them to cooperate and govern energetically. In the words of Publius (the pen name of the authors of the *Federalist Papers*), they advocated republican remedies for republican diseases.

In organizational terms, the perennial tug-of-war between centralization and decentralization was to be avoided by the introduction of the principle of noncentralization. The difference is a crucial one. Decentralization, even as it implies local control, assumes the existence of a central authority that has the power to concentrate, devolve, or reconcentrate power more or less at will. Noncentralization assumes that there is no central authority as such but that power is granted to several authorities, national and regional, directly by the people and, even though the national authority may enjoy an ultimate preeminence that is very real indeed, that those authorities cannot legitimately take basic power away from each other.

True federal systems must be noncentralized systems. Even when, in practical situation, there seems to be only the thin line of the spirit between noncentralization and decentralization, it is that thin line which determines the extent and character of the diffusion of power in a particular regime.

The American people and their leaders were to extend this aspect of federalism, which is partially described in common parlance as the "checks and balances" system, into most other areas of their political life. Both the state governments and the national government have powers which cannot be taken from one another, even when both planes share in their exercise. The principle was further applied to relations between the various branches of government—executive, legislative, and judicial—within each plane even before the invention of federalism. It was subsequently applied to the structure and organization of the party system, which consists of two national coalitions of substantially independent state and local party organizations further checked by the independence of action reserved to the "congressional parties" within each of the two coalitions. It was applied to the other process of politics and even to the nation's economic system in ways too numerous to mention here.

The federal principle sets the tone for American civil society, making it a society of balanced interests with egalitarian overtones, just as the monarchist principle makes British civil society class- and elite-oriented despite democratic pressures, and the collectivist principle sets the tone for Chinese civil society, making it antiindividualistic even when equalitarian. In political terms, this is because the federal principle establishes the basic power relationships and sets the basic terms for the processes of distributing power within American civil society. The founders understood the role of such central principles in setting the framework for the development of a political system. They knew that, while the roots of the fundamental principle of every civil society are embedded in its culture, constitution-makers do have a significant opportunity to sharpen the principle's application and the direction of its future growth.

In sum, federalism as the founders conceived it was an effort to protect the rights of men by consciously creating institutions and procedures that would give government adequate powers while, at the same time, forcing the governors to achieve a high level of consent from all segments of the public they served before acting in other than routine ways. Requiring extraordinary majorities for great actions, the Constitution was based on the idea that there is a qualitative difference between a simple majority formed for a specific issue and the larger consensus that allows governments to continue to function from generation to generation.

The Fullest Expression of Political Compact in the United States

Much of this has to be derived from the records of the debates surrounding the writing and ratifying of the federal Constitution of 1787. Because of the intensely practical character of the constitution and the previous half-generation of debate over the principles that undergirded it, the framers and ratifiers in general confined the debate to the very practical issues at hand. There was general agreement on principles, so the question before them was how to translate those principles into effective practice. This was the point at which other revolutions had foundered and still others were to founder in the future. Thus the Americans were not wrong in emphasizing the issue and deciding on their constitutional system, but this emphasis on the practical and effective has left the field open for the variety of interpretations given to the American founding by historians, political scientists, statesmen, and the American people as a whole.

Nevertheless, as the Constitution of 1787 was being written, the American people provided us with another authoritative statement of the American understanding of political compact and how it could be practically be applied, in the Northwest Ordinance of 1787, enacted by the Confederation Congress the same year that the new constitution was drafted. That act was one of the major achievements of the United States under the Articles of Confederation and, inter alia, should serve as a clue to the fact that despite its being discredited in the campaign for the ratification of the new constitution, which has left a historical legacy to this day, the United States under the Articles did not do so badly. Indeed, the Ordinance was readopted by the United States Congress after the new constitution went into effect.

The Northwest Ordinance of 1787 was the third such ordinance drafted. The first was enacted in 1784. The Northwest Ordinances of 1785 and 1787 were actually supplements to it.

The purpose of the ordinances was to organize the western lands, the territories ceded to the United States as a whole by the individual states as part of the bargain that led to the ratification of the Articles of Confederation and endowed the United States as a whole with a great patrimony and a great future, years before the federal constitution. The lands in question were those west of Pennsylvania and north of the Ohio river to the western border of the new country along the Mississippi river. While technically they applied only to those territories, in fact they set a precedent for the future development of the United States by providing that those new territories, when settled, presumably by Americans from the eastern states, at least predominantly, would be admitted to the new union as new states equal to the original thirteen.

This decision alone assured that the United States would be built by the development of a number of popular republics into which its whole territory ultimately would be divided. The Ordinance of 1787 provided that the way those republics would be organized would indeed be popular, democratic if you will, certainly by the standards of the time. In the end this democratic movement was set on the road to further democratization beyond the standards of the time. Government was to be organized on a popular basis by the settlers themselves under the aegis of the Congress of the United States and the officials it appointed for the territory to administer their initial settlement and transition to full republican status. Slavery was prohibited throughout the territory, not only taking American democracy a major step farther than was possible in the original states but making it clear what the American founders really wanted and hoped to achieve in the future regarding that issue. Most important of all for our purposes, the Northwest Ordinance was explicitly a political compact, the one national document that explicitly embodies the theory of political compact regnant in the United States during the revolutionary and early constitutional periods.

The compact is presented in Section 14 of the ordinance as a separate set of articles that go beyond the ordinance itself to bind the new states to be admitted under it.

ARTICLE I

No person, demeaning himself in a peaceable and orderly manner, shall ever be molested on account of his mode of worship, or religious sentiments, in the said territory.

ARTICLE II

The inhabitants of the said territory shall always be entitled to the benefits of the writs of habeas corpus and of the trial by jury, of a proportionate representation of the people in the legislature, and of judicial proceedings according to the course of the common law. All persons shall be bailable, unless for capital offenses, where the proof shall be evident, or the presumption great. All fines shall be moderate; and no cruel or unusual punishment shall be inflicted. No man shall be deprived of his liberty or property, but by the judgment of his peers, or the law of the land, and, should the public exigencies make it necessary, for the common preservation, to take any person's property, or to demand his particular services, full compensation shall be made for the same. And, in the just preservation of rights and property, it is understood and declared that no law ought ever to be made or have force in the said territory shall, in any manner whatever, interfere with or affect private contracts, or engagements, bona fide, and without fraud previously formed.

ARTICLE III

Religion, morality, and knowledge being necessary to good government and the happiness of mankind, schools and the means of education shall forever be encouraged. The utmost good faith shall always be observed toward the Indians; their lands and property shall never be taken from them without their consent; and in their property, rights, and liberty they never shall be invaded or disturbed unless in just and lawful wars authorized by congress; but laws founded in justice and humanity shall, from time to time, be made, for preventing wrongs being done to them and for preserving peace and friendship with them.

ARTICLE IV

The said territory, and the states which may be formed therein, shall forever remain a part of this confederacy of the United States of America, subject to the Articles of Confederation, and to such alterations therein as shall be constitutionally made; and to all the acts and ordinances of the United States in Congress assembled, conformable thereto. The inhabitants and settlers in the said territory shall be subject to pay a part of the federal debts contracted, or to be contracted, and a proportional part of the expenses of government to be apportioned on them by Congress, according to the same common rule and measure by which apportionments thereof shall be made on the other states; and the taxes for paying their proportion shall be laid and levied by the authority and direction of the legislatures of the district, or districts, or new states, as in the original states, within the time agreed upon by the United States in Congress assembled. The legislatures of those districts, or new states, shall never interfere with the primary disposal of the soil by the United States in Congress assembled, nor with any regulations Congress may find necessary for securing the title in such soil to the bona fide purchasers. No tax shall be imposed on lands the property of the United States; and in no case shall nonresident proprietors be taxed higher than residents. The navigable waters leading into the Mississippi and Saint Lawrence, and the carrying places between the same, shall be common highways, and forever free, as well to the inhabitants of the said territory as to the citizens of the United States, and those of any other states that may be admitted into the confederacy, without any tax, impost, or duty therefor.

ARTICLE V

There shall be formed in the said territory not less than three nor more than five states; and the boundaries of the states, as soon as Virginia shall alter her act of cession and consent to the same, shall become fixed and established as follows, to wit: The western state, in the said territory, shall be bounded by the Mississippi, the Ohio, and the Wabash rivers; a direct line drawn from the Wabash and Post Vincents, due north, to the territorial line between the United States and Canada; and by the said territorial line to the Lake of the Woods and Mississippi. The middle state shall be bounded by the said direct line, the Wabash from Post Vincents to the Ohio, by the Ohio, by a direct line drawn due north from the mouth of the Great Miami to the said territorial line, and by the said territorial line. The eastern state shall be bounded by the last-mentioned direct line, the Ohio, Pennsylvania, and the said territorial line: *Provided, However,* and it is further understood and declared, that the boundaries of these three states shall be subject so far to be altered, that, if Congress shall hereafter find it expedient, they shall have authority to form one or two states in that part of the said territory which lies north of an east and west line drawn through the southerly bend or extreme of Lake Michigan. And whenever any of the said states shall have sixty thousand free inhabitants therein, such state shall be admitted by its delegates into the Congress of the United States, on an equal footing with the original states, in all respects whatever; and shall be at liberty to form a permanent constitution and state government: *Provided*, The constitution and government, so to be formed, shall be republican, and in conformity to the principles contained in these articles, and, so far as it can be consistent with the general interest of the confederacy, such admission shall be allowed at an earlier period, and when there may be a less number of free inhabitants in the state than sixty thousand.

ARTICLE VI

There shall be neither slavery not involuntary servitude in the said territory, otherwise than in the punishment of crimes, whereof the party shall have been duly convicted: *Provided always*, That any person escaping into the same, from whom labor or service is lawfully claimed in any one of the original states, such fugitive may be lawfully reclaimed, and conveyed to the person claiming his or her labor or service as aforesaid.

Be it ordained by the authority aforesaid, That the resolutions of the 23d of April, 1784, relative to the subject of this ordinance, be, and the same are hereby, repealed, and declared null and void.

Done by the United States, in Congress assembled, the 13th day of July, in the year of our Lord 1787, and of their sovereignty and independence the twelfth.

The compact consists of a series of commitments to human rights and religious and civil freedom. It promises statehood for the territory yet requires the states to remain parts of the United States unless the latter be dissolved by mutual consent. It provides that the new states shall be free and republican.

In essence, the compact is a summation of the political, covenantal, and constitutional principles and doctrines that predominated in the United States at the time of the writing of the American federal constitution. The covenantal tradition had already been so secularized that the document was called a political compact. Nevertheless, the tradition was powerful enough to secure a special status for religion and morality in the public institutions to be established in the new territories. It was republican through and through. It sought the protection of the basic human rights spelled out in the Declaration of Independence as one of its major tasks.[16]

The Northwest Ordinance worked, with some modifications in practice derived from the settlement experience. Five entire states (Ohio, Indiana, Illinois, Michigan, Wisconsin) were admitted from the Northwest Territory and the eastern part of a sixth (Minnesota) included the north-westernmost part of it. All of these states still include the ordinance among their founding documents. More important, they all share a certain esprit derived from being part of the old Northwest, not only part of America's original trans-Appalachian West but the first states in which the American ideal in its entirety was translated into practice. Their subsequent history, which cannot concern us here, also marks the unfolding of that ideal through the section's frontier period of settlement and admission to the Union as individual states, the Civil War when the men and boys of the old Northwest played a decisive role in saving the Union, through the era of industrialization and influx of European immigrants and later southern blacks into those territories, and on to the present.

The States and the Nation: A Second Shift in Modern Constitutionalism

Even the most conventional histories of the United States indicate that American constitutionalism began with the constitutions of the states and then shifted its emphasis to providing constitutions for the United States. While these conventional histories are not exactly incorrect, they tend to overlook three important dimensions. One is the age of the state constitutional tradition. The documents did not simply spring into existence out of the blue at the time of the American Revolution but rested on histories of constitutionalism dating back to the very beginnings of British settlement in North America. Indeed, two states, Connecticut and Rhode Island, simply adapted their seventeenth-century charters to drop references to the monarchy, made necessary by the American Revolution and the independence that it produced, and continued with them well into the nineteenth century before the need arose for them to write new constitutions.

Two, state constitution-making in the revolutionary era paralleled constitution-making for the United States as a whole. The first Revolutionary era state constitution was written and adopted in 1776 and the last in 1790. The Articles of Confederation, the first federal constitution of the United States, was written in 1777 (although not ratified until 1781), and the Constitution of the United States, written in 1787 to supersede it, did not begin to function until early in 1789. Overlooking the Articles of Confederation in the history of American constitutionalism is a mistake.

Three, state and federal constitutions were grounded on different premises: the state constitutions on republican virtue and the federal on interest, utility, and commerce. In this respect, state constitutions continued earlier traditions of covenant and compact to provide a continued intertwining of the two and at the same time defend the moral basis for the United States as a whole. As Lutz has pointed out, the federal constitution rests upon the state constitutions and requires their existence in order to be complete. The federal constitution could be grounded in commerce not because the founders of the United States abjured a moral basis for their civil society but because they left that task to the states and entrusted them with it in their new constitutional order.

The federal constitution was understood to be of limited scope and, while comprehensive in its sphere, that sphere was quite narrow relative to that of government generally at the time. Indeed, Lutz has argued, this writer believes quite accurately, that the federal constitution can be read only in light of the state constitutions, that the former was grounded in the latter and designed to fill in with regard to those matters in which its framers felt the state constitutions needed to be supplemented or certain federal standards established.[17] The states could easily, in fact naturally, be expected to play the role of moral guardians and they did so unchallenged until the Civil War, when the United States seized the moral leadership on the slavery issue and began a process of acquiring a moral basis for itself, at times at the expense of the states and the state constitutions. Nevertheless, the conventional wisdom today that sees the federal constitution as overarching and all-encompassing and the state constitutions as playing their role only within that federal framework and limited in their ability to promote republican virtue or any other kind of morality by the decisions of an activist United States Supreme Court, would have been incomprehensible to the founders (Even if some of the framers would have liked that, they knew they had not gotten it.)

Thus it is not surprising that the great strength of the states lay in their police powers which, as understood at the time, involved the protection and advancement of the states' moral expectations as matters of public policy and private adherence. That is why the political compact in the Northwest Ordinance speaks directly to that state task in its discussion of religion, morality, and knowledge, and the states' responsibility for that triad. By contrast, the federal constitution was responsible for the protection and fostering of commerce, not only interstate but nationally, if such distinction can be made, and not only in goods but in goods, services, and ideas. That was a very important but still limited task. In the intervening years the U.S. Supreme Court has built it into a comprehensive one, but even John Marshall, the great chief justice of the United States who did so much to expand federal powers under the constitution, in the early days of the generation after 1789, enunciated a doctrine giving the states substantial powers with great scope and reach through their police powers, just as the federal government was given substantial powers with great scope and reach through its commerce powers.

Despite their differences in scope, this fostering of interest, utility and commerce was the essential purpose of the Articles of Confederation as well. This is reflected in the purposes of the confederation stated in Article 3 of the Articles: "For their common defense, the security of their liberties, and their mutual and general welfare" while Article 4 specifies the ways in which these goals are to be secured. In this respect the second tradition is as much embodied in the Articles of Confederation as in the later constitution.

Moreover, the distinction between the primary grounding of the state constitutions and that of the federal ones was clear from the first. Thus the state constitutions reflect more of the covenantal dimension, albeit secularized, and the federal constitutions are more reflective of political compacts, albeit in the covenantal tradition. See, for example, the last paragraph of Article 13, the last article of the Articles of Confederation.

And whereas it has pleased the Great Governor of the world to incline the hearts of the Legislatures we respectively represent in Congress, to approve of, and to authorize us to ratify the said articles of confederation and perpetual union. Know ye that we the undersigned delegates, by virtue of the power and authority to us given for that purpose, do by these presents, in the name and in behalf of our respective constituents, fully and entirely ratify and confirm each and every of the said articles of confederation and perpetual union, and all and singular the matters and things therein contained: and we do further solemnly plight and engage the faith of our respective constituents that they shall abide by the determinations of the United States in Congress assembled, on all questions, which by the said confederation are submitted to them. And that the articles thereof shall be inviolably observed by the States we respectively represent, and that the Union shall be perpetuated.[18]

Two Traditions: The 1787 Constitution Compared

The years 1787–1789 marked a second sea change in the history of the development of modern constitutionalism. If the first sea change moved constitutionalism from the service of the covenanted commonwealth to a combination of religiously grounded commonwealth and civil society, the second sea change left civil society in a very dominant if not exclusive position. This is evident in the fact that state constitutions written after the ratification of the federal constitution increasingly become like it, that is to say, they reduce their emphasis on republican virtue, albeit not below the minimum that they must maintain in order for their constitutions to function at all, and increasingly imitate the utilitarian constitution of the United States. Still, each genre must stick to its last, at least minimally, and state constitutions still emphasize that moral dimension of virtue while the federal constitution has simply expanded its powers, principally through extending the definition of what constitutes commerce and interstate commerce at that.

By the beginning of the nineteenth century, then, constitutionalism had essentially replaced covenantalism as the operative idea of civil society, not only in the United States but in spreading ripples throughout the world, first in Europe and Latin America through their respective revolutions and, later, beyond. It is interesting to note that during the same period Americans abandoned direct appeals to natural law as well, turning them into appeals to the Constitution.[19]

It was as though, once they had their constitution, the American people could abandon the more theoretical, not to speak of philosophic, arguments about the basis for constitutionalism in covenant or natural law or some combination of the two and could concentrate on the more practical issues of interpreting their written documents.

In time this view spread worldwide. While it was eminently successful in making constitutionalism practical, not merely a matter of theory, in time it served to detach the people who might otherwise have been open to it, from systematic speculative thinking about the foundations of constitutionalism and to which constitutions must ultimately and indeed periodically be related. Unquestionably this has led to distortions in constitutional interpretation without their being perceived as such.

The difference between the state and federal constitutions in the United States was a constitutional manifestation of another major change in political thinking in the modern epoch: the shift from virtue to interest as the foundation for the good regime. This was the result of the shift in the theory of political behavior. Classical political theory emphasized virtue as the basis for cultivating proper political behavior; that is to say, the success of a particular form of polity depended upon the cultivation of the virtue properly associated with that form. Classic republics rested upon the cultivation of republican virtues, and political institutions were to be designed to foster and cultivate such virtues.[20] Implicitly this was true of the classic covenantal tradition as well.[21]

Modern political science, despairing of the effectiveness of virtue as the principal way to foster the good polity, shifted its emphasis from virtue to interest. The concern with interest flowed directly from the foundations of the new political science in natural right, human psychology, and the methodological individualism on which both rested. Every individual by virtue of his or her humanity has interests.

This shift was part of the revolution of sober expectations that was characteristic of the first half of the modern epoch, cresting in the American constitution of 1787. The new political science, by viewing all humans as equal in their basic psychology, that is, their passions, desires, and interests, rejected the possibility that any significant number of humans could rise above their passions and interests sufficiently to form an elite of any kind. Hence "all men are created equal" and any political system in order to succeed must be based on a proper understanding of and harnessing of those passions and interests. Thus interest became the basis of political organization rather than virtue or expectations of virtue.

While the sources of this new political science are to be found in Hobbes and were further developed by a more optimistic Harrington, the framers of the U.S. Constitution of 1787 were the first to actually turn theory into meaningful practice and *The Federalist* is the great work of political philosophy that best states their understanding. It does so most pointedly in *Federalist* nos. 10 and 51 in Madison's argument for the extended republic and for the constitutional distribution of powers ("ambition must counter ambition"). The state constitutions with all their realism in matters of institutional design still implicitly relied upon virtue to sustain the regimes that they framed. The U.S. Constitution of 1787 relied upon interests.

It should be added that, following Harrington, the federal constitution emphasized the public interest and the necessity to cultivate it, something like a halfway position between virtue and interest simply, but it was not precisely halfway because even concern with the public interest as distinct from private interests had crossed the line from reliance on virtue to reliance on interests, only with the hope that a common public interest could be cultivated along with (not in place of) the myriad private interests with which all humans begin.

In the wake of that change, the shift from covenant to compact and from commonwealth to civil society was unavoidable. Covenant and commonwealth in their classic meaning relied upon the cultivation of particular virtues based upon a commitment to that cultivation. Civil society was based on the recognition of the fundamentality of interests and their redirection for purposes of achieving or, better, protecting human happiness.

Later, as the modern epoch continued, the struggle between the two categories of virtue and interest was to continue but in different ways. New ideas of virtue emerged as "true interest." These were far from classical conceptions of virtue and almost invariably led to totalitarianism in the end, precisely because they rested on a combination of modern populism and unrealistic expectations of people.

On the other hand, private interests, once they were recognized as legitimate, became ever more important in the overall scheme of things, finally to triumph over even the idea of the public interest in the postmodern epoch. As privatism grew, public standards as well a sense of the public interest lost their legitimacy. True covenants became ever harder to establish and even political compacts became more difficult because they, too, required a sense of public interest. Instead, the ordering of life became reduced to being a matter of contracts. After the 1960s even marriage, long viewed in the West as a covenant based upon moral as well as material pledges, was entirely redefined as a matter of contract and began to disintegrate as an institution wherever that happened. To bring matters full circle, political theorists began exploring the possibilities of salvaging society through the resurrection of the idea of private virtue.[22]

Notes

1. Ronald Peters, *The Massachusetts Constitution of 1780: A Social Compact* (Amherst: University of Massachusetts Press, 1974).
2. John Adams, *The Political Writings of John Adams* (Indianapolis, IN: The Liberal Arts Press, 1954); Donald Lutz, *The Origins of American Constitutionalism* (Baton Rouge, LA: Louisiana State University Press, 1988); Daniel J. Elazar, "The Constitution, The Union, and the Liberties of the People," *Publius*, vol. 8, no. 3 (Summer 1978).
3. Cf. Daniel J. Elazar, *The Politics of American Federalism* (Lexington, MA: D.C. Health, 1969), Introduction.
4. William C. Morey, "The Sources of American Federalism," *Annals of the American Academy of Political and Social Science*, vol. 6, no. 2 (1895), pp. 197–226.

5. Harry M. Ward, *The United Colonies of New England, 1643–90* (New York: Vantage Press, 1961).
6. For a discussion of the larger meaning of compound republic, see Vincent Ostrom, *The Political Theory of the Compound Republic* (Lincoln: University of Nebraska Press, 1987).
7. Arthur Schlesinger, *Congress and the Presidency* (Washington, D.C.: American Enterise Institute, 1967).
8. Cf. Gary Wills, *Inventing America* (New York: Vantage Press, 1979).
9. Charles S. Hyneman and Donald S. Lutz, *American Political Writing During the Founding Era, 1760–1805* (Indianapolis, IN: Liberty Press, 1983).
10. Contemporary political scientist Robert Licht has analyzed the adoption of the U.S. Constitution as the result of a successful collaboration between secular and religious moderates—the former influenced by the political compact ideas of the new political science and the latter by the covenantal political theology of Reformed Protestantism in which both were able to find common ground and thus push to the periphery while they harmonized the two more moderate positions. Subsequently, Licht argues, especially in the twentieth century, the extreme wings of both became dominant, engendering a tension between the two positions that is presently gripping the United States. See Robert Licht, "Church-State Relations: End of the American Jewish Consensus?" Paper presented Dec. 13, 1993 at the 25th Annual Conference of the Association for Jewish Studies.
11. For a recent exposition of the nationalist view of American federalism which argues that federalism was a concomitant part of the origins of American nationalism, see Samuel Beer, *To Make a Nation* (Cambridge, MA: The Belknap Press, 1993).
12. Martin Diamond, *The Democratic Republic* (Chicago: Rand McNally, 1970).
13. *Esther* 1:2.
14. *The Complete Anti-Federalist,* Herbert J. Storing, ed. (Chicago: University of Chicago Press, 1981); Jackson Turner Main, *The Anti-Federalists: Critics of the Constitution 1781–1788* (Chicago: Quadrangle Books, 1961); Cecilia Kenyon, *The Anti-Federalists* (Indianapolis, IN: Bobbs-Merrill, 1966).
15. Martin Diamond, "The Federalist's View of Federalism," in *Essays on Federalism*, Benson, Diamond, et al., eds. (Claremont, CA: Institute for Studies in Federalism, Claremont Men's College, 1961); Forrest MacDonald, *Alexander Hamilton* (New York: Norton, 1979); Gary W. Carey, *The Federalist* (Chicago: University of Illinois Press, 1989); James Madison, *The Mind of the Founder,* Marvin Meyers, ed. (Hanover, NH: University Press of New England, 1981).
16. Peter S. Onuf, *Statehood and Union* (Bloomington: Indiana University Press, 1987); Gordon S. Wood, *The Creation of the American Republic, 1776–1787* (Chapel Hill: University of North Carolina Press, 1969); and Jack N. Rakove, *The Beginnings of National Politics: An Interpretive History of the Continental Congress* (New York: Alfred A. Knopf, 1979)
17. Donald Lutz, *The Origins of American Constiutionalism.*
18. France Newton Thorpe, ed., *The Federal and State Constitutions, Colonial Charters, and Other Organic Laws* (Washington, DC: Government Printing Office, 1909), vol. 1, pp. 15–16.
19. Edward Corwin, *The Higher Law Background of American Constitutionalism* (Ithaca, NY: Cornell University Press, 1967).
20. Leo Strauss and Joseph Cropsey, eds., *History of Political Philosophy* (Chicago: Rand McNally, 1972); Donald Lutz, *Popular Control and Popular Control: Whig*

Political Theory in the Early State Constitutions (Baton Rouge: Louisiana State University Press, 1980).

21. Daniel Elazar, "The Book of Judges: The Israelite Tribal Federation and Its Discontents," *Interpretation* (forthcoming).

22. Robert N. Bellah et al. *Habits of the Heart: Individualism and Commitment in America* (Berkeley: University of California Press, 1985).

Part II

The United States:
The Covenant Challenged

4

Covenant and Contending Principles in the Expansion of the United States

Federal Democracy and the Jacobin Challenge

The establishment of the American federal system was, at one and the same time, a new political invention and a reasonable extension of an old political principle; a considerable change in the American status quo and a step fully consonant with the particular political genius of the American people. Partly because of their experiences with the model before them and partly because of the theoretical principles they had derived from the philosophic traditions surrounding them, the American people rejected the notions of the general will and the organic state common among their European contemporaries. Instead, they built their constitutions and institutions on the covenant principle, a very different conception of the political order.[1]

Because it was based on the covenantal model (in its secular form), the United States embraced manifold uses of the covenant idea. The American "instinct" for federalism was extended into most areas of human relationships, shaping American notions of individualism, human rights and obligations, divine expectations, business organization, civic association and church structure as well as their notions of politics. While there were differences in interpretation of the covenant principle among theologians, political leaders directly motivated by religious principles and those within a secular political outlook; among New Englanders, residents of the Middle States, and Southerners; and from generation to generation, there was also a broad area of general agreement that unified all who subscribed to the principle and that set them and their doctrine apart within the larger realm of political theory. All agreed on the importance of popular or republican government, the necessity to diffuse power, and the importance of individual rights and dignity as the foundation of any genuinely good political system. At the same time, all agreed that the existence of inalienable rights was not an excuse for anarchy, just as the existence of ineradicable human passions was not an excuse for tyranny. For them, the covenant provided a means for free men to form political communities without sacrificing their essential freedom and without making energetic government impossible.

The implications of the federal principle are brought home forcefully when it is contrasted with the other conceptions of popular government developed in the modern era. Other revolutionaries in the "Age of Revolutions" that has existed since the late eighteenth century—most prominent among them the Jacobins—also sought solutions to some of the same problems of despotism that perturbed the Americans. But, in their efforts to hurry the achievement of the millennium, they rejected what they believed to be the highly pessimistic assumptions of the American constitution-makers that unlimited political power could corrupt even "the people" and considered only the problem of autocratic despotism. They looked upon federalism and its principles of checks and balances as subversive of the "general will," their way for expressing a commitment to the organic unity of society, which, like their premodern predecessors, they saw as superior to the mere interests of individuals. They argued that, since their "new society" was to be based on "the general will" as a more democratic principle, any element subversive of its organic unity would be, ipso facto, antidemocratic.[2]

By retaining notions of the organic society, the Jacobins and their revolutionary heirs were forced to rely upon transient majorities to claim the establishment of consensus or to concentrate power in the hands of an elite that claimed to do the same thing. The first course invariably led to anarchy and the second to the kind of totalitarian democracy that has become the essence of modern dictatorship.[3] While the "general will" was undoubtedly a more democratic concept than the "will of the monarch," in the last analysis it has proved to be no less despotic and usually even more subversive of liberty.

The history of the extension of democratic government since the eighteenth century has been a history of the rivalry between these two conceptions of democracy. Because of the challenge of Jacobinism, the meaning of the American idea of federal democracy takes on increased importance.

Jacobinism was the first European theory of polity and society that rejected covenantal compact to cross the ocean. The French Revolution began in 1789, in the same year that the new government of the United States was inaugurated under the federal Constitution. Jacobin emphasis on the general will led to the development of an alternative conception of democracy to that of the Federalists. The Reign of Terror and subsequent tyrannies in France, culminating in Bonapartism, did not keep Jacobin democracy from becoming the darling idea of European intellectuals. At the same time, the very fact of the French Revolution attracted many Americans to its support in the 1790s, including Thomas Jefferson. In a sense, Jefferson's support for that revolution was a prevision of what happened in the 1920s and 1930s in the United States, after the Bolshevik Revolution in Russia, when even people who were not communists sympathized with what they accepted at face value as a progressive step in the unfolding history of liberty. While the direct consequences of sympathies for France in the 1790s on American federal democracy were minimal—Jefferson, after all, remained, as he said, both a federalist and a republican, faithful to the U.S. Constitution and the theory behind it—it was to have later repercussions in American society, after the European revolutions of 1848 led to an influx of continental European intellectuals into the United States and into positions in American institutions of higher education.

Forging a Federal Consensus

The framers of the Constitution capitalized on the American instinct for federalism which had already revealed itself in the nationwide organization for the revolutionary struggle and in the first constitution of the United States. In one sense, they simply tried to improve the American political system within the framework of the covenant idea by creating—as they phrased it—a "more perfect union." The results of their work were not accepted uncritically at the time, nor did the results remain unmodified after the ratification of the Constitution. Their emphasis on the "national" as distinct from "federal" aspects of the new Union (the terms are those of *The Federalist*) did not sit well with the majority of the American people, who felt keenly that emphasis on the federal aspects was necessary to keep government limited, taxes low, and liberties secure.

The antifederalists lost their fight to prevent ratification of the constitution but, by immediately accepting the verdict and entering into the spirit of the new consensus, they soon won over a majority of the American people. After the Jeffersonian victory in 1800, the dominant theoretical emphasis around the nation was to be on the primacy of the states as custodians of the nation's political power, an emphasis that was to be dented from time to time—substantially between 1861 and 1876—but not altered until the twentieth century. This emphasis provided a very hospitable environment for the development of the "states' rights" perspective that colored the actions of Southerners during the Civil War generation.[4]

In reality, the debate over the meaning of the American covenant and its federal principles began anew under the Constitution, has continued ever since, and will no doubt continue as long as the American people remain concerned with constitutional government as an essential element of the American mystique. Its very existence adds to the health of the body politic. Yet, from first to last, it has remained a debate over the interpretation of the meaning of the federal principle and not over the validity of the principle as such.

Though the debate has involved vital questions of the first magnitude, it has been carried on within the context of a basic political consensus regarding what constitutes a properly constructed republic that is all the more remarkable for having changed relatively so little for some two hundred years. Rarely, if ever, given verbal expression as a whole, the existence of this consensus is attested to by scores of commentators on the American scene from Crevecouer to Max Lerner and from de Tocqueville to D.W. Brogan, and from Orestes Brownson to Samuel Beer.[5] More impressive testimony is found in the behavior of the American people when that consensus has been threatened. Abandoning their more transient allegiances, they have invariably responded to the call, changing their "normal" patterns of behavior—often to the amazement of observers lacking historical perspective—for others more appropriate to the situation. It is this instinctive understanding of the basics of the American political system that sustains popular government despite the mistakes of transient majorities. The consensus itself is imbued with the spirit of federalism through and through, though it extends much beyond a concern with the strict institutional aspects of the federal system to embrace the ideas of partnership and balance which, put together, gave birth to the federal principle.

This emphasis on the basic covenantal consensus certainly is not a suggestion that conflict was absent in the nineteenth century, which would be patently absurd in the face of the struggle over slavery and states' rights which culminated in civil war. However, the conflicts, including the Civil War itself, were conflicts over the interpretation and application of shared principles. History has often demonstrated that such conflicts are as bloody as conflicts between ideologies. How much blood was shed in the Middle Ages over what today we all would consider minor points of Christian doctrine by Christians otherwise united in their fervent Christianity?

The federal constitution rapidly became the symbol of that consensus, replacing the Whig constitutional models when it came to the essentials of constitution-making in the American states. To this day Americans, almost without exception, accept as givens the basic inventions of the Federal Constitutional Convention such as the separation of powers, an independent chief executive, democratic bicameralism, and judicial review. State constitutions depart from this model only in questions of detail on substantive rather than structural matters. Those details reflect the products of political conflict, but conflict within the framework of covenantal consensus.

Abraham Lincoln was the last great exponent of American covenantalism in the nineteenth century, presenting the Declaration of Independence as a covenant precisely in order to counteract the Southern contract theory and the Northern abolitionist view that the Constitution was a pact with the devil. The Civil War, in the agonies it brought about, brought Americans back to the covenantal sense of being under judgment. Abraham Lincoln summed this up best in his second inaugural address:

Neither party expected for the war the magnitude, or the duration, which it has already attained. Neither anticipated that the *cause* of the conflict might cease with, or even before, the conflict itself should cease. Each looked for an easier triumph, and a result less fundamental and astounding. Both read the same Bible, and pray to the same God; and each invokes His aid against the other. It may seem strange that any man should dare to ask a just god's assistance in wringing their bread from the sweat of other men's faces; but let us judge not that we be not judged. The prayers of both could not be answered; that of neither has been answered fully. The Almighty has His own purposes. "Woe unto the world because of offences! for it must needs be that offences come; but woe to that man by whom the offence cometh!" If we shall suppose that American Slavery is one of those offences which, in the providence of God, must needs come, but which, having continued through His appointed time, He now wills to remove, and that He gives to both North and South this terrible war, as the woe due to those by whom the offence came, shall we discern therein any departure from those divine attributes which the believers in a Living God always ascribe to Him? Fondly do we hope— fervently do we pray—that this mighty scourge of war may speedily pass away. Yet, if God wills that it continue, until all the wealth piled by the bondman's two hundred and fifty years of unrequited toil shall be sunk, and until every drop of blood drawn with the last, shall be paid by another drawn with the sword, as was said three thousand years ago, so still it must be said "the judgements of the Lord, are true and righteous altogether.

He was but one of many who echoed that theme. As always, it was reality that stimulated covenantal concern.

After the Civil War, however, Lincoln's views ceased to be intellectually modish. They continued to exist and to influence a postwar generation of reformers, but more as a call for activism than as an intellectual system. The idea of contract as the central principle of social order was shifted from the public to the private sphere.[6]

Later in the century there were clashes, at times bloody, between labor and capital, at times suggesting that a new civil war based on the class struggle was in the making. Yet socialism as an ideological movement was decisively rejected by American labor as much as by anyone else. This was true even though groups far more "American" in the eyes of the public, such as the Populists and Progressives, advocated public policies that were very similar if not identical to those advocated by European and American socialists, including nationalization of the railroads and basic industries.

I would submit that the difference is that socialism, being Jacobin in character, clearly departed from the federal consensus and demanded a sharp break with it, whereas indigenous American radicalism could argue for similar programs while supporting the consensus. Those commentators on the American scene who suggested that the twentieth-century American adopted a socialist platform while rejecting socialism and are at a loss to explain why might well look in this direction. Nor is this merely a distinction without a difference. There really is a difference between a welfare state that seeks to preserve federal democratic individualism and partnership and one which seeks to emphasize statist or collectivist goals.

Subsequent Uses of Covenanting: Settling the West

The constitutions of the American states in the founding era were perhaps the greatest products of the American covenant tradition. But just as they were not the first expressions of that tradition, they were by no means the last. Covenant-making remained a part of the settlement process throughout the days of the land frontier. Adapting the law of the sea, most of the westward wagon trains were internally governed by compactual or contractual arrangements established at the outset.[7] The founding of new states, even new towns, across the United States throughout the nineteenth century reflected the covenanting impulse. People gathered together in every one of the thirty-seven states admitted to the Union after the original thirteen to frame constitutions for their governance.[8] Cities and towns were founded by compact whenever bodies of people joined together to establish communities devoted to common ends.[9]

As they recede in history, these covenantal phenomena of an earlier America can easily be downplayed in their importance, but we need to recall how important they were in the years of the settlement of the United States and the completion of its continental expansion. Because of Americans' romance with the West and its history, there may remain some public consciousness of wagon trains and even of their democratic character, although the myth does not necessarily focus on their compactual dimensions. Hence, even people who understand the myth of wagons westward have little or no idea of the constitutional basis for those wagon trains that enabled them to cross that vast territory with its hostile elements, human and natural, to reach their destinations relatively intact. It was the American ability for constitutional organization that flowed from the covenantal tradition which enabled any group of Americans to come together and organize themselves to undertake common tasks even under very difficult conditions.

If Americans have lost cognizance of the reality behind the romance of the wagon trains, most never really knew much about the formation of the American states beyond the original thirteen. If they were fortunate, they may have learned something about the settlement of their state in public school and even some of the relevant dates in their state's constitutional history. These were rarely put together with what to every democrat should be the magnificent story of founding and polity-building in each state.

While each state has its own history of polity-building, there were two essential patterns. In one, the settlers of the new territories took the lead, organized themselves into states, and secured recognition from Congress. Occasionally this pattern even began from scratch, as in the case of Texas and Hawaii where settlers went beyond the reach of American authority to organize themselves originally as Texans or Hawaiian and, only after doing so entirely independently, petitioned for admission to the Union.[10]

Vermont represented a variant of this.[11] While in the larger sense under British colonial control, the settlers of Vermont, mostly from Connecticut, had to fight off the claims of New York and New Hampshire to gain control over the territory of their future state. They then joined with the rest of the embryonic United States to fight off the British during the American Revolution, in the process organizing their own state, initially outside of the United States of America, and then, like Texas and Hawaii, petitioning the United States to join it and being accepted.

Periodically other concentrations of settlers tried to do the same, such as those led by John Sevier in what is today eastern Tennessee who tried to organize a state to secede from North Carolina, or the settlers along the front range of the Colorado Rockies, who came west as a result of the Gold Rush of 1859 and tried to organize themselves as the Territory of Jefferson to secure recognition from Congress.[12] While those two and other similar efforts did not immediately succeed, the settlers achieved their goals shortly thereafter in other ways, as the existence of the states of Tennessee and Colorado indicate. California may also be considered in the first group, although the role of the United States in its achieving statehood is more ambiguous and complex.[13]

In most other cases, the United States first established the territorial status of the future state or some larger area that contained the future state—and established a preliminary territorial government, with or without the involvement of the local residents and settlers, and thus initiated the process of state-building. However, no later than at that point the inhabitants of the new territory took over. They were the ones who petitioned for statehood, organizing territorial conventions to do so. Often they not only petitioned for Congress to enact enabling legislation so that they could proceed down the road to statehood through calling a constitutional convention, writing a constitution for themselves, and getting it accepted by Congress, but they took the initiative to write a constitution and establish the state before petitioning Congress for recognition.[14]

In every case these were genuinely popular movements in which the people of a given territory saw themselves at some point as thrown back to the state of nature, from which they convened their representatives and organized themselves into a polity with a constitution and a government. While in every case it was their intention to become part of the

United States, they saw themselves as requiring statehood to become equal members of the American commonwealth and so they were seen by the rest of the American nation.

Only the Mormons who settled Utah can be seen as harboring ideas of settlement in order to separate from the United States. To avoid persecution in Illinois and Missouri, their leaders took them out far beyond the edge of American settlement in the 1840s and may indeed have harbored ideas of building a separate and independent existence on more than a temporary basis, but they soon were overtaken by American westward expansion and their people, as Americans, even though they were adherents of a then unpopular religion, did not seem to object to becoming part of the American union. In the end, they even gave up their cherished doctrine of polygamy in order to achieve statehood, since that was the price that Congress exacted from them. Today they are among the most patriotic of Americans, having identified their religion with their country.[15]

In every case, whether according to the first or the second model or any variation thereof, the new settlers of the new territories continued the covenantal tradition in its compactual form to found civil societies and become part of a larger union of civil societies. They did this by holding elections, calling conventions, writing constitutions, submitting same to the voters for approval, and negotiating with the Congress of the United States for their admission to the Union as states.[16]

Every state has its story and every story is of interest, at the very least to the citizens of the state involved. All are major contributions to the development of democratic theory and practice, especially within the covenantal tradition. Take Minnesota, for example. Immediately prior to 1849, the area that is now Minnesota was divided between Iowa and Wisconsin Territories. Although dotted with tens of fur trading posts, the area west of the Mississippi was essentially unsettled by Americans and thus did not require civil government. After Iowa became a state in 1846, it reverted to unorganized territory with no difficulty.

That part east of the Mississippi to the St. Croix River, however, did have several hundred permanent American settlers and in due course the Wisconsin territorial legislature established St. Croix country to provide it with civil government in a local government framework. Wisconsin was admitted as a state in 1848 with the St. Croix river its western boundary, thus leaving St. Croix county to its own devices. Eighteen of the region's leading men held preliminary discussions which led to their signing a call for a convention to be held at Stillwater, the country seat. They described themselves as "citizens of Minnesota Territory." They invited people from all the settlements east and west of the Mississippi to send delegates to the convention whose main task would be to secure the organization of the territory, which was now a clear idea in their minds. On August 26, 1848, just after Wisconsin's admission, sixty-one delegates residing in all parts of what is today Minnesota assembled in convention in Stillwater.

It is important to note that this step was taken at the settlers' (embryonic Minnesotans') own initiative. The Stillwater Convention and passed resolutions calling for Congress to establish a new territory to be named Minnesota. To strengthen their claim, one delegate came up with the ingenious idea that the parts Wisconsin Territory left out of the new state of Wisconsin still constituted Wisconsin Territory. The former governor of the territory had been elected as a senator from the new state so, under this theory, the Secretary of Wisconsin Territory, John Catlin, assumed the mantle of acting governor and in that capacity called an election to choose a new territorial delegate to Congress. The election actually was held on October 30, and Henry Hastings Sibley was elected delegate to Congress for the territory in the making.

Once Catlin certified Sibley's election, he disappeared from the scene, but Sibley, who was already becoming recognized as the leading founding father of the state-in-the-making, went to Congress legitimated by two quasi-legitimate acts. To everyone's surprise, Congress seated him as delegate from Wisconsin Territory, in part because of his own impressive mein. They were not willing to do more than seat Sibley, however, and would not provide for the continuation of territorial government.

After a certain amount of lobbying and negotiation on Sibley's part, on March 3, 1849, hardly six months from the convening of the Stillwater Convention, Congress enacted an Organic Act establishing Minnesota Territory providing for its government, and applying the laws of the recently extinct Wisconsin Territory to it so that it would not be without law before its governor and legislature could act.

Minnesota territory was proclaimed on June 1. Its first legislature convened that September. Eight years later the people of the territory petitioned Congress for an enabling act to enable them to take the next step toward statehood. They secured passage in March 1857. The constitutional convention was called, delegates were elected, a constitution written, ratified by Minnesota's voters, and the new state entered the Union on May 11, 1858.

What is important to note in this process is that the initiative for the founding of Minnesota came from the newly minted Minnesotans themselves, following the classic American theory that civil societies are established by covenant or compact among their members who come together in convention to do so. As individual settlers they may have reached Minnesota by accident but their political community was established as an act of will and consent.

The last two examples of this process occurred in 1958 and 1959 with Alaska and Hawaii respectively, when those two territories were admitted to the Union as states as a result of the pressures of their respective populations on the federal government. Consciously and deliberately following the pattern of earlier states of forcing the hand of Congress, both convened territorial conventions to write state constitutions and petition Congress for statehood, and both lobbied hard in the country as a whole for support, in the end successfully.

While those were the last two territories to be admitted as full states to the American union, a new status was developed for Puerto Rico and the Northern Marianas Islands, a status that Americans refer to as commonwealth; the Puerto Ricans as a free associated state (*eitado libre associato*); and political scientists, a federacy; an asymmetrical federal relationship involving the United States as the federate power and the two commonwealths as offshore federal partners, to guarantee them greater internal autonomy, especially in the preservation of their indigenous cultures, in return for accepting less of a role in the constitution and governing of the union as a whole. Initiated with Puerto Rico after World War II, this commonwealth arrangement was extended to the Northern Marianas by their choice in the 1970s.

In both cases the initiative rested with the locals, who followed procedures similar to state formation to gain their new status. In both, the locals first had to indicate that they preferred to stay within the United States rather than become independent. In the case of Puerto Rico, a commonwealth since 1952, there have been periodic referenda on the subject, the most recent in 1993, offering choices of continuation of commonwealth status, full statehood, or independence, and in every case the largest vote has been for the continuation of commonwealth status with statehood a close second and independence very far behind. Thus the covenantal tradition is preserved through a different form of political compacting more attuned to the diversity of the world in which the United States now finds itself.[17]

Meanwhile, constitutional choice in the United States has been institutionalized in new ways. As Americans completed the division of their national territory into states or the equivalent, two new steps were taken which demonstrated that the American people did not want to give up their rights of constitutional design and choice. The introduction of initiative, referendum, and recall in many states, whereby their citizens could vote on whether or not to accept particular constitutional changes and even initiate such changes when they so desired, came at the end of the nineteenth century, on the heels of the end of the state formation period, as a device to enable the people in a majority of the states plus their localities to continue to be involved in the constitution-making process, not only when new constitutions were proposed but when any constitutional change was on the agenda. Of course every state had to adopt these measures on its own as an act of constitutional reform in and of itself and there are no national devices of this type, but these devices, in all or part, became an increasingly popular feature of state constitutionalism in the twentieth century and were extended to localities almost from the first.

In regard to cities and other local governments, this process has gone even more unnoticed. Initially, every local government that was not simply established by the state for reasons of governing convenience as were counties, and often townships, had to petition the colonial, territorial, or state legislature for a separate corporate charter if it wanted to become even formally self-governing. Those charters were tailored by the legislature to each individual case. By the mid-nineteenth century this pattern of case-by-case action was replaced in the case of cities and similar local governments by general incorporation laws whereby standard procedures were established and municipal corporate status could be gained through ministerial procedures; that is, if a community qualified, the matter could be handled administratively without special state legislative action.

While in every case there had to be a local initiative to set the process in motion, the fact that these were formally in the realm of charters granted rather than local self-governing acts had to their covenantal or compactual character often being overlooked. As the procedure was made more ministerial and came under general state law rather than special charters, that became even more the case. Only in the matter of town foundings were any overt covenantal or compactual acts taken and then only in those cases where towns were founded outside of the normal state process and not pursuant to it.

Thus communities like Excelsior, Minnesota, established by covenant of the original settlers in New England before embarking on their migration to Minnesota, while Minnesota was still a territory, was a covenanting in the most original sense. In that case, a community of people of like religion and likeminded moral or social aspirations organized themselves into a town company before occupying the lands they acquired and planted a town with its own government on those lands before turning to territorial or state authorities for recognition.[18] Similar examples can be found throughout the country from Oberlin, Ohio, to Zion, Illinois; from the Amana colonies in Iowa (Amana is the English version of *amanah*, a biblical word for covenant), to Greeley, Colorado, to Salem, Oregon, to name only a few examples.

The device for continuing the process of constitutional choice for localities was home rule. Normally this was constitutional home rule, whereby state constitutions were amended to give, first municipal governments and then counties as well, the power to adopt home rule charters (i.e., constitutions of their own), written and ratified locally within the broad confines of state law, to organize their own forms of government. Some 90 percent of the states have adopted home rule provisions either by statute or by constitutional amendment since the plan was inaugurated by the state of Missouri in the 1880s. While the extent to which these home rule provisions are controlling has been a matter of some legal and political dispute, they are available to the vast majority of municipal governments in the United States so that the local citizenry, too, is involved in the continuing process of constitutional design and redesign.[19] In this way the covenantal tradition has achieved another measure of institutionalization even if the tradition itself is not explicitly recalled in the process.

With the rise of modern organizations (which was coincident with the settlement of the United States) the federal principle of compacting was given new purpose. Scientific and reform societies, labor unions, and professional associations as well as business corporations were formed on the basis of compacts or contracts.[20] In many cases, the noncommercial ones also contracted with one another to form larger organizations while preserving their own integrities, while the owners of commercial or industrial corporations organized mergers that did the same.[21] Virtually every nationwide voluntary association in the United States is federal insofar as it consists of local, state, and sometimes regional chapters that usually have a high degree of autonomy.

Most religious denominations are organized federally or confederally in the United States, with greater or lesser degrees of congregational autonomy and regional or national authority.[22] As such, these voluntary associations have extended federalization into new nongovernmental areas, a pattern that continues to this day. Each step brings lasting, but limited, linkages designed to make possible cooperative activity in ever larger arenas without reducing the members of each union to mere cogs within it.

That is why, for Americans, federalism is ultimately more than a governmental arrangement between the states. It is, rather, the basis of a way of life, or at least, a way of political life. Ironically, it has been easier for Europeans to recognize this than for Americans themselves. Perhaps it is too deeply embedded in the American way of life to occasion much notice.[23]

The Recession of Covenantal Thinking in the Nineteenth Century

The covenant idea reached the point of its greatest conscious influence in the first two or three generations of English, Dutch, and French Huguenot settlement in British North America and had already passed its peak by the end of the historical seventeenth century (roughly 1713).[24] After that, it was challenged and partially replaced by theories of political compact closely related to it, as part of the process of secularization then occurring in the modern world, including the American colonies.[25] Nevertheless, throughout the eighteenth century the two ideas of covenant and compact lived side by side, were often closely intertwined, and both permeated the mindsets of the leading figures of that century. Together they were unchallenged as the intellectual sources of the American Revolution and the federal state constitutions.[26]

At the same time, covenant as an explicit concept began to recede from public consciousness as the language of constitutionalism and contractualism superseded it after the Revolutionary era. This was partly reflected in the behavior of the U.S. Supreme Court in the late nineteenth century. The justices elevated contracts to a level of near sanctity and replaced the covenantal principles of cooperation and shared sovereignty with the theory of dual federalism involving separate and distinct state and federal sovereignties.

The major question that must be posed in any inquiry into the covenant idea as a seminal idea in politics is how use of the idea was lost to view between the time of the American Revolution and our time. The answer to that lies in the intellectual pacesetters' abandonment of covenantal and contractual thinking in the mid-nineteenth century and its replacement by organic and biological analogies derived first from romantic and then from Darwinian ideas. The history of that transformation worldwide needs to be studied carefully.

In intellectual history as well as in life it is easy to be misled by a change in stylish or "in" ideas and to assume that they permeated all of society without exception. Yet there is evidence that even after the intellectual "establishment" shifted from covenantal to organic models, other sectors of the society continued to be rooted in covenantal thinking. While that does not change the basic thrust of the argument presented here, it has implications which need to be considered.

Indeed, subsequent to the conclusion of the Revolutionary generation, there was actually a revival of covenantal thinking in many circles. The secular trends of the eighteenth-century Enlightenment were replaced by neo-Calvinism, the linking of Baconian science and Calvinist religion, and the emergence of reform movements grounded in covenantal ideas.[27] This revival required a synthesis between modernity and what had become traditional religious thought. It never quite came off because of the worldwide emergence of romanticism and Darwinism.[28] The watershed came in the generation between 1848 and 1876, during which time the covenant idea was progressively eclipsed by organic thought, which then became dominant as Social Darwinism and its offshoot, racism.[29]

Covenant Religion and Baconian Science

The crisis of confrontation between religion and science was decisive here. The operative synthesis between religion and science at the beginning of the nineteenth century was the one which had been developed by the self-same people who developed federal theology in the sixteenth and seventeenth centuries.[30] It persisted until Charles Darwin published *The Origin of the Species* in 1859, after which it, too, unravelled.

The neo-covenantalists of the early nineteenth century sought to base their new theology on an acceptable relationship with scientific ideas. In doing so, they were reflecting the modern temper. Humans have sought to maintain harmony between religion and science since earliest times, but that necessity became even greater from the mid-seventeenth century onward as a result of the emergence of a new and more independent body of scientific thought which claimed its own sources of validation. In the course of time, religion became more dependent on scientific validation rather than what had been true in pre-modern times, when science was dependent on religious validation.

While the initial scientific challenge to religion came in the seventeenth century, it was reconciled through the application of the principles of Baconian science, which could be understood as demonstrating the basic harmony between at least Reformed Protestantism and the new scientific knowledge. Hence it was to Baconian science that the nineteenth century leaders in the reconstruction of covenantal thought turned. In the first half of the nineteenth century, Baconian science could still be considered part of God's great scheme of things, but with the emergence of Darwinism, God's creation went by the boards to be replaced by an often vulgar evolutionism which became the dominant intellectual current of the times. When Baconian science collapsed under the onslaught of Darwinism and the related biological discoveries of the mid-century, religion and science seemed to be placed in conflict with one another with no room left for their reconciliation except on the basis of the jettisoning of old religious ideas and the adaptation of religion to new scientific truths.

The progression followed a clear generational pattern. The generation of 1789 to 1815 brought with it the culmination of eighteenth century thought. Then between 1816 and 1848 there were the aforementioned efforts at covenantal revival. We have already noted that the next generation (1848–1876) saw the development of Darwinism, while the last generation of the nineteenth century, from 1877 to 1914, witnessed its triumph.[31]

World War I brought with it the end of the nineteenth and the beginning of the twentieth century. The sense of inevitable progress implied in Social Darwinism was challenged by the realities of a world in regression. For the next two generations, the world was to struggle with the conflict between expectation and reality. In the latter part of the second generation, the old order of modernity was shattered and covenant resurfaced as an idea whose time had come back as people searched for ways to rebuild the social consensus.

With the adoption of the Constitution, American political thought was refocused away from the questions of natural law to questions of constitutionalism. On the one hand, this meant that references to first principles, including covenants, diminished. On the other, it represented a triumph for the concretization of the covenant idea in the constitutional thought of the new federal republic. While the history of federal thought in the United States was not to be a smooth one, it did replace political concern with the covenant idea until, in our time, thoughtful Americans have found it necessary to go back to first principles, originally those of the Founding Fathers, and then beyond even the period of constitution-making to the intellectual roots of the founders of the United States.

Similarly, new political theories emerged to rival federal democracy. The covenant theology held up until the mid-nineteenth century, although it was under increasing challenge from the end of the eighteenth century onward. The challenge was provoked by the new optimism of Americans that rejected the Calvinistic pessimism of the federal theology that saw most humans as damned by predestination. While the Puritan theologians had worked out an elaborate system to denude predestination of its full meaning, in the simple preaching of the church pastors it still carried a heavy message; and in increasingly optimistic America that message no longer reflected the spiritual expectations of the people.

An abortive effort was made to revive a more palatable Calvinism in the 1830s and 1840s but it did not succeed in holding the intellectual leadership among religionists. While Calvinism certainly did not disappear, it retreated from the public sphere to become a matter of revivalism and individual salvation, while new public theologies were developed by the religious establishment. The covenantal churches and their theologians moved away from covenant to other theological concepts. The covenant foundations of American Puritanism virtually disappeared from public view by the end of the nineteenth century and were only later rediscovered by Perry Miller.[32]

So, too, the synthesis between religion and science that had been developed by the selfsame people who developed federal theology persisted until Charles Darwin published *The Origin of Species* in 1859, after which it, too, unravelled. In the first half of the nineteenth century,

Baconian science could still be considered part of God's great scheme of things, but with the emergence of Darwinism, God's creation went by the boards, to be replaced by an often vulgar evolutionism that became the dominant intellectual current of the times.[33] In the years between the Civil War and World War I, Darwin's ideas were transformed into Social Darwinism, the idea that survival of the fittest was nature's way and that the human race progressed best by allowing nature to take its course. Connected with that harsh social theory were new theories of racial superiority and inferiority which soon became simple, even vulgar, racism according to which the northwest Europeans of Anglo-Saxon and German stock were racially superior to all others by evolution or whatever.

It was only after World War II, with the beginning of the postmodern epoch, that racism was formally challenged and rejected in American society and Social Darwinism was finally abandoned, although both had been seriously challenged from the 1920s onward. Those challenges came at the same time that the modern synthesis itself was being challenged by new and not necessarily more felicitous understandings of community and civil society. Throughout all of this there were those groups that held tenaciously to one or another aspect of the covenantal worldview and there were those who less consciously continued within that worldview. The former were involved in what appeared to be a life and death struggle with the new trends of the postmodern 'epoch, while the latter still sought, if only subconsciously, to harmonize the covenantal spirit with it.

Covenant and Organized Reform

Considerably more successful was the emergence of organized reform as secularized or semi-secularized covenantalism.[34] The institutionalization of reform is one of the great achievements of covenantal societies. A strong case can be made that the very idea of reform emerges from the covenant world view and is only possible where that world view exists. In the United States, the first efforts at organized reform emerged as part of the Revolutionary epoch and led to, among other things, the ending of slavery in the northern states and the reform of the criminal law (including such "achievements" as the introduction of prisons in place of public punishment such as whipping and stocks), as well as vital legal reforms, such as the elimination of primogeniture and entail.

The emergence of continuous organized reform efforts, whereby one specialized reform movement would follow upon another generation after generation, with each using the most sophisticated available organization techniques to mobilize support and achieve its goals, can be dated to the 1830s. A group of New England reformers, including Horace Mann in education, Dorothea Dix in mental health, the abolitionists, and various others devoted to different causes, led the way. In virtually every case, these reform efforts represented a secularized covenantal impulse.[35] This network of reform movements achieved substantial success in the state and local arenas in the 1840s and 1850s and reached a climax during the Civil War with the emancipation of the slaves and the enactment of much of the reformers' program by the federal government.[36] Lincoln gave reform new meaning, moral, humanitarian, and covenantal, by both integrating and modifying the impact of Yankee reformers on the American body-politic, reflecting his broadly humanitarian ethic.[37]

Reform lost momentum after the Civil War as the new conservatism of the Gilded Age came to dominate American public concerns. The 1870s and the 1880s were dry times for these covenant-grounded reformers, but their impulse reemerged in the 1890s and led to great achievements of a new generation of reformers, particularly in those states where the New England tradition was strongest.[38] The degree to which there was a direct concern with or reliance on covenantal ideas on the part of these reformers has yet to be explored. We have random expressions of such concern in which covenantal terms have become part of the common understanding of American history; these can be seen as indicators of what may lie beneath the surface.

Notes

1. Daniel J. Elazar, *The American Constitutional Tradition* (Lincoln: University of Nebraska Press, 1988).
2. Denis de Rougemont, "Etat-Nation," *Dictionnaire International de Federalism,* Denis de Rougemont, ed. (Bruxelles: Bruylant, 1994).
3. Jacob Talmon, *The Origins of Totalitarian Democracy* (Boulder, CO: Westview Press, 1985).
4. Carl Brent Swisher, *American Constitutional Development* (Cambridge, MA: The Riverside Press, 1954); *idem., The Growth of Constitutional Power in the United States* (Chicago: University of Chicago Press, 1963); Ralph Henry Gabriel, *The Course of American Democratic Thought* (New York: Ronald Press Co., 1956); Paul L. Murphy, *The Shaping of the First Amendment, 1791 to the Present* (Oxford: Oxford University Press, 1992).
5. Hector St. John Crevecoeur, *Letters From an American Farmer* (London: J. M. Dent and Sons, 1926); Alexis de Tocqueville, *Democracy in America* (New York: Alfred A. Knopf, 1993); Orestes Brownson, *Selected Essays* (New York: Henry Regnery Co., 1955); James Bryce, *The American Commonwealth* (New York:

Putnam, 1959); Dennis W. Brogan, *The American Political System* (London: H. Hamilton, 1947); Louis Hartz, *The Liberal Tradition in America* (New York: Harcourt, Brace, 1955); Max Lerner, *America as a Civilization* (New York: Simon and Schuster, 1957); Seymour Martin Lipset, *The First New Nation: The United States in Historical and Comparative Perspective* (New York: Basic Books, 1963); Vincent Ostrom, *The Political Theory of a Compound Republic* (Lincoln: University of Nebraska Press, 1987); Samuel Beer, *To Make a Nation* (Cambridge, MA: The Belknap Press, 1993).

6. Samuel Krislov, "Property as a Constitutional Right in the Nineteenth Century: or What Have We Learned Since Corwin?" *Publius*, vol. 22, no. 2 (Spring 1992).

7. Bernard DeVoto, *The Year of Decision* (Boston: Little, Brown, 1943); Ray Allen Billington, *The Far Western Frontier* (New York: Harper and Row, 1956); Josiah Gregg, *Commerce of the Prairies* (Ann Arbor, MI: University Microfilms, 1966).

8. *State Constitutional Designs in Federal Systems, Publius*, vol. 12, no. 1 (Winter 1982).

9. Page Smith, *As a City Upon a Hill: The Town in American History* (New York: Alfred A. Knopf, 1966).

10. Julius William Pratt, *The Acquisition of Hawaii and the Spanish Islands* (Chicago: Quadrangle Books, 1964); Mark E. Nackman, *A Nation Within a Nation: The Rise of Texas Nationalism* (Port Washington, NY: Kennikat Press, 1975).

11. Ralph Nading Hill, *Yankee Kingdom: Vermont and New Hampshire* (New York: Harper and Row, 1960).

12. LeRoy Reuben Hafen et al., *Western America* (Englewood Cliifs, NJ: Prentice-Hall, 1970).

13. Robert Glass Cleland, *From Wilderness to Empire: A History of California* (New York: Alfred A. Knopf, 1959).

14. *State Constitutional Designs.*

15. Leonard James, *The Mormon Experience: A History of the Latter-Day Saints* (New York: Vintage Books, 1980).

16. *State Constitutional Designs.*

17. Juan Torruella, *The Supreme Court and Puerto Rico: The Doctrine of Separate and Unequal* (Raio Piedras, P.R.: University of Puerto Rico, 1985); Truman R. Clark, *Puerto Rico and the United States* (Pittsburgh: University of Pittsburgh Press, 1975).

18. *The Lake, The Land, and The People: A Historical Portrait of the City of Excelsior as Seen in its Buildings and Sites: The Great Historical Survey* (Excelsior, MN: Lake Minnetonka Historical Society and the Excelsior City Council, 1978; Grace Knowlton, *Historic Excelsior* (Excelsior, MN: The Excelsior Heritage Preservation Committee under Auspices of the Excelsior City Council, 1982).

19. Daniel J. Elazar, "State-Local Relations: Reviving Old Theory for New Practice," in Stephen Cole, ed., *Partnership within the States: Local Self-Government in the Federal System* (Urbana: University of Illinois, 1976).

20. On the organization of commercial/professional associations, see Corrine Gelb, *Hidden Hierarchies* (New York: Harper and Row, 1966).

21. Harold Underwood Faulkner, *American Economic History* (New York: Harper and Row, 1960).

22. On the organization and governance of religious bodies, see Edwin Scott Gaustad, *A Religious History of America* (New York: Harper and Row, 1966); Will Herberg, *Protestant-Catholic-Jew* (Garden City, NY: Doubleday, 1960).

23. Alexandre Marc, "New and Old Federalism: Faithful to the Origins," *Publius*, vol. 9, no. 4 (Fall 1974); *Federalism as Grand Design.*

24. On seventeenth century covenantalism, see Patrick Riley, "Three Seventeenth-Century German Theorists of Federalism: Althusius, Hugo, Leibniz" in *Publius*, vol. 6, no. 3 (Summer, 1976); Donald Lutz and Jack D. Warden, *A Covenanted People: The Religious Traditions and the Origins of American Constitutionalism* (Providence, RI: John Carter Brown Library, 1987). For Althusius' works in the original and in translation, see Carl J. Friedrich (ed.), *The Politica Methodice Digesta of Johannes Althusius* (Cambridge, MA: Harvard University Press, 1932) and Frederick S. Carney (ed. and trans.), *The Politics of Johannes Althusius* (Boston: Beacon Press, 1964).

25. Cf. Donald S. Lutz and Jack D. Warden, *A Covenanted People: The Religious Tradition and the Origins of American Constitutionalism* (Providence, RI: John Carter Brown Library, 1987); Donald Lutz, ed., *Documents of Political Foundation Written by Colonial Americans* (Philadelphia, PA: Institute for the Study of Human Issues, 1986); and Charles Hyneman and Donald Lutz (eds.), *American Political Writing During the Founding Era, 1760–1805* (Indianapolis, IN: Liberty Fund, 1983).

26. On the American Founding, cf. Daniel J. Elazar and John Kincaid, *The Declaration of Independence: The Founding Covenant of the American People* (Philadelphia, PA: Center for the Study of Federalism, 1982); Daniel J. Elazar, *The American Constitutional Tradition* (Lincoln: University of Nebraska Press, 1988); Hyneman and Lutz, *American Political Writing During the Founding Era, 1760–1805*; and Lutz and Warden, *A Covenanted People: The Religious Traditions and the Origins of American Constitutionalism.*

27. For a discussion of Neo-Calvinism in colonial America, see W.A. Speck and L. Billington, "Calvinism in Colonial North America," in Menna Prestwick, ed., *International Calvinism, 1541–1715* (Oxford: Clarendon Press, 1985).

   For a discussion of Calvinist and Neo-Calvinist thought, see Robert McCune Kingdon, ed., *Calvin and Calvinism: Sources of Democracy?* (Lexington, MA: D.C. Heath, 1970) and George Laird Hunt, ed., *Calvinism and the Political Order*, essays prepared for the Woodrow Wilson Lectureship of the National Presbyterian Center (Philadelphia, PA: Westminster Press, 1965).

   For a historical discussion of Neo-Calvinism, see John T. McNeill, *The History and Character of Calvinism* (New York: Oxford, 1954).

28. On the emergence of Romanticism worldwide, see e.g. Morse Peckham, *The Birth of Romanticism* (Greenwood, FL: Morse Peckham, 1986); Howard M. Jones, *Revolution and Romanticism* (Cambridge, MA: Harvard University Press, 1974); and John C. Greene, *Darwin and the Modern World View* (New York: New American Library, 1963).

29. On the intellectual history of the nineteenth century, see Maurice Bruce, *The Shaping of the Modern World* (London: Hutchinson, 1958) and John Morris Roberts, *Revolution and Improvement: The Western World, 1775–1847* (London: Weidenfeld, 1976).

   On the intellectual history of nineteenth century America, see Vernon L. Parrington, *Main Currents in American Thought* (New York: Harcourt, Brace and Co., 1930) and Ralph Henry Gabriel, *The Course of American Democratic Thought* (New York: Ronald Press Co., 1940); cf. also Catherine Zuckert, *Natural Right in American Imagination* (Lanham, MD: Rowland and Mitchell, 1990).

30. On the early nineteenth-century synthesis of religion and science, see John Cogley, *Religion in a Secular Age* (London: Pall Mall Press, 1968), especially "Religion and Modernity," pp. 71–114 and "The Religious Response to Modernity," pp. 115–42. On the relation of Darwin to Bacon's thought on science and religion, cf. Maurice Mandelbaum, History, Man and Reason: A Study in Nineteenth Century Thought (Baltimore, MD: Johns Hopkins Press, 1971), especially p. 86.

31. Daniel J. Elazar, "Generational Breaks," in Nissan Oren, ed., *When Patterns Change: Turning Points in International Politics* (New York: St. Martin's Press and Magnes Press, 1984); "The Generational Rhythm of American Politics" in *American Politics Quarterly* no. 6 (January, 1978), pp. 55–94; *American Federalism: A View from the States*, 3rd edition, (New York: Harper and Row, 1986); and *American Mosaic*, (Boulder, CO: Westview Press, 1992).

32. Daniel J. Elazar, ed., *Covenant in the Nineteenth Century* (Lanham, MD: Rowman and Littlefield, 1994).

33. Gaustad, *A Religous History of America.*

34. On the institutionalization of reform in the nineteenth century, see Daniel J. Elazar, *Building Toward Civil War* (Lanham, MD: Center for the Study of Federalism and University Press of America, 1992) and Robert E. Brown, *Charles Beard and the Constitution: A Critical Analysis of "An Economic Interpretation of the Constitution"* (Princeton, NJ: Princeton University Press, 1956). Cf. also Richard Abrams, ed., *The Shaping of Twentieth Century America* (Boston: Little Brown, 1965); Richard Abrams, ed., *The Issues of the Populist and Progressive Eras, 1892-1912* (New York: Harper and Row, 1969); J. David Greenstone, "The Transient and the Permanent in American Politics" in J. David Greenstone, ed., *Public Values and Private Power in American Politics* (Chicago: University of Chicago Press, 1982); and J. David Greenstone, "Political Culture and American Political Development: Liberty, Union, and the Liberal Bipolarity" in *Studies in American Political Development*, vol. I (New Haven, CT: Yale University Press, 1986).

35. On the New England reform impulse of the pre-Civil War years, see Van Wyck Brooks, *The Flowering of New England* (New York: Dutton, 1936).

36. Allan Nevins, *The War for the Union: War Becomes Revolution*, vol. 2 (New York: C. Scribner, 1947).

37. Thomas Harry Williams, *Lincoln and the Radicals* (Madison: University of Wisconsin Press, 1960); Greenstone, *Lincoln's Political Humanitarianism*, pp. 187-88.

38. Richard M. Abrams, *Conservatism in a Progressive Era: Massachusetts Politics, 1900-1912* (Cambridge, MA: Harvard University Press, 1964).

5

Slavery and Secession:
Covenant versus Compact

Early in the nineteenth century the American covenantal world view met its first great, one might even say potentially deadly, challenge: the struggle over slavery. At the time of the American Revolution and the adoption of the United States Constitution, enlightened opinion had turned against slavery precisely for covenantal reasons, at least as they were filtered through the idea of inalienable rights embodied in a natural rights view of humanity. Hence, the American founders could abolish slavery in all of the Northern half the country, already embracing the majority of the American population, and treat slavery where it remained in the Southern states as an evil that would wither on the vine of its own accord if it were simply contained. To that end, the U.S. Constitution authorized Congress to prohibit the slave trade after 1808. Slaves were delicately referred to in the constitution as "other persons" and whatever steps possible were taken to demonstrate disapproval of slavery under conditions that would allow union of the states.

Within a few years of the adoption of the constitution, however, technological change, beginning with the invention of the cotton gin, made slavery economically profitable once again and hence desirable to the slave owners where it existed. Since the slave owners were also the political and social leaders, they had relatively little difficulty in overcoming Southern abolitionism and making slavery first a desideratum and then the foundation stone of Southern society and its ideology. To do so they had to launch a major assault on the doctrine of inalienable human rights, in order to dehumanize blacks. They also had to attack the covenantal basis of society, not only as part of their assault on universal human equality but also to justify organically social hierarchy which placed the slave owners on the top and the slaves on the bottom of the

123

social order. Finally they had to attack the basic theory of American federalism to divert it from the notion of a political compact among equals to that of a political compact among equal states.

All of this took place over a period of a generation, but by the late 1830s the conflict was prepared to erupt in earnest. As we all know, it led politically and militarily to a great Civil War in which the long and bloody military conflict overshadowed the very serious intellectual and ideological dimensions of the struggle. The latter bear serious consideration, however, both for the role they played and for what they yet have to offer in the development of American civil society.

Politically, the slavery issue fractured the original American covenant. Southern whites, in order to maintain what they considered their right to preserve slavery in their states, increasingly defined the Constitution as a compact among sovereign states which could be renounced by any party to it if it felt the terms of the compact were being violated. On the other hand, radical antislavery forces responded by defining the Constitution as what their leader, William Lloyd Garrison, termed a "covenant with hell" because it allowed slavery to continue. The Civil War discredited the Southern compact theory even though its proponents argued, as did Alexander Stevens, former vice president of the Confederacy, that force of arms may have decided the issue but could not change the validity of the idea.[1]

It is helpful to recapitulate the difference between the Southern compact theory, especially as articulated by its foremost exponent, John C. Calhoun, and the covenantal theory of the Union, especially as articulated by Abraham Lincoln, its great expositor. In one of those all too frequent endeavors made by the public, even the presumably educated public, throughout history to understand its past, their "dialogue" has been neglected of recent, most unfortunately for the American people. Since both were political leaders of the first rank as well as political theorists, Americans can learn from them in both the theoretical and practical dimensions.

Southern statesman and political philosopher John C. Calhoun, for many years United States senator from South Carolina and also secretary of war and vice president of the United States, formulated his theory in an effort to defend the rights of the South to preserve their "peculiar institution," slavery, and the social system that flowed from it through the structure and relationships of American federalism. In order to do so,

Calhoun developed a sophisticated political theory that sought to move Americans from their covenantal origins, even in secularized compact form, to a new understanding of the nature of civil society.[2]

Calhoun argued that civil society was basically an organic phenomenon and that only organic societies could be true primary polities. The states, he argued, were the organic primary societies and polities of the United States and as such had primacy within the Union, however desirable the Union was for its purposes. Calhoun was a Unionist, not a secessionist. He believed in a strong Union within its sphere, and as secretary of war even argued that any time 50 percent plus one of the states wanted to undertake a project and it could be done more effectively through the federal government, the federal government should be called upon to do it.[3] But Calhoun argued that the Union was still one of limited purposes, established by a compact among the states, and that the states retained primacy because they were organic societies and the Union was not, nor could it ever be without transforming the whole political-social structure of the United States.

This view had already been visible at the time of the American founding during the Revolutionary War. Only the agreement on immediate ends, namely the declaring of independence and the organization of the Union, enabled the representatives of the Southern states who held this view and those of the Northern states who held a more covenantal view of the United States, seeing both the states and the nation as emerging simultaneously and equally from the covenants of the American people, to come together and agree on specific steps to be taken at the time. Even with regard to compromise over the slavery issue, the Northern states had used the Revolution as an opportunity to emancipate their slaves. Slavery was formally ended everywhere north of the Mason-Dixon line in the revolutionary era. Moreover, the Northern states secured the end of slavery in the territories of the Old Northwest—that is to say, west of the Appalachians and north of the Ohio River—and clearly indicated what they thought would be the future direction of the United States. At the same time they compromised with the Southern states, allowing the latter to continue slavery within their boundaries for the sake of union and then a more perfect union.

Changing technologies and economic circumstances led to a resurgence of the profitability of slavery in the Southern states at the end of the eighteenth century. This precipitated intersectional conflict and led

the South to seek a theory of union compatible with its position on slavery. Unfortunately, Calhoun's theory of union, rejected by the North at
the time, later came to be assumed to be the original American theory of
federalism and was so closely identified with slavery (and later, segregation) from the 1840s onward and even more so after the Civil War, that
American federalism, especially as a compact theory, was badly tarred
with its brush.

Meanwhile Northerners like Lincoln went back to the covenant theory,
not only to justify Northern coercion of the South to remain in the Union
but because of what they saw as the Union's higher purposes. Abraham
Lincoln was the majesterial voice here. He was probably the greatest
American exponent of covenantalism in the sense that he integrated both
the religious and secular liberal strands of covenantalism, covenant, and
political compact into one unified whole on the basis of his understanding of the meaning of the American founding. This was an extraordinary
achievement that few in American history have been able to reach. This
writer would suggest that this is another, albeit less clearly perceived,
reason why Lincoln has become in so many ways the quintessential
American prophet in the biblical sense of the term.

W. Lloyd Warner, the first great anthropologist to apply the tools of
his discipline to examining American society, held that Americans saw
Lincoln as a Christlike figure; that is to say, one who brought salvation
to the American people and then died for their sins. He understood this to
be the American popular view of Lincoln, at least into the 1960s.[4] I
prefer to think of Lincoln in the prophetic mold of Moses, and there are
some indications that he saw himself in the same way or at least understood his role in that way; that is to say, someone who founds or, in his
case, refounds a regime on the basis of its fundamental principles in
response to a great crisis.

Like Moses, Lincoln was a prophet-founder rather than a prophet-
critic or a prophet-bringer-of-hope like the classic but lesser prophets of
the Bible. He, indeed, forecast the necessity for this role in his well-
known speech to the Young Men's Lyceum in Springfield, Illinois in
1838, when he identified those special leaders who appear in the world
so often and are of "the race of lions and the tribe of eagles" and need
challenges of sufficient greatness to satisfy them. At that time his thoughts,
still mostly unformed, led him to the examples of Alexander, Caesar, and
Napoleon along with George Washington. At that time, he already sensed

that the first three were deficient and certainly not appropriate for a democratic republic. For that, a Lincoln was needed and he appeared not only to save the Union, which he did in the manner of Isaiah's suffering servant, but to articulate its meaning and vision as well.

Lincoln articulated the American vision for all Americans "unto the latest generation," as Lincoln was so frequently wont to say. He did so by taking American civil society and holding it under judgment even as he tried to save it, articulating the Americans' vision yet not neglecting for a moment to point out Americans' flaws. In speech after speech whose words have become immortal, he drove home both perspectives. Lincoln best summed it up in his second inaugural address, quoted earlier. He was but one of many who echoed that theme. As always, it was reality which stimulated covenantal concern.

In the mid-twentieth century, the American people abandoned the American vision and replaced it with the American dream, essentially a dream of material prosperity and well-being. Lincoln certainly could understand the second aspect of American aspirations since he shared it, but he would not have accepted Americans' rejection of the first. Perhaps that is why, to him, Americans were only the "almost-chosen people."

Not only were Lincoln's ideas covenantal but his language and cadences were biblical. Nor was his thought partial, but rather comprehensive, touching on every facet of human life and not afraid to recognize change and even encourage it where change was appropriate. Perhaps Lincoln's finest and most comprehensive statement of his prophecy was to be found in that series of remarks and speeches which he gave shortly after his election to the presidency of the United States, when he took what later came to be called a whistlestop tour by train from Springfield to Washington by a circuitous route designed to bring him to at least touch every section of the country, from the West in Illinois and the old Northwest, to the gateway to the South in Kentucky, to the industrial East in Pittsburgh, to the North and greater New England in upstate New York, and to the Middle States in New Jersey and Pennsylvania. To each he delivered the same message or a variant thereof, a message whose political vision was encapsulated in the phrase "the constitution, the Union, and the liberties of the people," all or some part of which he elaborated on at every stop.[5]

...to the salvation of this Union there needs but one single thing—the hearts of a people like yours. When the people rise in masses in behalf of the Union and the liberties of their country, truly may it be said, "The gates of hell shall not prevail against them."...I wish you to remember now and forever, that it is your business, and not mine; that if the union of these states, and the liberties of this people, shall be lost, it is but little to any one man of fifty-two years of age, but a great deal to the thirty millions of people who inhabit these United States, and to their posterity in all coming time. It is your business to rise up and preserve the Union and liberty, for yourselves, and not for me.... I...am but an accidental instrument, temporary, and to serve but for a limited time...with you, and not with politicians, not with presidents, not with office-seekers, but with you, is the question, "Shall the Union and shall the liberties of this country be preserved to the latest generation?" (Reply to Gov. Oliver P. Morton at Indianapolis, Indiana, February 11, 1861)[6]

I am exceedingly anxious that this Union, the Constitution, and the liberties of the people shall be perpetuated in accordance with the original idea for which that struggle was made, and I shall be most happy indeed if I shall be an humble instrument in the hands of the Almighty, and of this His almost chosen people, for perpetuating the object of that great struggle. (Address to the New Jersey State Senate at Trenton, February 21, 1861)[7]

In contrast to Calhoun, Lincoln argued that the federal constitution was based upon a covenant uniting all the American people and their states into "a new nation conceived in liberty and dedicated to the proposition that all men are created equal." That covenant was the Declaration of Independence. If that covenant could be dissolved at all, it could be dissolved only by mutual agreement precisely because it was a covenant; that is to say, it rested on a moral basis and had moral ends. In that light, Southern secession was not only a violation of a political compact but the breaking of a covenant with all the moral implications that that held.

From this flowed Lincoln's position that it was the leaders of the Southern states' "slave power" who were in rebellion, not the Southern people (this was the most tenuous part of his theory), and therefore it was the legitimate right of the American people (read the North) to suppress the usurpation of those leaders and the rebellion which followed in the name of the American covenant, and to enable that covenant to survive and its moral purposes to triumph. All of this was encapsulated in Lincoln's Gettysburg Address:

Four score and seven years ago our fathers brought forth on this continent, a new nation, conceived in Liberty, and dedicated to the proposition that all men are created equal.

Now we are engaged in a great civil war, testing whether that nation, or any nation so conceived and so dedicated, can long endure. We are met on a great battle-field of that war. We have come to dedicate a portion of that field, as a final resting place for those who here gave their lives that that nation might live. It is alto-gether fitting and proper that we should do this.

But, in a larger sense, we can not dedicate—we can not consecrate—we can not hallow—this ground. The brave men, living and dead, who struggled here, have consecrated it, far above our poor power to add or detract. The world will little note, nor long remember what we say here, but it can never forget what they did here. It is for us the living, rather, to be dedicated here to the unfinished work which they who fought here have thus far so nobly advanced. It is rather for us to be here dedicated to the great task remaining before us—that from these honored dead we take increased devotion to that cause for which they gave the last full measure of devotion—that we here highly resolve that these dead shall not have died in vain—that this nation, under God, shall have a new birth of freedom—and that government of the people, by the people, for the people, shall not perish from the earth. (Address delivered at the dedication of the cemetery at Gettysburg, November 19, 1863)[8]

As David Greenstone has argued, on that rock Lincoln erected a new political humanitarianism, based on his understanding of the American founding as filtered through the leading political and intellectual figures whose ideas he had encountered in his younger years, Daniel Webster and Henry Clay, who had begun to articulate both the moral and political meaning of the United States as a new covenanted nation in direct oppo-sition to the theories of Calhoun.[9]

Unlike Calhoun's compact theory, which died with the collapse of the Southern Confederacy and survived only in a negative sense (to be re-ferred to as not being the underlying theory of the American Union and hence a negative on the whole idea of American federalism), Lincoln's political humanitarianism survived to positively influence subsequent generations of reformers, especially in the Progressive Era. In fact, the latter idea, too, suffered eclipse in the minds of Americans grown tired of the sacrifices called for in that theory. Those who were willing to make those sacrifices and urge on their fellow Americans to do the same kept Lincoln's political humanitarianism alive and the force of varying im-pact until it was superseded in American public life first in the 1930s by Franklin Delano Roosevelt's New Deal social democracy and finally in the 1960s by the "New Age" thinking of the early postmodern epoch.

The heart of Lincoln's political humanitarianism was the idea and practice of moral reform. Greenstone summarizes it as follows.

1. Like that of the abolitionists, Lincoln's position on slavery reflected a broadly humanitarian ethic. But unlike the abolitionists', Lincoln's humanitarianism was political rather than personal; it required dedicat-

ing and, when necessary, rededicating the American regime—the nation's political institution—to the moral, material and intellectual self-improvement of every citizen.

2. This political humanitarianism achieved coherence and intelligibility—and could attract so much popular support—because it drew upon beliefs and practices deeply rooted in American culture. While the abolitionists' personal humanitarianism expressed a tradition of Protestant separatism and piety, Lincoln's ethic asserted "a union of piety and prudential rationality, of sainthood and citizenship." Initially articulated in America by New England's colonial orthodoxy, this outlook was developed in the nineteenth century by Lincoln's Whiggish political culture.

Together, these two claims offer limited but important support for a much more general proposition: in American political culture, the humanitarian tradition has been a major liberal alternative to the dominant version of American liberalism. Whereas the dominant tradition focuses on the satisfying of each person's individually determined objectives—whether rather directly through some form of utilitarianism, or more indirectly through a commitment to individual rights—humanitarianism focuses on the development of human faculties.

Lincoln anchored his thought not only in the Declaration of Independence and subsequent works of American political importance but in the Bible. His speeches, particularly his various confrontations with Stephen Douglas, his great Illinois political rival, are filled with such references, sometimes cited, sometimes not.[10]

In all of these references and his effort to relate them to the American scene it should be recalled that Lincoln was from the Middle Border, in Lincoln's case Kentucky, Indiana and Illinois, and hence a moralist in an individualist region. Consequently, since his preserved thoughts on this are almost entirely in his public political speeches, he was very careful in his phrasing so as not to alienate his audience while making his point. For example, in his great speech in Peoria in 1854 he stated: "My faith in the proposition that each man should do precisely as he pleases with that which is exclusively his own, lies at the foundation of…[my] sense of justice."[11]

Lincoln did indeed support the Whig economic program which was based upon capitalist entrepreneurship, but the addition of the word "exclusively" to that passage, while allowing his audience to think that he identified with their ideas of natural liberty, indicated that he believed it necessary to restrict them by his ideas of federal liberty. Lincoln's position was strikingly Yankee, combining morality and ambition into a single engine designed to promote both moral and material progress.

Lincoln's derivation from the Middle Border plus his view of the American Union as a moral achievement combined to differentiate him from the abolitionists (who were greatly pained by those differences and usually misunderstood Lincoln as a result) and to view slavery as a grave issue but not always the decisive one for Americans' moral improvement. Lincoln's covenantal humanitarianism was prudential but always focused on the target. He justified his stance as necessary in order to be faithful to the political religion of the nation, which requires "reverence for the laws" (Address to the Young Men's Lyceum) as its foundation. Of course that reverence only belonged in a regime and under a constitution which promised popular republican institutions.

In all of this Lincoln was a Whig, not only in his original political party and fundamental political leanings, but in the larger sense of Whiggism as this had developed in Anglo-American civilization since the seventeenth century. Like all Whigs, prudence was not relativism but movement toward moral goals by carefully weighing the opportunities, limits, and possibilities, by keeping one's eye on the main chance—those things which were critical to the success of the movement—and adjusting the pace of change so as to avoid threatening the political-social order beyond what it could bear. Whiggism in this sense was the antithesis of aggressive self-righteousness linked to some immediate cause which, no matter how legitimate, threatened the whole fabric of the enterprise.

Greenstone painstakingly traces Lincoln's Whiggish beliefs back to their source in the Yankee religious tradition which he understands as covenantal, what he calls the New England Calvinist heritage.[12]

Lincoln's family settled in New England when they first came to North America in the seventeenth century, but his Massachusetts forebearers were Quakers who later moved to Virginia, became Baptists, and from there moved to Kentucky. The Baptist church of his father was antislavery; Lincoln himself did not join any organized denomination, although he found the Presbyterian church an appealing place in which to worship. Thus he was foursquare within the Reformed Protestant tradition, albeit toward the more radical wing of that tradition. Lincoln's Whiggism was strongly intertwined with these Reformed Protestant roots,[13] and identified fully with Whig concern for the community and its institutions.

As Greenstone commented "Lincoln's position drew upon a tradition of religious thought, a conception of sainthood and citizenship, that occupied a central place in New England culture. From this perspective, in other words, the Whigs' and Abolitionists' common religious heritage constituted a family of related belief systems. This point is not always well understood."[14]

In essence, Greenstone claims, they were united by the covenant idea and its tradition. The original mission of the Puritans was the reform of the whole national Church of England—that is, was of universalistic scope—but the Puritans held that this could be done only through separation in the form of a congregational church polity where the regenerate could prepare and sustain themselves while engaged in that mission. Thus separatism and evangelism went hand in hand.

By the same token, as Perry Miller has emphasized, the New England way insisted on maintaining both piety and rationalism. To reconcile these apparent contradictions, the Puritans relied upon covenant theology, having at least two sets of equally legitimate opposites to reconcile. Very early in New England's settlement, the idea of the national covenant of England was transformed into the idea of a national covenant uniting not only individual settlers and their families but all the community of New England, thereby reaffirming the communal dimensions of Puritan covenantalism through God's covenant of grace with the regenerate individuals and His national covenant with the community of saints.

Greenstone suggests a typology of nineteenth-century political and ethical positions that evolved out of colonial Calvinism. Like the seventeenth-century New England Puritans, Lincoln sought to develop positions that combined political and moral obligations, using instrumental rationality to move toward major ethical improvement if not perfection as the ultimate goal. In that connection, Lincoln contrasted his position, which looked upon slavery as morally wrong, with the position of Stephen Douglas and his followers, who did not, making that a major point of division. Even though instrumentally they were not very far apart in the short term, their long-term goals were different, since Lincoln believed that ultimately the Union would have to confront the issue of slavery as a moral one and should not confuse short-term tactics with long-term goals.

For Lincoln individual improvement, a humanitarian as well as an economic concern, went hand in hand with the improvement of the nation's social and political institutions. Lincoln recast this conventional Whig combination in progressive and egalitarian terms. For him, this was best done through preserving the Union. Lincoln embraced Madison's argument in *Federalist,* No. 10 that the Union was itself a "good" to be preserved, but as a moral as well as a political Union, which meant that its stand on slavery had to be clearly against that institution.

This defines not only Lincoln's politics but also his legacy for subsequent generations of Americans. Lincoln's assassination ended his ability to implement his political moral agenda and, while his successors initially tried to do so, they lacked his understanding both of that agenda and of how to implement it, in part because they lacked his rootedness in the covenant tradition. While he remained the ideal for many who gained high office in the Republic, both for those who came from that tradition and for others who did not, another generation had to pass before a new group of reformers rose up through an attempt to articulate the Lincoln tradition as the basis for their humanitarianism. In the meantime, the thrust of intellectual and political life in the United States had moved in different directions.

Nevertheless, for reasons involving the continued conflict between the moral demands of covenant theory and the much looser and more pluralistic aspirations of the society, the former could be activated only to advance specifically morally grounded crusades—against slavery, later against political corruption, still later against the deficiencies of nineteenth-century capitalism, and most recently against the exclusion of certain groups from full participation in American society—but it could not win reinstatement as a general theory without making greater moral demands upon the American people than they were prepared to accept or even to acknowledge as legitimate. What emerged out of the Civil War use of the covenant theory was a new sense of American nationalism that rejected the compact theory of federalism on the one hand but did not turn to the covenant theory, rather to new theories of Darwinism and pluralism that flowed from the Civil War experience to define American nationalism.

The most popular intellectuals of the time, including the first professor of political science in the United States, Frances Lieber, a distinguished and enormously influential German refugee who had been educated on Hegelian organic theories of the state that fit in well with the Darwinism that burst upon the world scene a decade later, were Jacobins by political instinct. In reaction to Southern secession and under Lieber's influence, they turned to the theory of the organic state. They challenged the idea of the political compact and the checks and balances of American constitutionalism on both philosophic and ideological grounds. A generation later, their students came to dominate American intellectual life. Lieber, appointed professor of political economy at Columbia University, soon became the center of a group of New York intellectuals and a guiding influence at *The Nation*, the journal founded by that group in 1865 in the closing months of the Civil War to articulate this new philosophy and ideology of Union.[15]

Ironically, it was Woodrow Wilson, a Presbyterian and son of a Presbyterian minister, who, as a political scientist educated according to the new doctrines, did more to undermine the principles of federal democracy among his countrymen than any other single person, even though he continued to see federalism as vitally important in the American system and to use covenantal terminology in his public political rhetoric. In his classic work, *Congressional Government*, published in 1886, Wilson argued that rather than the "paper theories" of separation of powers, in the real world there is always a single center of power in any regime and that, in the United States, that center of power is lodged in Congress.[16] In this Wilson was influenced both by organic theories of the state and by the British parliamentary system. He also became a proponent of modern bureaucracy as a necessary hierarchy imposed upon the body politic.[17] Before he became president, he developed a counter-theory to federal democracy that suited the new spirit of the dawning managerial age.

Those Americans not moved by Germanic theories of the organic state in the late nineteenth century were much influenced by the British system. The American "establishment" of the time had become very Anglophile. A century after the American Revolution, they turned to their English heritage as the major source for American democracy, perhaps in reaction to all the non-Anglo-Saxon immigrants flooding into the United States at the time. Part of that Anglophilism was an excessive admiration for British parliamentary institutions (which, incidentally, were always referred to as English institutions, ignoring the Scots and Welsh in Britain) as well as a desire to ignore immigrants not of English origin in the United States.

This outlook offered the theories of Woodrow Wilson and others such as A. Lawrence Lowell, a Boston Brahmin of the same generation, fertile ground in which to flourish.[18] The combination of Social Darwinism, a philosophy that had its roots in a vulgar application of Darwinian theories, Anglophilism, admiration for German order and bureaucracy, and the racism of northwestern Europeans, including those who had settled in the United States, left no room for covenantal systems. Indeed, it may be to the great credit of the covenant idea that it could not survive as a dominant one in a racist society looking for justifications for the maintenance of white rule at home and abroad.[19]

Meanwhile, on the left, Marxism, which derived from those same Germanic organic and hierarchical foundations, began to become a major influence. It, too, was the very opposite of covenantalism in its approach. As deterministic as the most deterministic Calvinism, its historic determinism offered no room for covenants of salvation and hence no room for political covenants. While much less of a force in the United States in the nineteenth century, it was to become an intellectual force in the twentieth century, especially after the Russian Revolution.[20]

Marxist ideas became an even greater challenge to federal democracy than organic ones. The exponents of the latter, perhaps because they were still close enough to their American origins, still held that the federal system itself was a good idea. The Marxist intellectuals of twentieth-century America, most of whom came from the later immigrant groups, had no commitment to American institutions. Standing in the Jacobin tradition, they viewed federal political organization as ideologically a wrong turn on the road to secular salvation. Nurtured on the economic crises of the twentieth century that culminated in the Great Depression, they sought collectivist solutions to deal with all social problems. For those intellectuals, the federal system was simply a network of barriers designed to help the entrenched classes and to prevent the oppressed classes from achieving what was their due. Thus, they not only became foes of federalism in every respect, but argued that there could be no real democracy with federalism.

Out of all this a liberalism developed at the beginning of the twentieth century whose program was based on principles enunciated by people such as Charles E. Beard, Herbert Croly, John Dewey, and J. Adam Smith. Its starting premise was that the federal Constitution of 1787 was the product of the economic interests of capitalists, and thus a conservative reaction to the liberal Declaration of Independence. Federalism, checks and balances, and all those constraints which the founders viewed as necessary for the maintenance of a proper democratic republic, they saw as devices imposed by reactionary elites interested in protecting their economic and social interests. For this group, the subsequent political struggle in American history was to undo the damage done by the Constitution and make operative the principles of the Declaration of Independence.[21]

This task was particularly important in the twentieth century, they continued, after industrialization had brought about the demise of the small community as the basis for social and political organization and introduced instead the "great society" (John Dewey's term), which required the transformation of the whole nation into a single community through a "new nationalism" (Croly's term) based upon heavy federal government intervention that essentially amounted to statism. This could be achieved if simple popular majorities would be mobilized on behalf of national government intervention and empowered to overcome existing constitutional barriers to enable the national government to carry out the popular will. Needless to say, nothing could have been further from the principles of covenant and federal democracy than this approach, which was originally labeled Progressivism (although it represented only one school of progressivism) and later liberalism. It was given great impetus by the Great Depression and the New Deal to become the intellectually dominant current in the United States by the late 1930s, and popularly dominant a generation later.[22]

The Persistence of the Covenant Tradition

Throughout all of this, covenantalism and federal democracy persisted as an active force in American life and no less than a secondary theme in American thought, at times latent but never insignificant, especially in the realm of action. The generation of reformers who had real grassroots impact took their ideas from Lincoln, the hero of their childhood. Thus Lincoln Steffens and Ida Tarbell sought to reform American cities, not to transfer cities' powers elsewhere.[23]

John Peter Altgeld served as governor of the State of Illinois in the same spirit, opposing federal intervention which he saw as serving plutocratic interests, and mobilizing the power of his state on behalf of the people.[24] Governors Hazen S. Pingree of Michigan, John Lind of Minnesota, Robert LaFollette of Wisconsin and Herman Johnson of California, to mention only a few names, sustained covenantalism in the same way and on the same principle over the next two decades.[25] Jane Addams went further.

Through Hull House she sought to demonstrate how the old covenantal communitarian ideas of the Puritans and Yankees could be applied to the latest waves of immigrants to bring them into the community.[26]

They did so even as the better recognized theoreticians of Progressivism formulated their ideas of the Great Society which were far from being covenantal in their approach. The Midwestern and Western Progressive politicians enunciated a different Progressivism, one which accepted the federal democratic principles of the U.S. Constitution and simply sought to implement them more fully. Senators George Norris of Nebraska, Robert M. LaFollette, Jr. of Wisconsin, William E. Borah of Idaho and Burton K. Wheeler of Montana, among others, demonstrated this not only in their efforts on behalf of progressive government intervention, but in their later rejection of New Deal liberalism as it veered from their Progressive program into the quest for the Great Society.[27]

It hardly need be said that the division was never quite as simple as the foregoing paragraphs might suggest. There continued to be covenantal-communitarian elements among the proponents of the Great Society, if only out of nostalgia, while the Progressive leaders often showed impatience with the checks and balances of federal democracy. Indeed, the New Deal synthesized the two to the nation's advantage.[28] But overall, the division was clear.

The triumph of the Great Society in the 1960s led to the imperial presidency, but it was top-heavy and collapsed under its own weight within a decade. The failure of the War on Poverty, the excesses of Johnson's Great Society programs, the war in Vietnam, and finally Watergate, brought about great disillusionment with what was in any case an impossible dream, that is to say, the creation of artificial community on a continent-wide scale.

Efforts at Covenant Revival Outside of Politics (1818–1848)

Paralleling these trends were a number of efforts at reviving or restructuring the earlier covenantal synthesis in American thought so that it would continue to influence American life by confronting the new problems of the nineteenth century. These efforts included a covenantal revival in religion, an attempt to reinterpret Calvinism in a more optimistic manner better suited to the nineteenth century; the effort to develop a new synthesis of science and religion through Baconian science; the emergence of reform movements reflecting secularized or semi-secularized expressions of covenantalism and the covenantal impulse; and the literary discovery of the deeper meaning of covenantalism. This led to the transformation of late eighteenth and early nineteenth century Protestant covenantalism into an American civil religion which, in turn, lost much of the "bite" of its covenantalism as a result of the impact of romanticism.

The eighteenth-century restructuring of covenant theology held up until the mid-nineteenth century, although it was under increasing challenge from the end of the eighteenth century onward. The challenge was provoked by the new optimism of Americans, which rejected the Calvinistic pessimism of the federal theology that saw most humans as damned by predestination. While the Puritan theologians had worked out an elaborate system to denude predestination of its full meaning, in the simple preaching of the church pastors it still carried a heavy message and in increasingly optimistic America that message no longer reflected the spiritual expectations of people.[29]

The beginning of the nineteenth century saw a dual crisis in the Reformed churches. On the one hand, the "modern" wings of those churches broke away from traditional doctrines—in the most extreme cases of the Unitarians and the Universalists, from the trinitarian idea itself. They and others broke away from the church polities themselves to form new denominations. These changes were both symptoms of and catalysts for internal theological controversies.

As the eighteenth century witnessed a growing secularization of society and separation between the religious and civil dimensions of life, the dynamic wing of Calvinism turned increasingly toward individual salvation as its concern and away from the construction of the holy commonwealth. This, in turn, led to the development of religious methods that emphasized "fire and brimstone" for the damned. Out of this experience, inaugurated by Jonathan Edwards, American revivalism emerged to become a permanent feature of the American religious and social landscape. By its very nature, this revivalism moved away from covenantal categories to emphasize God's awesome power yet his loving willingness to be gracious to individual believers who confessed their sins. This approach became less and less satisfactory for the modernists. It also shattered the unity of the church and contributed, along with the overall secularizing trend, to its final disestablishment in the New England states at the beginning of the new century, an event which further severed the ties between congregation and commonwealth as well as church and state.

Some of the modernists, having abandoned covenant to traditional Calvinism, pursued new noncovenantal theologies. Others, however, sought to create a new synthesis of the nineteenth century ideas and traditional covenantal religion; an abortive effort was even made to develop a more palatable Calvinism in the 1830s and 1840s. These new covenantalists nearly succeeded in holding onto the bulk of the adherents of the Reformed Protestant religion. In the end, they failed because of the new scientific theories which emerged in the second generation of the nineteenth century, particularly Darwinism, which challenged the intellectual underpinnings of their modernized covenantal thinking. Nevertheless, that thinking did continue to influence a significant segment of the American public and continues to do so.

This covenantally rooted effort reappeared among the Progressives at the turn of the century, among the Christian realists epitomized by Reinhold Niebuhr after World War I, and with renewed vigor among contemporaries such as Robert Bellah, Charles McCoy, Max Stackhouse, Douglas Sturm, and William Everett.[30] It can still be found as a strong current in American religious thought. However, because it ceased to be in vogue with the American intellectual "establishment," even those who are rooted in that style of covenantal thinking have rarely participated in the principal intellectual debates of their times unless they have been brought to do so as a result of the efforts of the few brave ones who were prepared to put forward such ideas as respectable theology.

While Calvinism certainly did not disappear, it retreated from the public sphere to become a matter of revivalism and individual salvation, while new theologies were developed by the religious establishment. The covenantal churches and their theologians moved away from the covenant to other theological concepts. Even the covenantal foundations of American Puritanism virtually disappeared from public view by the end of the nineteenth century and had to be rediscovered by Perry Miller in the 1930s.[31] In the interim, most Americans have drifted off into their intellectual systems even in the religious sphere or have simply ignored their own ideational heritage in the pursuit of ideas more in style.

A Sea Change in Legal Theory

Legal theory also took several turns away from covenant and compact in the nineteenth century. The first turn, early in the century, raised the private right of contract to the status of higher law. Then, at the end of the century, in reaction to excessive contractualism, there emerged the beginnings of a legal positivism which, in rejecting the absolute right of contract, ultimately threw out the baby with the bath water.[32]

By the end of the eighteenth century, the idea of law as public compact had become well-nigh pervasive. In a now forgotten flowering of compact-based public law, Americans developed a body of legal theory which deserves to be rediscovered. By the 1840s, the last generation to be educated in that doctrine began to leave the scene, to be replaced by a generation educated in its perversion, the principle of the sacred character of private contract above all. For a generation there was a combination between the two principles, with advocates of the former trying hard to come to grips with the demands of a new industrial society whose ideology in any case favored the latter.

The U.S. Supreme Court gave up the ghost in the 1870s after the retirement of Chief Justice Waite.[33] For the next two generations the contractarians were to be in charge. Before the nineteenth century was out they were to be challenged in the law schools by legal positivism.

Indeed, it was the development of law schools helped undercut the theory of public compact, for reasons which seem to have to do with the combination of the scientific study of the law on one hand and the increasingly narrow and specialized training for the legal profession on the other. The older system, whereby the academic study of the law was essentially related to philosophy and the more narrow vocational aspects of legal training were acquired by "reading law" in a law office without professors and their intellectual trappings, provided a deeper grounding and broader focus but was abandoned by century's end.

Transcendentalism: A New Romantic Philosophy

Another major intellectual change was the rise of Transcendentalism, an American intellectual version of romanticism, all the more potent because it arose in the heart of the old Puritan commonwealth.[34] The Transcendentalists' vague, pantheistic deity could hardly be a partner to the covenant in the manner of the Puritans' living god. In common with other romantic ideologies, Transcendentalism diminished the distinctions in the universe necessary for the establishment of covenantal relationships. Even a superficial reading shows the direction of Transcendentalist thought. Ralph Waldo Emerson, the founder and leader of the Transcendentalist school for nearly half a century until well after the Civil War, reflects this diminution of distinctions in his thought. In a sense he is also a transitional figure like the neo-Baconians, more reflecting thought patterns of the first stage of the modern epoch rather than the "hard" and "scientific" ideologies of the second.

The romantic Emerson was active through the Civil War generation and well into the 1880s, at which point he can be said to have been succeeded as New England's archetypical intellectual by Henry Adams, who was so prominent in American intellectual life in the last generation of the nineteenth century. Adams was in many respects Emerson's opposite—pessimistic, realistic, distinctly unromantic, even bitter about his fate and that of his family and his country. In one thing they were the same, however. They both saw the ideal society as an organic society, perhaps because they were so well rooted in over 200 years of New England society and were part of its elite. The organic model appealed to them and they rejected, even despised what they saw as mechanical departures from it.

Adams's *Autobiography* treats the issue in his famous chapter on "The Virgin and the Dynamo," in which he contrasts the organic unity of the high middle ages, when Christianity emphasized paying homage to the Virgin and the building of great cathedrals, to the disorganized helterskelter, crass, commercialized period of industrial development and money-making in which he lived.[35] While this theme does not touch upon covenant per se it is a rejection of the egalitarian impulses contained in nineteenth century society in favor of an organic society with a clear hierarchy of goods and people; there is no room for covenant or compact in Adams's world view. In a sense Henry Adams's rejections of what Sir Henry Maine at the time described as a society based on contract as distinct from one based on status reflected the failure of Transcendentalism, which was optimistic in thrust. It was replaced by a perspective which looked backward to a golden age and no longer had the hopes for the future which Emerson had propounded.

The Decline and Survival of the Covenant Idea

In the end, it was a combination of Darwin and Thomas Huxley, German political thought and English political institutions, Romantic religion and personalistic revivalism, that unravelled the covenantal system that had dominated American life and thought for two centuries. A new synthesis came into being after the Civil War and Reconstruction. Darwinism became Social Darwinism and organic thinking came to justify dog-eat-dog behavior.[36] Organic theories of nation and state contributed to the new racism that came to dominate the United States and the rest of the Western world in the last decades of the nineteenth century and joined with hierarchic theories of bureaucratic organization to begin the transformation of American government in ways that would not become fully apparent until the twentieth century.[37]

In the sphere of religion, both conservative religion and the social gospel drew upon organic models. While there were countertrends in operation in the form of the Lincoln tradition of reform and segments of the Progressive movement, it would be three generations until the covenant idea would be revived as a major force in American life.[38]

Throughout all of this, covenantalism and federal democracy persisted as an undercurrent in American thought, at times latent but never insignificant, especially in the realm of action. The generation of reformers who had their impact at the time that the theoreticians of Populism and Progressivism were formulating the idea of the Great Society were far more covenantal in their approach, taking their cues from Lincoln, the hero of their childhood.

Notes

1. John C. Calhoun, *A Disquisition on Government and Selections from the Discourses*, C. Gordon Post, ed. (New York: Liberal Arts Press, 1953); *idem., Union and Liberty: The Political Philosophy of John C. Calhoun*, Ross M. Lence, ed. (Indianapolis, IN: Liberty Classics, 1992); *idem , Calhoun:Basic Documents*, John M. Anderson, ed. (State College, PA: Bald Eagle Press, 1952).
2. Ibid.
3. *Union and Liberty*, ibid.; Calhoun, ibid.
4. W. Lloyd Warner, *American Life: Dream and Reality* (Chicago: University of Chicago Press, 1964).
5. Daniel J. Elazar, "The Constitution, the Union, and the Liberties of the People," in *The American Constitutional Tradition* (Lincoln: University of Nebraska Press, 1988).
6. Roy P. Basler, ed., *The Collected Works of Abraham Lincoln*, 8 vols. (New Brunswick, NJ: Rutgers University Press, 1953–55), vol. 4, pp. 193–94.
7. Ibid., p. 236.
8. Andrew Delbanco, ed., *The Portable Abraham Lincoln* (New York: Viking Penguin, 1992), p. 295.

9. J. David Greenstone, "Lincoln's Political Humanitarianism: Moral Reform and the Covenant Tradition in American Political Culture," in *Covenant in the Nineteenth Century*, Daniel J. Elazar, ed. (Lanham, MD: Rowman and Littlefield, 1994).
10. Basler, *The Collected Works,* particularly vol. 2, p. 278; vol. 3, pp. 368–70, 310.
11. Ibid., vol. 2, p. 265.
12. Greenstone, "Lincoln's Political Humanitarianism," especially pp. 160–79.
13. Daniel Walker Howe, *The Political Culture of the American Whigs* (Chicago: University of Chicago Press, 1979).
14. Greenstone, p. 168.
15. H.B. Adams, *The Study of History in American Universities*, Bureau of Education, Circular of Information, No. 2 (Washington, 1887), p. 21; Daniel W. Hallis, *University of South Carolina* (Columbia: University of South Carolina Press, 1951), Vol. 1, pp. 120–23.
16. Woodrow Wilson, *Congressional Government* (Cleveland, OH: Merdian Books, 1965).
17. Woodrow Wilson, "The Study of Public Administration," The Political Science Quarterly, vol. 2, no. 1 (June 1987): 197–222.
18. A. Lawrence Lowell, *Essays on Government* (New York: Johnson Reprint Co., 1968); *idem., Public Opinion and Popular Government* (New York: Johnson Reprint Co., 1969); Harry Cranbrook Allen, *Great Britain and the United States* (London: Odhams Press, 1954).
19. John Higham, *Ethnic Leadership in America* (Baltimore, MD: Johns Hopkins University Press, 1978); *idem, The Reconstruction of American History* (New York: Harper and Row, 1962).
20. Paul Buhle, *Marxism in the United States* (London: Verso, 1987).
21. Charles E. Beard, *An Economic Interpretation of the Constitution of the United States* (New York: Free Press, 1969); Herbert Croly, *Progressive Democracy* (New York: Macmillan, 1914); John Dewey, *The Public and Its Problems* (New York: Holt, 1927); Martin Diamond et al., *The Democratic Republic* (Chicago: Rand McNally, 1966).
22. Ralph Henry Gabriel, *The Course of American Democratic Thought* (New York: Ronald Press Co., 1956); Louis Hartz, *The Liberal Tradition in America* (New York: Harcourt, Brace, 1955).
23. *The Muckrakers: The Era in Journalism that Moved America to Reform*, Arthur and Lila Weinberg, eds. (New York: Simon and Schuster, 1961); Louis Filler, *The Muckrakers* (University Park: Pennsylvania State University Press, 1976); Lincoln Steffens, *The Shame of the Cities* (New York: Hill and Wang, 1987).
24. Ray Ginger, *Altgeld's America* (New York: Funk and Wagnalls, 1958).
25. Russel Nye, *Midwestern Progressive Politics* (New York: Harper and Row, 1965).
26. Jane Addams, *The Social Thought of Jane Addams,* Christopher Lasch, ed. (Indianapolis, IN: Bobbs-Merrill, 1965); *idem, Twenty Years at Hull House* (New York: Macmillan, 1911).
27. Nye, *Midwestern Progressive Politics;* George Mowry, *The California Progressives* (Chicago: Quadrangle Books, 1963); Richard Lowitt, *George W. Norris: The Making of a Progressive, 1861–1912* (Westport, CT: Greenwood Press, 1980); Allen Freeman Davis, *Spearheads for Reform* (New York: Oxford University Press, 1967); Richard Hofstadter, *The Progressive Movement 1900–1915* (Englewood Cliffs, NJ: Prentice-Hall, 1963); David P. Thelen, *Robert M.*

La Follette and the Insurgent Spirit (Boston: Little Brown, 1976); James Leonard Bates, *The United States, 1898–1928: Progressivism and a Society in Transition* (New York: McGraw-Hill, 1976).

28. Arthur Schlesinger, *The Age of Roosevelt* (Boston: Houghton Mifflin, 1957–1960).

29. On eighteenth-century covenant theology and its decline, see Sydney E. Ahlstrom, *A Religious History of the American People* (New Haven, CT: Yale University Press, 1972); Edwin Gaustad, *A Religious History of America* (New York: Harper and Row, 1966); H. Richard Niebuhr, *The Kingdom of God in America* (New York: Harper and Row, 1959); and H. Richard Niebuhr, "The Idea of Covenant and American Democracy" in *Church History*, No. 23 (1954), pp. 126–35.

30. Robert N. Bellah, *The Broken Covenant: American Civil Religion in Time of Trial* (New York: Seabury Press, 1975); William Everett, *God's Federal Republic* (New York/Mahwah, NJ: Paulist Press, 1988); and Douglas Sturm, *Corporations, Constitutions, and Covenants: On Forms of Human Relations and the Problem of Legitimacy* (Philadelphia: Center for the Study of Federalism, 1980).

31. Perry Miller, *The New England Mind: From Colony to Province* (Cambridge, MA: Harvard University Press, 1953); *Errand Into the Wilderness* (Cambridge, MA: Harvard University Press, 1956); and *The American Puritans: Their Prose and Poetry* (Garden City, NY: Doubleday, 1956).

32. For the best statement of the idea of legal positivism in this century and its historical origins, see H.L.A. Hart, *The Concept of Law* (Oxford: Clarendon Press, 1961).

33. *Historic Decisions of the Supreme Court,* Carl Brent Swisher, ed. (Princeton, NJ: D. van Nostrand, 1958); *idem., The Supreme Court in Modern Role* (New York: New York University Press, 1958).

34. On Transcendentalism, see Perry Miller, *The Transcendentalists* (Cambridge, MA: Harvard University Press, 1950) and Perry Miller, ed., *The American Transcendentalists: Their Prose and Poetry* (Garden City, NY: Doubleday, 1957). Cf. also Anne C. Rose, *Transcendentalism as a Social Movement* (New Haven: Yale University Press, 1981); Brian M. Barbour, ed., *American Transcendentalism* (Notre Dame, IN: University of Notre Dame Press, 1973); and O. Brooks Frothingham, *Transcendentalism in New England*, introduced by Syndey E. Ahlstrom (Gloucester: P. Smith, 1965).

35. Henry Adams, *The Education of Henry Adams: An Autobiography* (Boston: Houghton, Mifflin, 1961), especially chap. 25, pp. 379–90.

36. Alfred Kelly, *The Descent of Darwin* (Chapel Hill: University of North Carolina Press, 1981).

37. Herbert Croly, *Progressive Democracy* (New York: Macmillan, 1914).

38. Arthur and Lila Weinberg, eds., *The Muckrakers.*

6

Covenant and the Challenges
of Human Nature

Changes in intellectual fashion could not alone have brought down the structure of the American covenantal system which was so deeply implanted in the American psyche, the American political culture, and the behavioral and institutional manifestations of that culture. There also had to be problems with the covenant idea itself. These did indeed occur in two ways, both stemming from the realities of human nature.

The first, in a sense, is the simplest. The covenant tradition suffered from the sanctimonious and oversimplistic thinking of some of its adherents, often those who most directly relied upon it in their interpersonal relations to justify what they believed and what they were doing. Both are normal human failings, but any system that offers or appears to offer the keys to the kingdom of heaven is likely to suffer particularly from sanctimoniousness as those of its adherents who do not recognize their own weaknesses and failings easily find ways to be sanctimonious in relation to others.

We can also expect that some people will be more intelligent or better educated than others and that those with more limited intelligence or less education are prone to accept oversimple explanations for complex questions based upon the superstructure of ideas and behavior that they have erected for themselves. At the very least this is off-putting for people who are not satisfied with those oversimple explanations. At worst it can be a threat to the entire structure, however that structure is misunderstood by those seeking simplistic solutions to difficult and complex problems.

The second source of the problem is related to the first, that is to say, it is simply deficiencies, weaknesses, and failings in human nature that make the covenantal system and its tradition in its pure forms impossible

145

of realization in this world. Even those who strive most diligently to live up to the terms of their covenantal tradition will at some point or another fail and leave themselves open to those who will charge them with hypocrisy and the system with failure. For those who accept the tradition and the problems of human nature and who approach both with the kind of understanding which the Bible itself manifests, these problems do not dissuade them from the essential validity and importance of the tradition. But for those who chafe under its restrictions, these failings supply or form a basis for their own personal rejection and a club with which to beat the tradition before the public as well.

In the nineteenth-century United States there were those who came out of the covenantal tradition and who remained within it or close to it in some way, who tried to deal with these problems of covenant and human nature in a critical yet sympathetic way. Aside from Lincoln, the rest of them made their mark in literature rather than philosophy or politics and indeed formed the constellation of nineteenth-century American literary greats. Three in particular stand out: Nathaniel Hawthorne, Herman Melville, and Mark Twain (Samuel Langhorn Clemens).

The American literary renaissance that began with the new century was heavily concentrated in the hands of New Englanders or transplanted Yankees. Thus, it is not surprising that the deep structure of their thought was covenantal. This finds expression in their writings, especially of Hawthorne and Melville, but also in those of Mark Twain.

In many respects it was through their great literature of the nineteenth century that Americans expressed all of these conflicts in science and religion, philanthropy and reform, law and the constitution. Covenantal modes are perhaps most visible in the works of Hawthorne and Melville, where they serve as vehicles for exploring conflicts between humanity and authority. Other examples can be found in the case of most of the others of the New England School as well, excepting perhaps Emerson, who deliberately explored other directions, and Thoreau, who reinterpreted the covenants of society as contracts between the individual and the state.[1]

Covenantal modes were not simply confined to New Englanders, however. Walt Whitman used secularized covenantal images throughout his writings. For example, *Leaves of Grass* is informed with imagery of the federal union similar to that used by Abraham Lincoln when he discussed the Union as a "regular marriage."

As the nineteenth century moved on, much of American literature picked up on the trends which included potshots at the covenant idea. The three great figures, however, stand out not for being unenticed but for being critical from a more sensitive and complex understanding. All three grew up within the covenantal tradition, but each in his own way. Hawthorne and Melville came from New England, the covenantal commonwealth. Hawthorne lived out his life in Massachusetts. Melville later moved to New York, to a more complex world in which covenant was not the dominant influence. Mark Twain, on the other hand, was born and raised in a world where covenantal thinking was but one strain. Their critiques of the covenantal system and tragic views of the human condition are similar yet reflect these differences.

Nathaniel Hawthorne

Nathaniel Hawthorne's works opened a new chapter in post-Puritan American thought, one of great importance in any proper consideration of covenant in theory and practice. Hawthorne was the first major American figure to address the problem of the failure of the Puritan solution to the problems of humanity, politics, and society. Thus his is a test of that solution. He presents a portrait of that test in *The Scarlet Letter.* Hawthorne understood himself as a descendent of the Puritans and one who was in many respects shaped by their attitudes, but who was also post-Puritan in that he looked to other approaches to deal with the fundamental dilemmas, one should say tragedies, of life. While he rarely wrote directly about matters political, his writing is highly political in the sense that he addresses the problems of humans living together in a society that is a civil society. While he does not see any solution to meeting the needs of humans within the framework of public life, preferring instead to direct his readers to cope with their problems in the private sphere, that in itself is a highly political statement.

Hawthorne examined the covenantal way in light of the Puritan solution, as he understood it, recognizing the limitations of the latter in trying to force humans to conform to the impossible standards that Puritans demanded of them. In *The Scarlet Letter* he pursues the weaknesses, hypocrisies, and inhumanities of the Puritan solution. Indeed he brings the reader to query how the Puritans, who believed so deeply in original sin and in the fact that only a few humans were among the elect, while the many were among the damned, could have expected such perfection in behavior from the human community. Of course, what Hawthorne omitted was the Puritan view of the matter, namely that those who could, would and the others had to be controlled.

Hawthorne's problem with the Puritan solution was not only that it expected too much from human beings, but was prepared to use public means to enforce their impossibly high standards. Everyone in *The Scarlet Letter* fails to measure up to those standards in some way, although most of the principal characters are otherwise fine people who make their own contribution to the community in which they live despite their all-too-human flaws. The community that Hawthorne portrays is a covenanted community. Moreover, his picture is not unfaithful to what one would have expected from a covenanted community in every sense, from the high expectations of the good to the use of shame to punish violators of the good. It is also a nurturing community for those who remain publicly committed to its standards. Even someone like Hester who has behaved in a most deviant manner on a matter of great concern in Puritan society and is otherwise excluded from that nurturing is not driven out, and if shunned, is also protected. Moreover, she has internalized the essence of the covenantal community and gives of herself extensively in atonement, thereby redeeming herself in the eyes of the community. If the community can be harsh in its punishments, it also provides a remedy and means for covenant. In exploring that community, Hawthorne presents us with both the strengths and the weaknesses of a community covenanted in the Puritan manner.

Hawthorne's contrasting model is of the nineteenth-century utopian colony presented in *The Blithedate Romance,* a thinly disguised version of Brook Farm, which the Transcendentalists of Massachusetts established near Concord. Hawthorne himself was involved with Brook Farm at one stage, but he soon came to realize what he presents in his novel, that it and its utopianism is more flawed than the covenanted community it attempted to replace, and cannot possibly be what it claims to be. It is flawed for the opposite reasons—because it is a community that permits anything and relies upon the natural goodness of human beings to keep some semblance of order.

Not surprisingly, since Hawthorne was very much aware of the importance of sexuality in human behavior, it is a community most opposite from the Puritans in matters sexual. If the Puritans have a rigorous code of sexual behavior, these utopian descendants of the Puritans allow something close to free love. Indeed, there are those who see in Zenobia Hester Prynne's daughter Pearl as an adult. Free love leads to its own deceits, manipulations, and exploitations that are not only destructive of public order—the colony cannot sustain itself after confronting those deceits—but also of private existence—Zenobia is driven to commit suicide. Since the community does not perceive sin, it does not provide for atonement, in the end, a situation much worse than the covenanted community, one that leaves its victims shattered.

Both the Puritan community and the utopian colony present public solutions to the problems of human existence and both fail. Hawthorne's third possible solution, presented in *The House of the Seven Gables,* emphasizes private ones. This seems to be by design, as Hawthorne tells us, through other means of expression, his disdain for public activity that is governmental. Hence, although we know that his *House of the Seven Gables* is a novel produced for his publisher who had told him to provide a happier tale than in his previous ones because the audience demanded it, Hawthorne has inserted in it enough of his tragic sense of life to treat the novel as a fair expression of his views.

Once again we are in the presence of the descendants of the Puritans whose ancestors had indeed been involved in an original sin of their own, namely, conquering and stealing the house they claim as their ancestral home (just as the Europeans conquered and stole America?). Qualified redemption comes only when a descendant of the Pynchon family, those who originally stole the property, unites in marriage with a descendant of the Marcle family, the victims whose property was taken. Both have been led by love to forgiveness. Hawthorne's solution is very much a private one and one very acceptable to the post-Puritan world of American Christianity. Unlike *The Blithedale Romance*, it is an ordered world, but unlike the original Puritan community portrayed in *The Scarlet Letter* is also allows everyone a degree of freedom achieved through privacy that the Puritan commonwealth could not accept.

Thus Hawthorne does not neglect the political, but he opts for the private over the public as a means of overcoming problems of human selfishness and sexuality which he sees as possible only through private connections and private acts of love, primarily in the family. Human weakness is great in both the public and private worlds, but can be limited and hence overcome in the private world, something which he does not believe can happen in the public world.

In his shorter pieces, Hawthorne addresses aspects of this problem more specifically, such as the limitations of both art and science and how human weakness can pervert both. He almost suggests that the greater the artist or the scientist, the more likely his devotion to his art or science is likely to lead him to do devilish things to the rest of humanity.

Hawthorne was frequently pressed by his publishers to provide happy endings, at least on the surface, to reflect traditional American optimism. He had, however, an overpowering, tragic sense of life. For him, only the covenant of love can overcome blind nature, either through understanding or transcending it. The covenant of love can bring the forgiveness needed for human survival in this world. The sense of love includes neighborliness and friendship. In that respect it is Christian rather than erotic love, this despite Hawthorne's penetrating understanding of human sexuality and its importance in human existence.

Hawthorne often portrays vice essentially as the excess of virtue. This is true in every one of his major books, with different virtues being practiced excessively and leading to vices in each—Puritan virtues in *The Scarlet Letter*, humanitarian virtues in *The Blithedale Romance*, both commercial virtues and the virtues of honor in *House of the Seven Gables*. In each case their excesses are due to human appetites and have led to their transformation into vices. Hawthorne portrays this as one of the dangers of a covenantal society because covenantal societies rely upon human virtue to exist and turning virtues into vices is an all-too-human failing.

Hawthorne tempered his emphasis on the private by an equivalent emphasis on the attachment of people to place and the social links that such attachments afford, if not the political ones. Hester Prynne, for example, survives her error, shaming and shunning because she has a place and the community of that place, however much they persecute her in punishment, still give her a certain acceptance and protection because she belongs. Within that lies the difference between Hawthorne's privatism and the privatism of today which is a privatism without place.

Hawthorne is the heir of the Puritans, as he, himself, indicates, and one may raise the question whether at some point he does not himself make a religious leap to enable his ideas to work. What he does not see as possible is reformation through moral legislation which was the Puritan way and the use of public shame to enforce that legislation, but in the end that is not as weak a reed as the expectations of the nineteenth-century utopians in *The Blithedale Romance*.

Herman Melville and *Moby Dick*

A good case can be made that these major changes that were taking place and uprooting the covenant idea were best challenged by Lincoln, not only in connection with his battle over slavery and the nature of the federal Union but in relation to his whole understanding of human beings and their humanness. His ideas were paralled by those of Herman Melville, along with Hawthorne and Mark Twain, the three principal American writers of his time.

Melville's sophisticated probing of the covenant idea and its tradition deserves a treatment on its own. Melville deepens our understanding of kinship, covenants, and contracts, properly seeing them as the three most important institutions of social connection. His novella *Billy Budd*, for example, which has been read as an American passion play, spends no little amount of time and space dwelling on how Billy can be seen as having violated his contract as a seaman signed on to serve on Captain Vere's ship in order to maintain his larger covenant with mankind, and the problem, among the rest of the ship's company, of using the freedom gained by covenant without sharing in the responsibility.

Melville goes on to suggest that there exist three models of human society: civilization, barbarism, and something mixed in between, and that individuals fall into three categories: inherently good, inherently corrupt, and normal in between. Each of his characters can be assigned to a position from the nine-cell matrix established by his model, as shown in figure 6.1.[2]

This model is most fully expressed in *Moby Dick*. There are various individuals and ships that figure in the story of the voyage and the hunt. Each represents another form of social and political expression, all tied together by the covenantal theme.

The principal character in *Moby Dick* is the white whale whom we never see as a whole, symbolically indicating that we cannot know the whole of the universe. The book is produced by a profoundly Calvinist mind. Although Melville is no longer a believer, he asks a fundamental Calvinistic question: Is there an order in the world? Is there a whole?

FIGURE 6.1
Melville's Models of Individuals and Society

Individuals	Civilization	Societies Mixed	Barbarism
Inherently Good			
Normal (Mixed)			
Inherently Corrupt			

The novel is the search for that whole and the order in it, and Melville's pursuit of it is an obsession. The effort to discover the whole has to be one of experience, not contemplation alone. Humans have to take risks, they have to "lower the boats," even though to successfully lower the boats they must be lowered in a balanced way, something which is done by ropes, and, as the book describes, the balance is not easily maintained and the ropes can often kill.

Ishmael is saved by losing his balance, but in a boat. Ishmael indeed is a wanderer; is rootless, cut loose, like Americans. He is someone who cannot rely upon organic ties but must forge his own ties with his comrades. He does so by daring to extend his trust. Indeed, Ishmael chooses a ship without seeing Ahab, who is to be his captain, as does the rest of the crew. He begins by signing on with Captain Ahab—a contract—accepts Ahab's covenant, which is a covenant with the devil, but works his way loose from it in time.

Ahab starts as a God-fearing person but becomes cut off because of his obsession. Melville is a modern man in that he goes back to biblical sources but goes forward beyond Christianity. The book is both about failed leadership and failed followership—the failure of covenants, however sincere, because of human flaws. Not only does Ahab go from being God-fearing to mad, but his crew joins him in the madness as they rally around him out of some combination of misplaced trust, ill-considered enthusiasm, and adventure-seeking, and are unable to become free men as a result.

Melville is an ambiguous democrat or perhaps just a realistic one. He describes ships as if they were models of states. There are eight ships described in *Moby Dick*, representing eight different kinds of states. With regard to Ahab's ship, the *Pequod*, everything is right about it except its intentions. The *Jungfrau* displays the failure of senior leadership, the

Rachel the failure of the crew. The *Jereboam* is a ship of sadness. The *Samuel Enderbe* is a good ship; it is good in the ways that the *Pequod* is good but it is even better because it gets on with life. The *Batchelor* is a ship pursuing pure commerce; it has no higher purpose, unlike the *Pequod* which has a higher purpose but a perverse one.

Ahab has gone beyond the pure commerce of whaling and offers a return to the spirit. The crew recognizes and wants this, but Ahab's mission is too perverse. It may be that Melville finds that this is a metaphor for the United States, which he sees as losing its original sense of purpose based upon its God-fearing character, and moving toward pure commerce. A society may only move beyond pure commerce by accepting a perverse return to the spirit. In one sense, then, Ahab's madness is better than the mere pursuit of commerce, but uncorrected it leads to doom.

The eight ships are never connected. That, indeed, is the human failure, the inability to bring the pieces together. But the *Samuel Enderbe* is also ultimately unsatisfactory; it becomes the comic side of the vision, that is, it is insufficient for a Calvinist who seeks a commonwealth committed to a higher moral purpose. In that respect it may be like the vision of the commercial evil society of John Locke, which would be equally insufficient. Still, democracy is middling. It usually misses the vision. Melville seems to be saying that ultimately the choices are between facing the abyss or making one of a variety of unsatisfactory choices.

Only Starbuck, the excellent first mate, seems able to transcend Ahab's madness, but his virtue, namely a sense of loyalty to his captain, prevents him from doing so, so he, too, is destroyed. The last thoughts of the three mates are revealing in this respect. Starbuck is portrayed as thinking of God, Stubbs of sex, and Flask of money in their last moments. Starbuck is a failure because he is bound by the conventional senses of responsibility and is unable to transcend them. He is too good a Christian. The fact that Starbuck is presented as a model citizen of New England may also be suggestive. Starbuck's fall is a sign of how frail even the best of us are and that this is the human condition. In the end, however, Ishmael, an ordinary seaman, a wanderer, survives and that is the best that there is.

The covenant Ahab makes with the crew is made after the ship has sailed, so the question can be raised: objectively, what choice was there? Still, the crew responds enthusiastically, subjectively making a choice. Ahab had his covenant ceremony in addition to the signing of the ship's articles. In other words, he changed the ship's articles from a contract to a covenant and had to get the consent of the crew to do so, so he convened this perverse covenant assembly and, appealing to their emotions, moved them into his camp. Ahab's crew follows him because they are all isolates. None of them have any roots; they are all alienated people seeking a vision to turn to and a superior leader provides them with that vision even if he is obsessed and the vision is evil.

In essence, Melville is making a critique of the covenanted society by someone who grew up within it and knows it first-hand and sees that humans cannot live up to its terms. It is too easy to put the blame on the covenant. Rather, the blame is on human nature, as each of his eight ships is designed to demonstrate.

In the meantime, Melville is post-Christian. He is open to paganism and its ability to influence. It is, after all, an idol that has led Ishmael to the *Pequod*. He sees Queequeg as the noble savage, but he also understands that paganism leads to hedonistic individualism that demands a heavy price no matter how attractive it may be.

The book is also about the covenanted society encountering wildness in the state of nature, at least potentially. The sea is permanent wildness and, as such, has no place for women, which may be one of the reasons why the Americans abandoned the sea as the source of their myth and turned to the West where everyone could participate. Also, the sea is where the horror is and Melville can use that truth and also criticize democracy. The West in American history is where the promise is, where the horrors exist (e.g., Indian raids outlaws, natural disasters) but can be overcome by human effort to make the West a place where democracy is celebrated.

The evil Melville addresses is one to which covenantal societies and the individuals who are bred in them may be particularly susceptible. Ahab is shown as needing a cause. Moreover, the sea, that is to say, nature, is the antithesis of covenant in that it is indifferent to human suffering. That is what enrages Ahab, but rather than look to other human beings for comfort he loses his mind and makes a pact with the devil to pursue the malevolence in nature even though it cannot avail him anything to do so. In his search for justice he refuses to recognize that he is seeking justice from a dumb beast. In that sense he is a heroic character who goes too far. He is not psychically whole and in the chaotic world that is self-defeating.

Psychic wholeness is dependent upon balance or, more accurately, the appropriate balance in each case. *Moby Dick* discusses different balances for different ships and different people. Ahab lacks one leg, which makes him physically imbalanced as well as mentally. Significantly, both Ahab and Ishmael are orphans.

Even the fact that ships are hierarchies does not make much of a difference on the *Pequod*. The captain sets policies but everyone knows his job and the captain needs to do little more than preside and intervene at critical moments. Moreover, when a policy departs from the normal commercial one of a voyage, the captain makes a new covenant with the crew.

The Christianity that Melville knows, Reformed Protestant Christianity, seeks to simply change nature, but that is impossible. Melville's attack, like Mark Twain's was later to be, is an attack on simplistic Christian pieties, although once again Melville is more sophisticated. He gives examples of different churches Ishmael visits or sees on his way to New Bedford, and Reverend Mapple is anything but simple.

Still, Melville portrays the minister's Calvinistic hebraism and the prophetic tradition he presents in his sermon as inadequate. The Reverend Mapple perverts Calvinist Christianity as Ahab perverts Puritanism. Queequeg's pagan god is nicer but no more effective. It is as though Melville is saying that Puritans or people of Puritan stock lose compassion in pursuing their vision, much like the Abolitionists did in his day.

The Reverend Mapple preaches a sermon contrasting federal and natural liberty. He calls upon congregants to follow God, not how they feel. Ishmael, on the other hand, follows how he feels and is saved. Ahab follows how he feels and is destroyed along with the crew and the ship. So both Christianity and hedonism can be right, according to Melville.

Part of the tragedy is that Ahab can make life meaningful, unlike the other captains who can only talk about shares; but, tragically, there is no alternative to Ahab's vision. Starbuck is a noble man but he cannot propose an alternate vision. Ishmael has a certain amount of common sense but he certainly cannot. It seems that Melville is more sympathetic to Hobbes than he is to Locke. The Hobbesian ship, after all, saves its crew but it has no vision.

In a sense Melville is opposing Emerson. If nature is indifferent to humans, humans still cannot be indifferent. Nature's indifference stems from the fact that it is either random or hostile, but liberty is not a condition where things are random. There must be some kind of order resting upon humans' understanding of the consequences and willingness to make choices. In this respect Ahab is a superior, though evil, man, while Starbuck is, as Ahab assesses him, "too good of a fellow." Therefore, the only way to deal with nature is through covenant, even if humans cannot keep to their covenants. God and humans together order nature for liberty by covenant and live in hope.

Mark Twain and *Huckleberry Finn*

Melville was committed to the effort to create the American myth, but, at the end of the time when the sea had been the great setting for adventure in the minds of settled Americans, he used the sea as his setting. He was too late since the scene of action was shifting from the sea to the prairie and the great rivers and mountains bisecting it. Hence, Mark Twain came closer to achieving what Melville sought in his works.

Mark Twain (Samuel Langhorn Clemens), who emerged as a major literary figure immediately after the Civil War, was perhaps the foremost example of Middle Border covenantalism and its problematics.[3] A close reading of Mark Twain reveals him to be a classic spokesman for the covenant tradition in American life as expressed in the Middle States, from the mid-Atlantic to the Middle Border. That tradition is rooted in Presbyterian religion and Whig politics. It differs from covenantalism in New England, where the churches remained congregational but the polity and society were entirely within the embrace of a covenantal people, in that the exponents of the covenantal tradition in the Middle States were members of federally structured churches but constituted a minority within a larger individualistic, market-oriented, or traditionalistic, slavery-accepting civil society, to which they had to respond as a minority. Middle States exponents of covenantalism differed from their Southern kin in that they were communitarian, as in New England, rather than individualistic in their understanding of God's covenant with man, seeking communal as well as individual salvation, yet, like the Southerners, often were traditionalistic in their attitudes toward civil society.

As Mark Twain's own writings reveal, the Middle States covenantalists were in a tragic position in the classic sense of the term. Longing for the covenantal community, they were forced to live and make their way in an individualistic society. Hence they often became cynical as they recognized the gap between their ideals and the reality around them. One as-

pect of Lincoln's greatness is that he, in the same situation, did not suc-
cumb to cynicism but transcended his environment without rejecting or
ignoring it.

Mark Twain is the perfect exemplar of this tragic position. He makes
a powerful argument for the covenanted community in his works, yet
ends up time after time refuting the possibility for such a community to
exist in a society of originally sinful and unredeemable humans, who are
either grasping individuals or pretentiously pious. As such, he represents
a very important strand in American covenantalism, one that has been all
too often ignored in the infatuation with the New England ideal and its
manifestations, or the romance of the Southern struggle with the covenant, with the South's fatal flaw. Yet, for many if not most Americans,
the problem of covenant as confronted in the Middle States is precisely
the one that they confront.

Mark Twain also begins with humans confronting nature and focuses
on the problems of humans' efforts to master their environment, beginning with *Life on the Mississippi*. In *Huckleberry Finn* he confronts the
problem of federal versus natural liberty and in *A Connecticut Yankee in
King Arthur's Court* the problem of the regime and the limits of politics
and technology. Both Melville and Mark Twain are very American, but
Mark Twain's Americanness is even more striking, in part because he
has shifted his effort to portray the American myth from the sea to the
West. His wilderness is a conquerable one, accessible to all people, men
and women, whites and blacks, natives and immigrants.

Twain, too, uses water, the Mississippi River, as a metaphor for life,
emphasizing the river's changing character and the need to take a pragmatic approach when trying to deal with it. Yet in the end, the river—
nature—dominates, it takes over, it alters; it is eccentric, in Mark Twain's
term, and its eccentricity wins. Humans never really become masters of
the river. Those who try may learn the intricacies of the river but they
must learn those intricacies to such a degree that, for them, the romance
of the river is gone. Then they find that what they have mastered is also
gone and that they must learn to master it again. In that sense the pilot is
like the governor, the statesman who must guide the ship of state under
similar circumstances.

Mark Twain essentially affirms the American idea of freedom as tied
to the frontier. The conflict between freedom and the limits imposed by
the river can be bridged by man through technology and technique only

to a degree. Hank Morgan, a Connecticut Yankee, is presented by Twain as moving from merely an economic man, but a sympathetic one, to a man with a political program, an Enlightenment one, which, reflecting Twain's tragic sense of life, fails. So Morgan, almost against his will, moves toward Jacobinism and terror, unable to avoid it.

Connecticut Yankee is much like a Puritan sermon. In a sense, Samuel Langhorn Clemens' whole career is a struggle with New England and its heritage, toward which he is profoundly ambivalent. Significantly, Hank Morgan is a Connecticut Yankee, not a Puritan. Mark Twain is another republican who can see the problems and failures of republicanism and critique them.

In *Huckleberry Finn*, Twain essentially sees Huckleberry as an exemplar of natural liberty who, out of necessity, must climb out of that to translate his natural instincts into decent acts; in other words, to assume the responsibility that must accompany freedom. The book begins with Huck and Tom united by political compact but its next step, and a vital one to the story, is Huck's covenant with the escaped slave Jim, promising to deliver him from slavery. Huck does this with foreboding because his background has taught him to look upon helping slaves escape to be wrong. He would just as soon "light out for the territories," that is, escape civilization, but he cannot. In the end, Jim's freedom only comes through law after the covenantal bond between Huck and Jim has brought them to a point where they can benefit from law.

In the end, Twain loses his sense of humor. Man and society are too corrupt and he is too disillusioned. All he can do is expose because he has no faith in institutions. Like all satirists, he becomes angry and embittered when too little change takes place. Twain values freedom but expects it to lead humans to responsibility. His disillusionment comes when he sees that it does not. In a sense, Clemens suffers not from persecution but from success. Indeed, he does not even publish many of his later writings because they are so bitter and cynical.

Clemens, after all, is of Whig stock. His father was a Whig, he himself was a Republican until 1884, when he refused to support Blaine and supported Cleveland instead, because by that time the Republicans had become far removed from their Whig antecedents. His problem is that he is a Whig moralist in a Jeffersonian environment, first in Hannibal, Missouri, and then in the Gilded Age. As one raised a Presbyterian, he appreciates original sin, but he must confront what he sees that confirms human failings without the hope of God.

Throughout all his works Twain makes favorable references to covenanted peoples—Jews, Scots, and Swiss—but he detests Protestant self-righteousness and Southern violence. Where both come together, as in American imperialism in the late nineteenth century, he is most enraged. In general, Mark Twain has difficulty contemplating the heroic. Because he has no confidence in institutions, he fails to fully address himself to them. The most he can do is try to bring people to see the consequences of their actions. Twain does have a Whiggish belief in law and order but implicitly sees that as grounded in covenant, not in any elaborate institutional apparatus.

In sum, the crises of the mid-nineteenth century shattered the Christian republican consensus, forged in the wake of the American Revolution, which combined covenant and compact theories into a "package" that included both Christian and republican virtues, including the virtues of scientific inquiry, along with a shared social morality. As Catherine Zuckert points out, this Christian republican order had a darker side in the form of the tyranny of the majority and a weak point in its embrace of economic achievement as a sign of moral success.[4] Hence, as both the dark side and the weak point became more pronounced after mid-century and found a new home in a burgeoning urban industrial America, critics began to question the nature of the covenant or compact that undergirded that consensus.

Mark Twain was particularly repelled by the dark side even as he was repeatedly tempted by the weak points in his own life. His own personal confrontation produced a literature that challenged the vulgar understanding of the whole package with humor, irony, and not a little bit of cynicism. As Zuckert shows, Twain not only punctures the myths of the Christian republican consensus but offers a different vision of humanity, one that is Puritan in its belief in human fallibility but very much against the smug spirit of much of nineteenth century Christianity (itself a radical departure from Puritanism) and offers in its place a secular solution, one in which humans rely entirely on their own fallible characters.

Unlike all too many twentieth-century humanists who followed their nineteenth-century predecessors in believing in the perfectibility of man, Twain's humanism follows the far more skeptical views of human nature of his Puritan forebears. His solution to the problem is threefold: sober expectations—not to expect too much from oneself or one's fellows; full disclosure—we all have to know what everyone is doing, at least in the public sphere; and, most important of all, laughter—the use of humor and laughter to censure those moral violations which stem from human smugness rather than mere venality. On this basis, Zuckert suggests that Mark Twain believes it is possible to establish a meaningful and effective political social compact.[5]

Melville and Mark Twain wrote in the latter days of the period when the American commonwealth was still very strongly influenced at the highest levels by covenantal thinking. Indeed, with their more profound understandings of the complexities of human nature and the environment, they sought to critique conventional covenantalism as too simple.

Thornton Wilder and *The Eighth Day*

This modified covenantal tradition was to continue into the twentieth century. Thornton Wilder, himself a Yankee who moved west to the Middle Border, was the last great exemplar of it to date.[6] Wilder wrote three generations later, when American civil society had already shed most of its conscious and overt covenantalism. Wilder wrote in a more optimistic vein than Twain, to raise American spirits during the years of the Great Depression, but the corpus of his work is far more complex than that; he exposes, like all these other great literary figures, the inherent difficulties in covenant as well as the great promise that it offers us. In a very real sense, he resynthesizes the American covenantal tradition for contemporaries and offers those who would take advantage of it a glimpse into how covenant confronts fate and, battered and bruised, can overcome it, at least to a sufficient degree to make life worthwhile.

Wilder felt the necessity to revive the American spirit and through it Americans' faith in themselves through a revival of covenantal thinking, which he tried to do in the most profound way through his writings. Wilder's most popular writings were his plays, especially *Our Town*, *The Matchmaker*, and *The Skin of Our Teeth*.[7] Each addressed a different aspect of the covenantal society and its worldview.

In *Our Town*, Wilder addressed the simple interpersonal covenants of individuals and families passing through life in a normal way with all its joys and tragedies exposed and managed or at least softened by the covenants that hold families and communities together. *Our Town* was the small New England community of the American vision and its families were the foundation for all of the edifice of civil society, a place where commonwealth still prevailed, but, like his predecessors, he understood that nature, including human nature, remained omnipresent, often as a threat, and could only be mastered some of the time. It would have to be accomodated within the covenantal community, even in times of tragedy.

The Matchmaker is concerned with the preservation of sufficient virtue in the commercial republic that still could be a civil society. The story takes place between medium-size and large cities, Yonkers and New York City, among people who do not have the intimate relationships of those who grew up with one another but whose ties to each other are essentially commercial. They are doing business. This gives Wilder the chance to set forth not only a covenantal business ethic but how people must relate to each other beyond that in a commercial world. In *The Matchmaker*, Wilder also lays out a theory of vice and how vices grow from people's virtues. Even while doing business, Wilder seems to say, there are interpersonal relations that must transcend the contractual and be made covenantal if they are to succeed. In contrasting New York and Yonkers, Wilder pays due attention to the excitements of New York and their possibilities and to the somnolent deficiencies and parochialism of Yonkers and their limitations, but still he seems to decide for Yonkers because in no larger communities can people achieve what they must achieve to live decently.

In *The Skin of Our Teeth*, Wilder goes to the largest canvas, the human family in its world environment. Here, too, he brings the action to the family level but on a world canvas and with the complexities of human nature exposed, demonstrating how, through covenant, the natural connections within families are able to grow to become larger and help fallible humans get through life by the skin of their teeth.

Wilder elaborated on these themes and deepened his presentation of them in his novels, always trying to raise questions of path and covenant as they affect and illuminate the human condition. He had the complex view and understood mixtures. Speaking to the Americans of the interwar and early postwar generations, his ideas are based on understandings derived from a Puritan America as tempered by the nineteenth century. It is hard to escape the conclusion that his books are Presbyterian books.

Wilder was concerned with location in three ways: geohistorical location, cultural location, and heredity, one's "house" in a biblical sense. He was concerned about family, the families of specific humans, and the family of man. In his expressions of the impact of location he broke out of the "either-or" model. He was concerned with the small town and the world, the particular and the universal, and the links between them.

Wilder dealt with the great covenantal problem of how human actions can be meaningful in a world driven by necessity. He presented the view that the actions of free human beings, even miniscule ones, can direct or redirect matters within broad limits, even though free will is in conflict with predestination and necessity can be turned into volition. At the same time, in *The Bridge of San Luis Rey* he emphasized how even what seemed like volition is in certain ways predestination.

Wilder was preoccupied with the differences between natural man and federal man. The Ashleys, Henry Antrobus, and Sabina are all examples of natural man, while the various chosen peoples he describes, the people of *Our Town* and even the people of Coal Town in *The Eighth Day* are examples of federal man. In connection with both types, there are people who are righteous, ordinary, and wicked. The Ashleys are naturally righteous just as chosen peoples are federally righteous. Sabina is naturally ordinary just as the people of *Our Town* are federally ordinary. Henry Antrobus is naturally wicked just as the people of Coal Town are federally wicked. The three acts of *The Skin of Our Teeth* portray, in order, man vs. nature, man vs. the moral law, and man vs. himself. Wilder seems to be raising the questions: What is common? Who is chosen? His three great soliloquy's in *The Matchmaker* raise these questions. The merchant Vandergelder soliloquizes as to why he is what he is; in another the alcoholic Malachi Stack soliloquizes to show why he is better than he seems, and the matchmaker Dolly soliloquizes as to why she accepts less than she deserves. All three represent necessary commitments to the bonds of society through their actions and they must explain why.

Wilder's communities are self-governing, especially *Our Town*, both as a civil community and through its Church of the Covenant. In all of them, the basis of society is the combination of kinship and consent which enables its people to be even more self-governing. Wilder wrote his plays at a time when other dramatists were being highly "political," that is to say, ideological, normally Communist, but he avoids all of that while being truly political; raising serious and sensitive political questions instead of writing about stock characters and stock situations. His silences are at times even more important than what he says, especially given when he is writing. He builds from the household and family through the town and the tribe and then to the rest, rather than starting with the universal and never getting to the particular. Wilder is a partisan of reform, as long as it is reform by an individual working in his or her community or some segment of it to fix it and him or herself. He understands the necessity in volition. He also understands authority, but he wants it to be democratic authority.

In the end, human beings cannot really overcome the fate which they are predestined, but they can live the right kind of human lives within the parameters of that fate and that is what is important to Wilder as one who believes in the covenanted community.

John Ford and John Wayne

In many respects, John Ford and his movies expressed the essence of American covenantalism in the twentieth century. They centered on individualists moving westward to found communities based on choice, mutuality, and trust. John Wayne, Gary Cooper, and others like them were portrayed as heroes who were aware that a heroic age demanded heroic action but only in such a way that it would recognize and build community, mobilizing natural liberty to insure federal liberty. As the character Wayne plays in *Chisholm* put it: "Prepare your heart to seek the law of the Lord and to live by it."

The apogee of this may have been Wayne's character in *The Man Who Shot Liberty Valance* who demonstrated that it was more important for law, order, and civil society to come to the West than for John Wayne, the old-style westerner, to win the girl, so the heroic expression of natural liberty hides in the shadows and when James Stewart, the very nonphysical newspaper editor and champion of federal liberty, goes out to face the brutal outlaw even though he has no skill with firearms, Wayne shoots Liberty Valance from the shadows and lets Stewart and the community think that Stewart did it so that he can become their new leader. Stewart leads the fight for statehood as befits the new more settled times and then is elected to the new state's highest offices while Wayne sinks into obscurity.

That, indeed, was the general theme of westerns throughout the first half of the twentieth century, those with the greatest western actors in them, most particularly the westerns produced by John Ford. The settlement of the West called for the expressions of natural liberty but only to bring about federal liberty. Contrast those moralistic westerns with more recent ones, the kind popularized and symbolized by Clint Eastwood. In the latter, natural liberty is the predominant style for everyone. Law and order only represent the success of some individuals in achieving their private agendas through public office, but they have no public spirit nor are they trying to build community. This new kind of Western was originated by Eastwood in his Italian filmmaking period, in the "spaghetti" Westerns that reflected Italian political culture—private, individualistic, and cynical—rather than American.

Significantly, in the older westerns natural liberty is always presented in two ways: one, as evil and represented by evil outlaws or Indians (not in John Wayne movies; Wayne consistently was notably understanding of Indians as a group although, naturally some Indians fit into the same category as white outlaws [that is to say, they were by nature bad guys], but also sympathetically as humans who could be heroes when that was appropriate.

The greatest heroes were those who rendered themselves obsolete by their actions, who struggled to replace the state of nature with liberal democratic civil society, even at their own expense. As another American folk figure, the longshoreman philosopher Eric Hoffer, who lived in the San Francisco Bay area and became both an intellectual and a popular hero during the first generation after World War II, put it: "Only a people that doesn't need leaders can produce great ones."[8] That is because covenant peoples can be roused but they cannot be commanded, at least not by any human agency (with the obvious exception that, if they are roused to fight, they can be commanded in military units).

Even military command among covenantal peoples is essentially a process of leadership by example, which involves the ability to rouse one's troops. That is another central theme of American Westerns. The hero-leader is the one who rouses rather than commands, who leads by example, whereas the leader of the bad guys invariably commands, often in the most brutal hierarchical manner by inspiring genuine fear among his "boys." It is no innovation to suggest that the American covenantal myth is embodied in the Western.

Notes

1. Catherine Zuckert, *Natural Right and the American Imagination: Political Philosophy in the American Novel* (Lanham, MD: Rowman & Littlefield, 1989), in the chapter on Melville.
2. Ibid.
3. On Mark Twain, see the author's notes from the Center for the Study of Federalism—Liberty Fund Colloquium on "Freedom and Responsibility in the Works of

Mark Twain," (Philadelphia, PA: January, 1985). Cf. also Justin Kaplan, *Mr. Clemens and Mark Twain: A Biography* (New York: Simon and Schuster, 1966).
4. Catherine Zuckert, "The Novelist Who 'Corrupted' American Mores," *Covenant in the Nineteenth Century,* Daniel J. Elazar, ed. (Lanham, MD: Rowman and Littlefield, 1994), pp. 211–13.
5. Ibid., pp. 221–24.
6. See the author's notes from the Center for the Study of Federalism—Liberty Fund Colloquium "Freedom and Responsibility in the Works of Thornton Wilder," (Philadelphia, PA: January, 1985).
7. Thornton Wilder, *Our Town; The Skin of Our Teeth; The Matchmaker* (Franklin Center, PA: Franklin Library, 1980).
8. Eric Severeid, Interview with Eric Hoffer, CBS Television, September 19, 1967.

7

The Sum of Covenantal Expressions

The Renewal of Interest in Covenant

In 1954, when life had many more certainties for Americans than it does today, the noted American theologian H. Richard Niebuhr wrote:

> One of the great common patterns that guided men in the period when American democracy was formed, that was present both in their understanding and in their action, and was used in psychology, sociology and metaphysics as in ethics, politics and religion, was the pattern of the covenant or of federal theology...
>
> [O]ne may raise the question whether our common life could have been established, could have been maintained and whether it can endure without the presence of the conviction that we live in a world that has the moral structure of a covenant.

This renewed concern with covenant could be found in circles at every level and segment of society, whether academics and intellectuals touched by the words of Robert Bellah or simple moviegoers touched by the Westerns of John Ford.

The Civil Rights Movement Begins with Covenant

Perhaps the most recent comprehensive public expression of the covenantal tradition in a proactive way, that is to say, as the source for improving American behavior, came with the civil rights revolution and the transformation of African-Americans and other colored peoples in the United States into full and equal citizens by law and to a substantial extent in behavior as well. The first part of the civil rights revolution was made overtly covenantal by the Reverend Dr. Martin Luther King. He and his colleagues built on a generation of the invocation of principles of federal liberty in fact, if not by name, to bring about a series of federal

government actions that made it clear to Americans that racial segregation and other forms of racial discrimination violated the constitution of
the United States, not only in the public sphere but even if they were
otherwise protected by private rights.

King and his colleagues realized that unless American blacks took
matters into their own hands, progress would not only be extremely slow
but the earlier Supreme Court rulings would for many years be honored
in the breach. The question was should this be done violently or nonvio-
lently. King's brilliant insight and understanding of the American psyche
concluded that if blacks would demonstrate by nonviolent means that
they were prepared to go to jail and even risk death under laws they
believed to be patently unconstitutional and unjust, they would awaken
the consciences of white Americans to step in and take appropriate action to transform the situation.

Given an opportunity by Rosa Parks' refusal to move to the back of
the bus in Birmingham, Alabama in 1958, King assumed leadership of
the movement and, in the covenantal manner, aroused people to follow
him and almost all to follow him in his way. As the highly prestigious
secular British journal, *The Economist* said of him many years later,
"King [was] thrust by his successful leadership of a bus boycott in Mont-
gomery, Alabama, into worldwide celebrity at the age of 27, in circumstances so bizarre that it could only be God's will."[1]

King thought of himself as a student of Reinhold Niebuhr and drew
his understanding of the divine character of social justice from Niebuhr,
drawing practical idealism from Mahatma Gandhi. In essence, he called
upon Americans to live up to the terms of their covenant and, slowly at
first but with increasing rapidity, they did.

In the wake of the disasters of the 1960s and 1970s, certain individuals and groups explicitly suggested that the United States had broken its
covenant and called for its renewal. Others called for "a renegotiation of
the social compact" upon which the United States was built. Some made
this demand as radicals who claimed to have abandoned American tradition, barely aware of how much they were within the historic framework
of American thought and rhetoric. Others, like President Lyndon Johnson,
who in his inaugural address spoke of the Americans' covenant with
their land, simply wanted to improve what was. Whatever the validity of
the specific demands of each, they stand as examples of how the covenant idea has permeated American culture and how despite its erosion

since the 1930s and especially the late 1960s, it offers a firm but flexible framework for political change.[2]

Curiously, Richard Nixon was the first president to be cognizant of the practical problem of overreliance on the theories and practices of the Great Society. He developed a program he called the New Federalism that pretended to deal with the problem. The nature of Nixon's personality was such that his program turned out to be a kind of personally selfish Great Society, in other words, as president, Nixon was willing to transfer anything that was likely to give him trouble to the states and localities and at the same time bring to Washington, and especially to the presidency, anything that was likely to strengthen his chances for public esteem or, at the very least, reelection. There was no compactual dimension to Nixon's New Federalism, much less covenantal. Indeed, whatever Nixon's abilities and his pragmatic successes, there was no moral tone in his message.[3]

Gerald Ford, who succeeded Nixon after the latter's resignation in 1974 in the wake of the Watergate scandal, was the first president ever to achieve office other than through the original forms of constitutional election. Hence, he felt it incumbent upon himself to pledge in his brief inaugural speech that he was entering into "an unprecedented compact with his countrymen" to return the presidency to first principles and uphold the Constitution.[4] In the brief time of his incumbency that, indeed, is what he tried to do, with no little success.

It remained for Jimmy Carter to be the first president to try to restore a sense of covenantal morality, if not of covenant itself. He did so in an uneasy synthesis between Great Society liberalism and his sense that the American people were looking for a restoration of a federal republic of smaller communities. In the end, the incompatibilities inherent in that synthesis, coupled with his personal inability to bridge those incompatibilities, led to his undoing, but not before he made the old religio-moral message of covenantalism once again part of the American political scene, albeit in somewhat new, revised garb.[5]

In that respect, Ronald Reagan was a more polished continuation of Jimmy Carter. Reagan was supported by an alliance of republican individualists and republican communitarians. Both groups rejected Great Society liberalism in the name of liberty. While in the course of his administration the two groups were to collide periodically, together they formed a coalition that had the potential of reshaping American politics.[6]

It is hard to say exactly where Reagan stood in all of this, since his forte was in instinctive judgments and not philosophic understanding. He articulated a straightforward, if unsophisticated, vision of American federalism and sought to implement that vision within the parameters of the contemporary presidency, in which there was still little hesitancy to centralize where the president was persuaded the federal government should intervene. Moreover, his vision of the states as primary communities at times conflicted with his vision of very limited government, so that he could endorse programs which weakened the government not only in Washington, but in the state houses as well. Perhaps the best way to describe Reagan's program was that it was designed to reflect the America that the president knew (or remembered) when he was a boy around the time of World War I; that is to say, an America at the very end of the nineteenth century, still informed by a latent covenantal idea that often continued to be made manifest in the Illinois Grand Prairie towns where Reagan was born and raised. This was vulgar covenantalism to be sure, but one untouched by organic or hierarchic theories of the state.

In any case, all of this was overwhelmed during the Reagan years by the passions of excess of the greedy 1980s and disappeared entirely in the administration of George Bush, a man who despite his own New England origins was singularly unmoved by such issues in the public sphere, however much he and his family preserved New England virtues in their private lives. With Bush's defeat and the election of Bill (William Jefferson) Clinton to the presidency, for a moment it seemed as if there would be a resurgence of overt concern with the covenantal tradition. Clinton, with his wife Hillary Rodham Clinton, gave every sign of being very concerned with an older American politics of meaning even as they prepared to march the United States into an uncertain future. It may not have been surprising that he tried to float the phrase "the new covenant" as the architectonic slogan of his campaign to "rebuild America."

The phrase "a new covenant to rebuild America" became part of Clinton's basic campaign speech.[7] A product of the 1960s generation, Clinton had to overcome a reputation of having actively avoided military service during the Vietnam War when he was associated with the radical student movements, albeit in a modest way. At the same time, he was also deeply rooted in American religious tradition. Both he and his wife, a northerner born in Illinois from a Pennsylvania family, found this new covenant theme expressive of their intentions in the White House. Candidate Clinton used this theme at least for the first half of his campaign. But despite Americns' increasing bewilderment, dissatisfaction, and demoralization with the world they saw emerging around them in the United States, the phrase had no resonance for the Americans of the 1990s. Clinton's pollsters undoubtedly told him so very quickly since the phrase surfaced very briefly and then dropped. After it did not resonate, no replacement for it was found.

Misled by his liberal advisors for whom a religiously laden term like covenant did not resonate, Clinton abandoned it. But that was not the end. Prior to the 1994 midterm Congressional elections, the resurgent Republicans promulgated a "Contract with America," a secular variant to the covenantal idea as a means of making their commitment to the American people. The Contract received wide publicity and helped the Republicans win a resounding victory in November which made the Contract headline news. In an effort to respond, Clinton dusted off his idea of a New Covenant which he presented as the central theme of his State of the Union address in January 1995 and of the second half of his administration:

> I call it the New Covenant but it is grounded in a very, very old idea that all Americans have not just the right but a solemn responsibility to rise as far as their God-given talents and determination can take them. And to give something back to their communities and their country in return. Opportunity and responsibility— they go hand in hand, we can't have one without the other, and our national community can't hold together without both. Our New Covenant is a new set of understandings for how we can equip our people to meet the challenges of the new economy, how we can change the way that our government works to fit a different time and, above all, how we can repair the damaged bonds in our society and come together behind our common purpose.

Once again, Clinton's liberal supporters missed the importance of the reference, but Clinton brought the American people full circle back to their covenantal beginnings at the beginning of the postmodern epoch. Lyndon Johnson would have approved.

This experience well summarizes the present state of the covenant tradition in American politics. Those who are politically involved and still knowledgeably rooted in the American tradition find resonances in traditional concepts while those who have lost that connection with their own past do not find resonance when those concepts are used to move them. The best that one who still finds resonance in those concepts can hope for is that the United States is at a crossroads and that a proper articulation of the covenant idea will still strike chords as it is better understood. If not, the new postmodern epoch will bring a sea change even greater than anticipated.

The Individual and Society: Contrasting Orientations

Implicit in the foregoing history is a specific conception of the proper relationship between the individual and society. Perhaps more than any other polity in human history the United States has consciously and explicitly focused upon that question as the cardinal question of politics. American history can be understood as a struggle between four major orientations toward the relationship between the individual and civil society (that by-now-slightly-archaic early modern term that conveys so well the way in which all comprehensive societies necessarily have a political form and the way all good societies keep that political form from becoming all-embracingly totalitarian and which was revived by the liberals in the Communist bloc countries for their revolt against Communism).

All four orientations can be traced back to the first foundings of American settlement and have continued to manifest themselves in the American experience ever since. One of these is individualism. It is perhaps the best known and most celebrated, so much so that it is often thought to be the *only* legitimate American orientation. Another is collectivism, viewed by most as the opposite of individualism and as a kind of bogeyman to be rejected by all right-thinking Americans. A third is corporatism, an orientation rarely identified in its own right yet a powerful influence on the course of American history. The fourth is federalism, a term as familiar to Americans as individualism, in its own way almost as hallowed and certainly as misunderstood.

Americans and foreign observers alike have tended to emphasize American individualism.[8] The American has been portrayed as the Lockean man, the solitary individual confronting a society he has made through his contract with other solitary individuals, assessing both his rights and duties within the society on the basis of individual self-interest, hopefully rightly understood. The society, in turn, confronts the individual with all its massiveness, uncushioned by mediating groups of other than transient character. At its best, America as an individualistic society emphasized the importance of individual rights, the limitations the existence of those rights places upon governments and the responsibility of government to preserve and protect those rights. On the other hand, individualism has also provided a cover for social irresponsibility, especially (but not exclusively) on the part of the rich and the powerful, and the fuel for an overwhelming alienation on the part of the detached individual.[9]

The rapacious, unregulated economic individualism of the late nineteenth and early twentieth centuries has gone by the wayside, restrained by government intervention, first in the name of an economic equity and more recently in the name of environmental protection.

On the other hand, social and moral individualism has taken a giant step forward since the end of World War II, most especially since the 1960s. The transfer of many social standards from the public to the private sphere has been an unending process since that time. More and more activities, ranging from the right to abortion to the right to have nude dancing in a bar have been defined as private and guaranteed constitiutional protection through rights to privacy or to freedom of expression developed by interpretation by the U.S. Supreme Court. The sum total of all of this is that it is almost impossible to establish or enforce public standards that might curb individual actions of self-expression in most social, moral, and religious spheres.

It was in answer to the latter strains within American individualism that collectivism emerged as a major force on the American scene. Collectivist strains can be found from the very beginnings of American society. The first efforts at colonization on the part of the English, both at Jamestown and Plymouth, were based on collective effort and ownership. In both cases, within a year or two the experiment with collectivism was abandoned as a failure in favor of the encouragement of individual enterprise, with far better results. The collectivist strain periodically resurfaced in other colonization efforts, particularly in the utopian colonies of the nineteenth century.[10] These experiments represented the first attempts to utilize collectivism as an antidote to what were considered the evils of individualism and were initiated for the best of reasons. As long as the collectivist impulse was confined to a few relatively small experiments and all of the colonies either disappeared or transformed themselves into noncollectivist communities, it had little influence on the body politic as such. Beginning with the New Deal, however, a collectivist approach began to be imposed on a national scale through massive government intervention.

The intellectual origins of this collectivist approach can be found in the post-Civil War years, in the last generation of the nineteenth century, when intellectual reformers seeking to eliminate the evils of industrial society while retaining the benefits of industrialization began to propose collectivist solutions to current social problems. Perhaps the foremost example of this new collectivist utopia was provided by Edward Bellamy in his novel, *Looking Backward.*[11] In it he describes a society organized on military principles in which every person is mobilized for the active adult portion of his or her life within one grand pyramid to undertake the tasks of society. At the time, Bellamy's utopia was widely admired and clubs were established all over the country to advance his scheme.[12] Today, in retrospect, with the experience of such utopias in other parts of the world before us, we are appropriately horrified by the collectivist regimentation involved and appalled at Bellamy's naivete regarding human nature when it comes to the exercise of power.

Less radical expressions of this collectivist impulse were expressed by people like Herbert Croly, often identified with the Progressive movement.[13] Croly's ideas had more of an impact in that he did not seek an utter transformation of American society but rather an amelioration of existing conditions through more national government effort on a collectivist basis. It was the Crolyan image which provided the basis for the kind of collectivism which emerged during the New Deal.

This is not to say that the New Deal was itself collectivist. It was far too unsystematic for that, and it is unlikely that Franklin D. Roosevelt wished to foster a collectivist America, but among those around him there were people who saw in collectivism—democratic collectivism to be sure—the only solution to the problems facing the country.[14] Capitalizing on the moralistic strain in American society which periodically encourages Americans to try to impose single standards of behavior, even in delicate areas, upon the American public, they and their heirs have succeeded in the intervening decades in creating a substantial collectivist thrust within the body politic. Needless to say, it is not known by that name. Sinclair Lewis wrote a novel to illustrate how fascism could only come to the United States in the name of liberty.[15] So, too, with collectivism.

Collectivism American style has often been encouraged by a third strain in American life, that of corporatism. In this context, corporatism may be defined as the organization of civil society through corporate structures which are able to efficiently focus considerable power and energy on the achievement of specific goals and which have a tendency to combine with one another to control common fields of endeavor, primarily economic but potentially political as well.[16] Such corporate bodies, while nominally broad-based, in fact are excellent devices for concentrating control in the hands of managers who are formally trustees for the broad group of owners (shareholders), but in fact have great freedom of maneuver. The shareholders, in return for relinquishing control to managers through the corporate framework, are in a position to gain profit without sharing responsibility since the corporation becomes a reified person standing apart from those who have combined to form, own and manage it.

It is easy to see how corporatism of this kind can be closely linked with a kind of collectivism. In fact, that linkage also began with the very first English settlements on American shores. The first settlers were sent out by the great trading companies of England and Holland, the predecessors of the modern corporation. It was those trading companies which sought to utilize collectivist mechanisms to build their colonies until those mechanisms proved themselves to be unprofitable. This phase of corporatism did not last much beyond the first generation of settlement in each of the colonies. But the mere fact that the original colonies tended to be settled through such corporate structures has often been overlooked in American history. It was only after corporate endeavors had laid the groundwork that other settlement agencies would pick up the momentum.

Much the same pattern recurred at each successive take-off point in the advance of the land frontier. Thus settlement of the trans-Appalachian West owed much to the initial work of fur and land corporations, while subsequent settlement of the trans-Mississippi West was in no small measure initiated by larger fur corporations and the great railroad corporations. Needless to say, the urban-industrial and the metropolitan-technological frontiers are closely related to corporatism. Even the initial wave of entrepreneurs on the urban-industrial frontier rapidly came to institutionalize their efforts in corporate structures. Indeed, the struggle in the Jacksonian era over the freedom to incorporate was crucial to the opening and development of the urban-industrial frontier. By the time of the opening of the metropolitan-technological frontier, pioneering was itself a corporate activity, in a matter reminiscent of the earliest days of land settlement, but even more so.

In the era of the land frontier, corporatism had strong competitors, so its role remained significant but not dominant, intervening at key junctures in American development, but then having to retreat before other factors. Even the nascent corporations were subject to other strong influences so that corporatism, as such, had less of an impact. It was only on the urban-industrial frontier that corporatism acquired a major role, but still by no means a dominant one. Corporations assumed significant economic roles and involved themselves in politics as a result, primarily to protect and advance their own interests. However, even the most ruthless among them did not seek to provide a model for organizing the polity. It was expected by all and sundry that corporate and political organizations existed for different purposes and hence drew from different models. Here, too, it was the intellectual reformers who borrowed corporate models in the last generation of the nineteenth century as the basis for many of their reform proposals. In the Progressive Era, they were joined by spokesmen for corporate interests, who saw in the smooth workings of the great business corporations models to be adopted by government, particularly municipal government, to improve their efficiency.

Still, it was only with the coming of the metropolitan-technological frontier in the generation following World War II that the corporate model became identified with progress in the political realm. In that generation, there was a movement towards linking corporatism and collectivism. This, in itself, marked a revolutionary shift. Collectivism was originally fostered in government to fight corporate power. In the end, however, the natural alliance between the two has tended to bring them together, at the expense of individualism.

The American people, who pride themselves on their individualism, are, for the most part, unaware of the role corporatism has played in their history, even though they have come to share many of its basic assumptions, often unbeknownst to them. Thus, for example, since Americans have inevitably defined efficiency in commercial terms (that is to say, what is efficient for the promotion of commerce is accepted as efficient for all purposes), they increasingly have come to accept corporate definitions of efficiency as corporations have become the dominant forces in commerce. Thus political life has also been pushed in the direction of corporatist ideas with little questioning as to whether the basic assumptions of corporatism are applicable or appropriate in a democratic political arena.

It has already been suggested in this volume that federalism, in the original covenantal sense, is a fourth orientation in American life, one which has so dominated the mainstream of the American experiment that it has been utterly taken for granted and often gone unrecognized.[17] Since the days of the Puritan and Revolutionary founders, when John Winthrop could still talk of federal liberty and Thomas Jefferson of ward republics, federalism in this sense has sunk so deeply into the American psyche. It is only in civil societies in which there are people searching for the federalist way—France, for example—that federalism is identified as a sociopolitical orientation in its own right. Intellectuals in those countries write about "integral federalism." In the United States, federalism has been integral to the American experience; hence, there has been no incentive to discuss integral federalism as a concept.

Federalism as an orientation emphasizes each individual's place in a network of cooperative communities where individualism is not defined through one's detachment but through partnership with others, a network in which the individual does not confront society alone but through such mediating institutions as the family, the religious community, an ethnic group, or the like. It is this federalist way that has limited the anarchic tendencies inherent in individualism to generate the kind of disciplined independence that has been characteristic of American society. It is this federalist way that has enabled Americans to undertake collective action without embracing collectivism. It is this federalist way which has provided both the political and social dimensions necessary to harness the power generated by corporatism and direct it towards the goals of justice that animate American civil society.

Judgment Under Covenant

One of the most impressive and significant dimensions of American covenantalism is the way in which the covenant idea is used to place the American people under judgment. We have seen how the idea of covenant implies a kind of chosenness which in a religious sense requires those who are accepted into partnership with God to accept a special vocation. The price of that chosenness is to be constantly under God's judgment. Like the ancient Israelites, the Puritans were experts in conveying that sense. As Winthrop declared in 1630:

> Wee must Consider that wee shall be as a Citty vpon a Hill, the eies of all people are vpon us;.... the Lord hath giuen us leave to drawe our own Articles...if wee shall neglect the observacion of these Articles...the Lord will surely break out in wrathe against vs, be revenged of such a periured people and make vs knowe the price of the breache of such a Covenant.[18]

Since the people of the New England colonies were as human as anyone else, there was always sufficient failure to live up to the rigorous terms of the covenant and to bring down the wrath of God. Recognizing this, the Puritans introduced the jeremiad, the sermon designed to recall to the people their sins and bring them to repentance. Named after the Hebrew prophet Jeremiah, who had brought biblical covenantal preaching to its highest form in the 6th century BCE, these jeremiads became a regular feature of the Puritan commonwealths, institutionalized means of encouraging repentance.[19]

While the jeremiad as a regular institution disappeared in the eighteenth century with the transformation of the Puritans into Yankees, the principle remained deeply embedded in the American way of life. No doubt hundreds of thousands of sermons equally entitled to the title "jeremiad" have been preached since, but the institution went beyond sermons. For example, from December 1864 to February 1865, in the latter days of the Civil War, the *Charleston Mercury*, the great secession newspaper, published a series of articles to explain why the South was suffering imminent defeat. In those articles, the newspaper's editorial staff invoked the covenant principle and confessed that apparently God had judged that the South had broken its covenant with Him and was punishing the Southern people accordingly. A month after the *Charleston Mercury* used covenantal conceptualizations to chastise the South, Abraham Lincoln used the same framework to chastise all of the American people in his Second Inaugural Address.[20]

One hundred years later theologian Robert Bellah, who was the first to systematically describe the American civil religion as such, published a book entitled *The Broken Covenant*, suggesting that the Vietnam War was a punishment for America's sins.[21] If American chosenness has sometimes led to the hubris of manifest destiny it has also had the redeeming feature of self-criticism. Americans have seen themselves as being under judgment and there have always been those who have been ready to judge themselves and their fellows, or at least their fellows, as wanting under the terms of the covenant.

Who is Bound by the Covenant?

From the earliest beginnings of American history, questions of who is included and who is excluded from the covenant have been troublesome, especially in relation to Native Americans (Indians) and African-Americans (blacks). Ironically, early relations with the confederal Iroquois and other Indian peoples in sections of the Northeast were mediated through "covenant chains" which, true to the federal idea, recognized the Indians as free people, treated their nations as polities in their own right, and required the Europeans to call them "brethren." When these covenant chains were broken and violated in the early eighteenth century, the Indians and Europeans ceased to be partners and became enemies.[22] The subsequent tragedy of the American Indian reflected the refusal of white Americans to associate with them federally.

Nevertheless, the Native American tribes were treated by the United States as sovereign nations well into the nineteenth century, finally being denied the right to exercise that sovereignty by an Act of Congress on March 3, 1871, which made all nonassimilated Indians except those remaining in the original thirteen states wards of the federal government. Even so, the U.S. Supreme Court refused to entirely abandon the principle that the tribes had residual sovereignty, a principle enunciated by Chief Justice John Marshall himself in 1832 in the *Worcester vs. Georgia* decision: "A weaker power does not surrender its independence, its rights to self-government, by associating with a stronger, and taking its protection. A weak state, in order to provide for its safety, may place itself under the protection of one more powerful, without stripping itself of the right of self-government, and ceasing to be a state.... The Cherokee Nation...is a distinct community occupying its own territory...in which the laws of Georgia can have no force, and which the citizens of Georgia has no right to enter but with the assent of the Cherokees themselves...." That principle began to receive some reinforcement after 1934 under the New Deal, when new leadership in the Federal Bureau of Indian Affairs reintroduced the notion of tribal self-government under American constitutional models.

The Native American revolt of the 1960s which, in a few cases, actually brought about the limited renewal of fighting between Native Americans and the federal government, introduced a new stage in the conflict over tribal sovereignty, principally fought out in the federal and state courts, the end result of which was not only to reaffirm tribal sovereignty but to make it operational in a number of crucial areas so that today the surviving tribes stand in an asymmetrical federal relationship to the United States, with a status resembling that of the commonwealths (federacies) of Puerto Rico and the Northern Marianas.[23]

The exclusion of African-Americans from the American covenant was a far harsher matter. The Native Americans were at least initially excluded because they were deemed independent; blacks were excluded because they were deemed permanent slaves. The matter also was not without its ironies, as in the case of the clauses of the U.S. constitution which counted each slave as three-fifths of a person for purposes of representation of Congressional apportionment.

Until 1858, the states had exclusive powers to determine the degree of black exclusion or acceptance. As a result, Northern states in which blacks had been emancipated during the Revolutionary era increasingly made them at least associate members if not full parties in the covenant and the commonwealth. Then in 1858 the U.S. Supreme Court handed down the Dred Scott decision, which depersonalized the slaves entirely in the eyes of American constitutional law. This was so unacceptable to such a high percentage of the American people that it was perhaps the proximate cause precipitating the Republican victory in the 1860 presidential elections and the subsequent Civil War.[24]

After the war, the federal Constitution was amended in such a way as to specifically reject the implications of the Dred Scott decision. The Thirteenth Amendment abolished slavery, the Fourteenth granted the ex-slaves their civil rights, and the Fifteenth granted them the right to vote so that they could protect those civil rights in the only way that people can, through the exercise of the political rights of citizenship. Those amendments formally inducted the blacks into the American covenant but, in fact, after a false start in the South under Reconstruction and perhaps for a decade thereafter, it would take another 100 years before the formal change would lead to a meaningful one in reality.[25]

In the late nineteenth century, when Social Darwinism and its byproduct, racism, were dominant throughout the world, Americans of European descent excluded other nonwhites from the American covenant as well, particularly the Chinese and Japanese who settled on the west coast and the Mexicans and Hispanics in the southwest. It was only after World War II had discredited racism worldwide and at the very least embarrassed Americans over their racist behavior during the war, that these groups were admitted into the American covenant, even though formally they had never been excluded. In this case, too, the 1960s was the watershed.[26]

Here too, the revival of covenantal thinking has been a significant factor in bringing about change. As indicated earlier, there seems to be an inverse correlation between covenantal thinking and racism, with the latter requiring organic conceptions of human relations that all too often end up being so hierarchical that they become castelike. Thus John C. Calhoun, arguing for a contract theory of the Constitution, emphasized his conception of the individual states as organic polities, with the federal union a mere contractual alliance among them and that their organic character rested upon what he argued was the natural relationship between whites as masters and blacks as slaves. Covenantal ideas, on the other hand, are strongly inclined to recognizing the equality of all humans, at least insofar as they are partners to a particular covenant.

Nineteenth-century Western racism led to Nazism and genocide, from which the world recoiled in revulsion, rejecting racist theories and the social Darwinism that went hand-in-hand with them in the post-World War II period. There is a chicken-and-egg question here as to whether new conceptions of human equality stimulated a renewal of covenantal thinking or vice versa. It is clear that the two have begun to march hand-in-hand.

In the United States covenantal thinking sooner or later finds expression in actual covenantal acts. The struggle against racism in the United States has stimulated several such acts. In 1979, for example, after the city of Boston had gone through several years of racial turmoil caused by efforts to break down de facto segregation of the public schools, the community's religious leadership convened an interfaith assembly to try to restore harmony. It drafted a Covenant of Justice, Equality, and Harmony which was proclaimed on the Boston Common and then signed by thousands of citizens in 1979–1980, and which had an extremely salutary effect on transforming the situation.[27]

The Spirit of Covenant in the Second Epoch

The Bible reminds us that the tenth generation brings with it a new epoch in human history. The first nine generations of American history constituted such an epoch, one in which the American people forged a unique covenantal-federal synthesis of constitutionalism, republicanism and democracy.[28]

The covenantal-federalist way is not dogma but rather a direction, a path. Thus federalism as a political way provided a basis for the secession of the Southern states on the one hand and, on the other, for their reintegration into the Union on an equal footing with their Northern sis-

ters once the Union forces won the Civil War.[29] Federalism has been
interpreted as limiting government action and as providing the basis for
government intervention to force private individuals to behave in a morally correct way. It is unfashionable for contemporary Americans to endorse John Winthrop's conception of federal liberty, which he defined as
the freedom to do what is right. But the recent history of government
enforcement of civil rights on the basis of U.S. Supreme Court decisions
is precisely an example of federal liberty, of the abridgement of the rights
of some individuals as well as polities to do wrongs to others.

For three and a half centuries, two under the same constitution, Americans have managed to follow the covenantal-federalist way, often without
being conscious that they were doing so except in the narrowest institutional sense. Now, however, that way has come under assault by the twin
pressures of corporatism and collectivism. These pressures developed in
no small measure in response to a radical individualistic heresy, no less
problematic than the collectivist and corporatist heresies now confronting
Americans. An understanding of organization based upon corporatist models
of efficiency coupled with a set of expectations from government based
upon collectivist models, which have come at the same time as a reorienta-
tion of individualism in the direction of license, have all combined to assault the covenantal mainstream of the American experiment.

The year 1976 marked the end of the tenth complete generation of
American history and the sixth generation of American independence. It
also marked the end of the first generation of the postmodern epoch. The
United States, aptly called by Seymour Martin Lipset the first new nation, was born at the beginning of the modern epoch, achieved its independence as that epoch reached its apex five generations later, and reached
maturity during the course of the next five generations until the modern
epoch came to an end.

Until the end of the modern epoch, when as much time separated the
founding of the American colonies from the Revolution as separated the
Revolution from them, it was still possible to talk about the United States
as being on the threshold of maturity. By 1976, Americans had actually
experienced a generation of maturity—of great world responsibility, of
tragic foreign involvement, of constitutional crisis at home derived from
the attempt to substitute imperial for republican styles of behavior in the
highest offices of the land. Today's Americans no longer have that luxury.
The United States has crossed a divide no less formidable than that which

Frederick Jackson Turner suggested was crossed when the era of the land frontier came to an end, and perhaps even more so.

In the postmodern epoch, ethnicity, an organic phenomenon, has increasingly become a legitimate expression of Americanism.[30] Indeed, its most extreme advocates have sought to replace the original American vision with a new myth of ethnicity and multiculturalism in a direct assault on the original foundations of the United States. This is a very new phenomenon.

Obviously Americans have always been aware of ethnic differences, even in the colonial period when those differences principally were between the peoples of the British Isles. Moreover, there were always those among them who sought to preserve their differences, but the overall and massive thrust of American society was toward the forging of a new American man and, indeed, mainstream American writing about what constitutes being American emphasized the newness of the American people with its strands from every part of Europe, a distinctly covenantal idea that individual humans were free to choose not only their allegiances but also their identities.

Ethnicity as a deliberate movement first appeared on the American scene in the late nineteenth century as Americans from northwest Europe not of English stock sought to set forth their claim to having contributed to the founding and development of the United States. After setting forth those claims, in a relatively short time most assimilated into the American mainstream. In retrospect, it seems that they simply wanted to do so as equals and not by sufferance of their English-descended compatriots.

This process was accelerated by the arrival of Eastern and Southern Europeans in large numbers, adding more visibly contrasting ethnic groups to American society. The new groups were told by older Americans that they were "hyphenated Americans" but that they could—and shall—assimilate and become just Americans like those who had arrived earlier if they were willing to assimilate into American culture. The vast majority did so with alacrity.

Then in the 1960s, as the race issue moved toward a more egalitarian resolution, the issue of ethnicity was raised again, this time by the descendants of those Eastern and Southern European immigrants. In the end their claim, too, was to have their nationalities' contributions to the United States recognized so that they could assimilate and become fully unhyphenated. Indeed, even as those most active in claiming their ethnicity did so, with one or two exceptions they did not have enough of their original group culture preserved, beyond a few foods and cultural habits, no longer consciously maintained, that they could use in order to distinguish themselves.

Multiculturalism received its push from those ethnic groups that were racially different in full or part.[31] Thus blacks, Native Americans, Hispanics (most of whom were amalgams of Hispanic, Native American, and African-American ancestry) and Asians had a sufficiently distinctive basis both racially and culturally to go beyond the simple demands that their contributions be equally recognized to ask for the right to preserve their cultures equally with the mainstream American culture. By doing so, they sought to transform the accepted rule of American civil society during its first epoch, namely that all or virtually all were welcome on American shores provided that they were willing to become new American men.

The multiculturalists launched the second epoch by insisting that the United States had to become the multicultural home for people who brought with them and wished to maintain their Old World cultures, for the most part coming out of very different cultural traditions from those of Northwestern Europe or even the rest of that continent. At the very least, the extreme manifestations of multiculturalism made serious challenges to the existence of a separately definable American culture with its own myths and heroes, language and habits to sustain it. All of these are under assault by multiculturalism, at least in its extreme form. Indeed, the struggle between advocates of the older and newer forms of American self-definition has been joined. It remains to be seen whether multiculturalism is simply another version of newer groups asking to be admitted as equals to the common American culture or whether they are really seeking separate maintenance on an equal footing.

In the last analysis, the covenant tradition survives in the contemporary United States, albeit sometimes in distorted ways. How, for example, do we describe the response of most residents of Los Angeles and evirons to the great 1994 earthquake that hit the western parts of their city. It is true that many or at least several thousands simply picked up and left the city for good, essentially disappearing without a trace (or at least without a trace until deliberately hunted), but the vast and overwhelming majority of Angelinos, residents of a city legendary for its kookiness and its commitment to the ultimate individualism—one might say to natural liberty with a vengeance to a point where, at times, the outside observer might wonder whether civil society even continued to exist—organized themselves to confront the challenge and did so with great success, restoring the city to working order in a matter of days and to full working order in a matter of months.

In a sense the Californians' response was typically American. First of all, the local authorities were there to take charge. Second, rescue and reconstruction was conducted in a federal way with both state and federal governments providing human services, technical and financial aid in a variety of ways. Third, it involved what seemed to that same outsider as a natural bent for cooperation, for people pulling together and knowing how to do so effectively. The response also involved contracts to pay for those things that had to be rebuilt that were made more lucrative if the work was done more expeditiously. That work was done within the framework of inventiveness, finding better ways to build in protections against earthquake destruction, and indeed the inventiveness produced good ideas for doing so which were implemented in the reconstruction.

All told, what emerged was not the kind of covenantalism that John Winthrop would have recognized but a covenantalism of technocratic humanism in a special California way, demonstrating great technological skills and great pride in those skills, combined with great concern for making life easier for the people affected. It is hard to think of many other civil societies that could have risen to the challenge the way those Californians did.

Where this leaves the American people is not at all clear. In the political arena, whenever Americans had the choice they have rejected Jacobinism and managerialism on behalf of federalism. Nevertheless, in the universities and those institutions most influenced by the universities, governmental, public, and private, one or the other or both nonfederalist ideologies remain strong; in some respects protected by the institutions they denounce since they can remain untested and hence their deficiencies remain unrevealed.

In the meantime, proponents of both communitarian federalism and Great Society liberalism have turned to covenantal arguments to buttress their positions. This is not the place to try to resolve the conflict between them. What is more important is that in doing so they have revived the debate in the right terms. As the United States enters its second historical epoch, with all the trauma and crisis that brings, it is not surprising that the appeal to covenant is once again becoming prominent among the American people. Thus, while the debate has involved vital questions of the first magnitude, it has been carried on within the context of a political tradition which has changed little in over 200 years and has helped to sustain popular government despite the mistakes of transient majorities.

While the methodology and technique of covenanting passed into the realm of American constitutionalism, the felicitous synthesis between the spirit of religion and the spirit of liberty came to be disrupted, most particularly in the twentieth century. That disruption was even canonized by the U.S. Supreme Court, especially from World War II to the end of the 1980s. The felt consequences were not long in coming and beginning in the 1970s a movement developed to challenge the direction that American society was taking.

At first ignored as a reflection of the crackpot Christian fundamentalist right, it took nearly two decades to gain the momentum and recognition that moved it toward the center. In November 1994 its voters were instrumental in bringing about a result in national and state elections that was widely hailed as revolutionary. Whether it will be or not remains to be seen, but what is certain is that it opened the center to a return to the beliefs that had made that earlier synthesis possible.

Perhaps nothing symbolized that more than the lead article in *Commentary* of January 1995 on "God and the Americans" by Paul Johnson, in which he restated the history of the United States from the perspective of that synthesis, showing how that synthesis was normative and that the twentieth century was the deviation.[32] The venue for that article, although already twenty years into a neoconservative path, had remained staunchly Jewish in the sense that it remained staunchly secular throughout the period since its transformation, as it had before, at most defending the rights of the Christian right to express a different view. Johnson's lead article elaborately presented an alternate thesis, abundantly illustrated with quotations from the days of the Puritans until the present including discussions of the Puritan idea of covenant, their vision of "a city upon a hill," and (although not by name) their leader John Winthrop's description of federal liberty.

In the interim, Governor Bill Clinton of Arkansas tried to build his presidential campaign around the theme of a "New Covenant" with the

American people.[34] While public response to the phrase was muted, at first pundit response was not, as, for example, in *The New Republic* after Clinton won the presidential election in November 1992.[35] Jesse Jackson and his Rainbow Coalition challenged Clinton to live up to his New Covenant, on one side, and John Barela, critiqued it on the other.[36] The influence of the American covenental tradition on Bill Clinton through his schooling was even discussed in educational circles.[37]

Apparently, however, the theme did not echo well enough in the polls because Clinton backed away from it in the middle of his campaign. Nevertheless, references to the idea kept appearing in the first year of his term.[38] Then came the 1994 off-year elections and the Republicans' Contract with America. In response, Clinton revived his covenental theme to contrast it with what he presented as the less-than-humane Republican contract.[39] Since then the term has cropped up from time to time and is clearly embedded in the president's consciousness.[40]

On November 6, 1995, as clouds began to cover the sun on a clear autumn day in Jerusalem in Israel's national cemetery on Mt. Herzl, the American and Jewish covenantal traditions came together as the President of the United States, William Jefferson "Bill" Clinton, eulogized the assassinated Prime Minister of Israel Yitzhak Rabin at a state funeral that combined the touching intimacy of a Jewish family gathering, the homage of a people, and the respectful recognition of Israel's world position and of its assassinated prime minister's world contribution before the Rabin family, the Israeli government, and representatives of 86 nations including the heads of state or government of Great Britain, France, Germany, Russia, Spain, the President of the European Union, King Hussein of Jordan, President Mubarak of Egypt, and representatives from the Gulf states and Morocco. In his eulogy, Clinton said:

> I ask you, the people of Israel, on behalf of my nation that knows its own long litany of loss—from Abraham Lincoln to President Kennedy to Martin Luther King—do not let that happen to you. In the Knesset, in your homes, in your places of worship, stay the righteous course.
> As Moses said to the children of Israel when he knew he would not cross over into the Promised Land: "Be strong and of good courage. Fear not, for God will go with you. He will not fail you. He will not forsake you."
> President Weizman, Acting Prime Minister Peres, to all the people of Israel, as you stay the course of peace, I make this pledge: Neither will America forsake you.
> Legend has it that in every generation of Jews from time immemorial, a just leader emerged to protect his people and show them the way to safety. Prime Minister Rabin was such a leader.

He knew, as he declared to the world on the White House lawn two years ago, that the time had come, in his words, "to begin a new reckoning in the relations between people, between parents tired of war, between children who will not know war."

Here in Jerusalem, I believe with perfect faith that he was leading his people to that Promised Land.

This week, Jews all around the world are studying the Torah portion in which God tests the faith of Abraham, Patriarch of the Jews and the Arabs. He commands Abraham to sacrifice Yitzhak, "Take your son, the one you love, Yitzhak."

As we all know, as Abraham in loyalty to God was about to kill his son, God spared Yitzhak. Now, God tests our faith even more terribly, for he has taken our Yitzhak.

But Israel's covenant with God—for freedom, for tolerance, for security, for peace—that covenant must hold. That covenant was Prime Minister Rabin's life's work, now we must make it his lasting legacy. His spirit must live on in us.[41]

Clinton brought matters full circle in the presence of the world, as the world and the Middle East gave every sign of entering a new era of peace that could bring with it its own opportunities for covenanting in the polities involved and challenges to covenanting in life.

Notes

1. *The Economist*, "Regions of the Mind," May 6, 1989.
2. Robert Bellah, *The Broken Covenant* (New York: Seabury Press, 1975).
3. Daniel J. Elazar, "The Resurgence of Federalism," *State Government,* Summer 1970; *idem., The Nixon Welfare-Manpower Proposals and the American Federal System* (Philadelphia, PA: Center for the Study of Federalism, Working Paper, 1970); titles and pseudonyms of papers: Publius, "New Federalist Paper, no. 1"; Cato, "Federalism: Old and New"; Johannes Althusius, "New Federalist, no. 3"; Polybius, "In Support of Strengthening the American Federal System," all appearing in *Publius*, vol. 2, no. 1 (Spring 1972).
4. *Swearing-In Ceremony of Gerald R. Ford as President, August 9, 1974* (Ann Arbor, MI: Gerald R. Ford Library, 1974).
5. Gaddis Smith, *Morality, Reason and Power: American Diplomacy in the Carter Years* (New York: Hill and Wang, 1986); Joshua Muravchik, *The Uncertain Crusade* (Washington, DC: American Enterprise Institute, 1986).
6. *Publius*, Special Issue, "Assessing the New Federalism," vol. 16, no. 1 (Winter 1986).
7. "The Basic Campaign Speech: Democratic Presidential Candidate Bill Clinton," *Albany Times Union*, February 13, 1992.
8. For example, Tocqueville, *Democracy in America* (New York: Alfred A. Knopf, 1993).
9. Allan Bloom, *The Closing of the American Mind* (New York: Simon and Schuster, 1988).
10. Charles Nordhoff, *The Communistic Societies of the United States* (New York: Schocken Books, 1970).
11. Edward Bellamy, *Looking Backward* (New York: Magnum Books, 1968).

12. See ibid., Introduction.
13. Herbert Croly, *Progressive Democracy* (New York: Macmillan, 1914).
14. William E. Leuchtenberg, *Franklin D. Roosevelt and the New Deal, 1932–1940* (New York: Harper and Row, 1963); Francis Perkins, *The Roosevelt I Knew* (New York: Viking Press, 1946).
15. Sinclair Lewis, *It Can't Happen Here* (Garden City, NY: Doubleday Doran, 1936).
16. John Kenneth Galbraith, *The New Industrial State* (New York: Signet Books, 1967); William H. Whyte, Jr., *The Organization Man* (Garden City, NY: Doubleday and Co., Inc., 1957).
17. Andrew McLaughlin, *The Confederation and the Constitution* (New York: Harper and Row, 1968); *idem., A Constitutional History of the United States* (New York: Appleton-Century-Crofts, 1963); Donald Lutz, *Popular Consent and Popular Control* (Baton Rouge: Louisiana State University Press, 1980).
18. John Winthrop, "A Modell of Christian Charity," in Perry Miller, ed., *The American Puritans: Their Prose and Poetry* (Garden City, NY: Doubleday Anchor Books, 1956).
19. Sacvan Bercovitch, *The American Jeremiad* (Madison: University of Wisconsin Press, 1978).
20. Abraham Lincoln, Second Inaugural Address, *The Portable Abraham Lincoln,* Andrew Delbanco, ed. (Harmondsworth, Middlesex: Penguin Books, 1992, pp. 320–321).
21. Robert Bellah, *The Broken Covenant.*
22. Alden T. Vaughan, *New England Frontier: Puritans and Indians 1620–1675* (Boston: Little, Brown and Co., 1965).
23. C. Matthew Snipp, *American Indians: The First of This Land* (New York: Russell Sage Foundation, 1989); Ralph K. Andrist, *The Long Death* (New York: Collier Books, 1964).
24. Dred Scott vs. Sanford (1865); Don Edward Fehrenbacher, *The Dred Scott Case* (New York: Oxford University Press, 1978).
25. John Hope Franklin, *From Slavery to Freedom* (New York: Alfred A. Knopf, 1967).
26. On the "2 cities," cf. Daniel J. Elazar, *Cities of the Prairie* (New York: Basic Books, 1970), 230–34 and *Cities of the Prairie Revisited* (Lincoln: University of Nebraska Press, 1986), chapters 2 and 3.
27. Lawrence W. Kennedy, *Planning the City Upon a Hill: Boston Since 1630* (Amherst: University of Massachusetts Press, 1992).
28. George Mendenhill, *The Tenth Generation: The Origins of the Biblical Tradition* (Baltimore, MD: Johns Hopkins University Press, 1973).
29. Daniel J. Elazar, *Building Toward Civil War* (Lanham, MD: Madison Books and the Center for the Study of Federalism, 1992); *idem.* "Federal-State Collaboration in the Nineteenth Century United States," *Political Science Quarterly* (June 1964).
30. Oscar Handlin, *Immigration as a Factor in American History* (Englewood Cliffs, NJ: Prentice-Hall, Inc., 1959); Louis Adamic, *A Nation of Nations* (New York: Harper and Bros., 1945); Carl Wittke, *We Who Built America* (Cleveland, OH: Case Western Reserve University Press, 1969).
31. Peter Schrag, *The Decline of the WASP* (New York: Simon and Schuster, 1970).
32. Paul Johnson, "God and the Americans," *Commentary*, vol. 99, no. 1 (January 1995):25–45.
33. Paul Johnson, "God and the Americans," *Commentary*, vol. 99, no. 1 (January 1995):25–45.

34. 1992 Democratic Platform, "A New Covenant with the American People" (Washington, D.C.: Democratic National Committee, 1992); "Excerpts from the Platform: A 'New Covenant' with Americans: Democratic Party Platform: From the Democratic National Convention," *New York Times*, July 15, 1992, P. A10; Amy Kaslow, "Democrats Fashion Broad Platform; Clinton and Party Offer 'New Covenant' to American Voters: Democratic Presidential Candidate Bill Clinton; Democratic National Convention Espouses Economic Growth in Lieu of Wealth Redistribution," *Christian Science Monitor*, July 14, 1992, p. 1.

35. Fred Barnes, "The New Covenant," *New Republic*, vol. 207, no. 20 (November 9, 1992).

36. Dan Balz, "Jackson Preaches the Challenger Clinton's New Covenant: Bill Clinton Attends a Sermon Delivered by Jesse Jackson," *Washington Post*, November 23, 1992, p. A1; John Barela, *The New Covenant of Bill Clinton and Al Gore: Neopagan Fundamentalism and the New Politics* (Tulsa, Oklahoma: Mark 4 Publications, 1992); Lynn Duke, "Minorities to Monitor 'Covenant': National Rainbow Coalition to Monitor President Bill Clinton's Campaign Promise of a 'New Covenant' with the American People," *Washington Post*, p. A16; Orlando Patterson, "Our History vs. Clinton's Covenant: President Elect Bill Clinton's Election Holds Hope for American Dream," *New York Times*, November 13, 1992, p. A15 (N), p. A29 (L).

37. Karen DeWitt, "Teacher Inspired Clinton's New Covenant: Bill Clinton's History Teacher Carol Quigley Helped Form His Political Ideas," *New York Times*, July 17, 1992, p. A12 (N) and p. A15.

38. William Galston, "Student Aid for National Service: President Clinton's New Covenant for Educating America," *AAHE Bulletin*, vol. 45, no. 9 (May 1993); Carl Tobias, "Keeping the Covenant on the Federal Courts: The Clinton Administration's Judicial Appointments," *Christian Science Monitor*, February 14, 1994, p. 23; Tom McNichol, "The New Co-Dependent Covenant: Reflections on Bill Clinton as Baby Boomer Covenant," *Washington Post*, February 28, 1993, p. C1; Carl Tobias, "President Clinton's Covenant and the Federal Courts," *Denver Law Review*, vol. 71, no. 1 (1993); Leon Wieseltier, "Washington Diarist: Covenant and Burling," *New Republic*, vol. 208, no. 5 (February 1, 1993).

39. "Covenant or Contract? Republican and Democratic Visions for the Future," *Christian Science Monitor*, January 26, 1995, p. 18; James P. Pinkerton, "Raiders of the Lost New Covenant: State of the Union Address by President Clinton," *Los Angeles Times*, January 26, 1995, p. B7; Todd S. Purdum, "Clinton Calls for Sharing Responsibility in Stressing Themes of G.O.P. and of '92; Few New Goals: State of the Union Talk Revives Notion of a 'New Covenant'," *New York Times*, January 25, 1995, p. A1; Paul Richter and Marc Lacey, "Clinton Calls for a 'New Covenant'," *Los Angeles Times*, January 17, 1995, p. B1.

40. Bill Clinton, *Empowerment, A New Covenant with America's Communities: President Clinton's National Urban Policy Report* (Washington, DC: U.S. Department of Housing and Urban Development, 1995); John F. Harris, "President Defends His Activism; Georgetown Speech Avoids Policy Details; Bill Clinton Declares a 'New Covenant' Between the Government and the People," *Washington Post*, July 7, 1995, p. A4.

41. "Words of Grief and Resolve from Friends and World Leaders, *New York Times International*, November 7, 1995.

Part III

Covenant on the Great Frontier

8

The Western Hemisphere:
False and Real Frontiers

Frontiers, out of necessity, generate the best conditions for the formation of covenanted peoples. The combination of people uprooted from their original locations, even if by choice, and forced to reconstitute themselves as peoples and not just to found new governing and social institutions, not only offers the largest opportunity for change by negotiation and choice but thrusts people in that direction. This is particularly true of land frontiers of the kind opened by Europeans at the end of the fifteenth century that became major arenas of human progress for the next 400 years.[1] The fact that the people in some new implantations formed covenant societies while others merely transport their older hierarchical patterns intact is in itself telling, teaching us that in addition to opportunity and necessity, culture and prior historic experience play a major role in the process.

The Covenantal Tradition and New Societies

We have seen how covenant in the direct sense is the animating force of certain polities, civil societies, and regimes. But however fundamental it may be, covenant rarely, if ever, stands alone as the basis of human association; perhaps that is in the nature of things. Thus biblical Israel was compounded out of a combination of covenant and kinship: a family or a putative family of tribes, believing that they were descended from the sons of a common father, became a nation as a result of a series of covenants with God and among themselves. To this day there is a basic tension in Jewish life between the two dimensions of covenant and kinship. In a somewhat similar way, the Scottish nation synthesized covenant and clan.

Iceland was built around the migration of Norse families fleeing attempts to impose a hierarchical regime upon them. While they organized covenantally from the first, they were for all intents and purposes one people (they did have some increase from the northern parts of the British Isles), who were merely faced with the necessity of establishing and to some extent restructuring their traditional institutions.

The Swiss, the second great covenanted people, built their polity on a synthesis of covenant and community, with "community" being confessional, linguistic and/or commercial. In the case of the Swiss, like the Scots and the Puritans of New England, their churches, guilds, and other commercial institutions as well as their polity were organized by covenant. Only their linguistic communities have an organic origin.

The United States is the closest to being fully covenantal in the sense that its synthesis is between covenant and compact. The American people were united as a people by those pacts. Their central myth begins by recognizing that all but the one percent of Native Americans were immigrants to new territory, and that they organized themselves into a new people through "reflection and choice," beginning with religiously based civil and political covenants of the seventeenth century and continuing through the political and social compacts influenced by Locke, Montesquieu, and the Scottish Enlightenment, which were introduced in the eighteenth. Because of the frontier character of American society, with its emphasis on the migration of individuals or covenanted communities of individuals, there is hardly any organic basis in the American political or social order, except in matters of race where it is deemed illegitimate because racism is in violation of the American first principles of equality that are so thoroughly covenantal.

Canada is a synthesis of compact and custom and rests on a compact between customary communities. Australia is a step even farther removed. Australian society is a synthesis of convicts and Chartists; that is to say, members of the lower or excluded classes in England who were shipped to Australia for offenses committed, plus those of similar background who emigrated in search of wealth at the time of the Chartist movement in England and who were much influenced by that idea of using covenantal means to reform English society from within.

The most difficult combination of all was to be found in South Africa, whose polity and society were, for three centuries, a combination of covenant and caste. For its Afrikaner founders, the covenant at Blood River was at the center of their national unity and identity. It was but one of several covenants that led to the development of the usual covenantal network. On the other hand, Afrikaner covenantalism was designed, among other things, to mark the sharp separation between whites and blacks and to ratify the inferior status and position of the latter. Hence the two stand in what has become unbearable tension.

We return finally to the new State of Israel, which continues the Jewish tradition of synthesizing covenant and kinship. The Zionist movement began its way with a series of covenants, large and small, that were necessary to unite the Jewish people in pursuit of the goal of a Jewish national home, even though Zionist theory followed the fashions of biological analogy of the late nineteenth century. At the same time, the state they sought to establish was designed for a people understood as an extended kinship group. The perennial issues confronting the Jewish state such as defining "Who is a Jew?," are reflections of that latter dimension. What is clear in all these cases is that the motivating intellectual content is covenantal, even if the motivating reality may partake of other characteristics.

All of the foregoing except perhaps Switzerland are or began as new societies, sharing a certain similarity of circumstances as well as the differences among each. The story of ancient Israel was explored in *Covenant and Polity in Biblical Israel*, the first book in this series. Those of Iceland and Switzerland were explored in *Covenant and Commonwealth*, the second. We have already examined the story of the United States. Now we will turn to the other new societies of the modern epoch.

It is in the nature of a land frontier that people move into empty areas, or at least areas that are empty to them, where they must establish new political and social institutions simply in order to survive. The possibilities inherent in the establishment of such new institutions by people who, by self-selection, are among the most adventurous and energetic of the race, are such that generate optimal conditions for the establishment of governments on the matrix model, on the basis of pacts, covenants, compacts, or contracts among the founders which, if they do not recognize the full social equality of the partners of those involved in the enterprise, create partnerships that recognize their underlying equality as humans. We have already seen how this was true of ships' companies who ventured out into unsettled areas every time a ship sailed from port, who organized governance relationships before the start of every voyage through ship's articles, a pact that offered every member of the ship's company a share in the voyage, in the most literal sense, while binding all to a system of discipline and command.

A False Start: The Caribbean and Latin America

The great frontier of Europe was the greatest of all human frontiers to date. In *Covenant and Commonwealth: From Christian Separation through the Protestant Reformation* we have already had a preview of the effects of that frontier on Iceland many centuries earlier, where the combination of free people fleeing the extension of hierarchical government in their original Norwegian homes capitalized on the settlement of the empty territory of Iceland to organize an oath society with all the republican accoutrements of late medieval northwestern Europe and to found a democratic republican polity and regime that has survived in that mold to this day.[2]

The next frontier opportunities were to occur to Europeans far to the south, the Portuguese and Spanish who came from a very different tradition, one in which hierarchy was predominant, despite earlier experiences with oaths and pacts within the context of the Christian reconquest of the Iberian peninsula. Moreover, the Castilians and the Portuguese, who came from that segment of Iberia that was most hierarchical culturally, took the lead in the expansion of the Hispano-Lusitanian Atlantic frontier. The more pact- and oath-oriented peoples from the northern part of the peninsula, especially from the Kingdom of Aragon, were turned eastward to the Mediterranean where they were primarily merchants and only secondarily colonists and conquerors, while the Castilians and the Portuguese turned westward and southward to the new worlds.[3]

The Portuguese settled the eastern Atlantic islands and those off the coast of Africa before reaching the Western Hemisphere, planting fourteenth- and fifteenth-century Portuguese civilization on them with a minimum of modifications.[4] The first new worlds to be discovered and occupied in the Western Hemisphere were the islands of the Caribbean. While most, if not all, had fairly extensive native populations, the Columbian transfer, which brought European diseases to populations that had never before experienced them and hence had no immunity or resistance, led to their disappearance.[5] The few who may have survived were enslaved by the conquering Spaniards and in no case were any seen as host societies

into which the Spanish settlers might merge. Thus the field was clear for
the Spaniards to build new societies on whatever model they chose.

They chose feudalism. Perhaps it was not so much a choice as acceptance of reality. In the last generation of the fifteenth century, modernity
was still four to six historical generations in the future. Even the Reformation, which in any case did not touch Spain directly, was two decades
ahead. Moreover, the Spaniards had developed a means of using feudal-
style arrangements to absorb conquered lands through the 700 years of
the *reconquista*, and so had ready-developed techniques that could be
simply transported across the ocean, lowering the incentive or the perceived necessity for developing new forms.[6]

Not only that, but the end of the fifteenth and the early sixteenth centuries were the late Middle Ages, when newly emerged monarchies had
begun to repress the contractual dimension of earlier feudalism. Spain
and Portugal themselves had emerged from the era of *fuero* (pact)-mak-
ing and indeed their kings were seeking ways to moderate or eliminate
the *fueros* then in existence in the Iberian peninsula to achieve more
hierarchical and centralized rule.[7] They certainly did not seek to introduce that system into the New World.

None of this might have worked sufficiently had the settlers been of
only Spanish descent. While it probably would have been possible to
impose a hierarchical society on the indigenous peoples, since their own
indigenous societies were largely hierarchical—as in the case of the Az-
tecs and Incas—to the extent that they were not small, primitive, and
tribal—as on the Caribbean islands—it might have taken the form of
earlier Iberian feudalism, which allowed for a great deal of contractually
based subsidiarity whose consequences led to a basic commitment to the
equality of all Spaniards, an outlook that permeates Spanish culture in
Spain to this day. But the Spanish settlers of the New World did not
come to do their own work but to get rich as quickly as possible. Hence
they needed slaves and instituted a society based on slaves and masters.
When the Indians proved to be poor slave material the Iberian conquerors began to import Africans. Within a relatively short time a completely
stratified society developed, in which the large bottom rung consisted of
people with no political rights or hope for political rights at all.[8]

Thus new society conditions really never existed in Ibero-America. In
their place came a feudalism worse than that of the mother country because of the racial element involved. Obviously under such conditions

covenantal relations were rejected, as it turned out, even for the relatively few Europeans who came to the New World.

Among the countries of Hispanic Latin America, Costa Rica stands out in its commitment to democratic republicanism which became a reality in 1889 and has remained one every since. Costa Ricans claim that their democratic origins go back further into colonial times. Not only is a very high percentage of Costa Rica's population of Spanish descent, there are relatively few Indians in the country so that a caste system was not established as a matter of course at the beginning of settlement.

There is a widespread local belief that a relatively high percentage of the original Spanish population were Sephardic Jews fleeing the Inquisition. As evidence they offer the many families in Costa Rica with family names derived from animals and plants rather than from christological symbols that reflect those Sephardic origins. Whether that is so or not we have no way of knowing, but we do know that many of the Spanish settlers came from the Basque country and Aragon, two of the centers of liberty (at least feudal-style liberty) in Spain at the time of settlement.

The constitutions of Costa Rica more than in its sister states reflect at least a theory of political compact. The first, adopted in December 1821, was the Pact of Concordance. It was to be an interim constitution proclaiming Costa Rica's independence from Spain. Included within it was an expression of the willingness of Costa Rica to be part of a confederation with other entities in Central America.

Unfortunately, Costa Rica's connections came as a result of its conquest for a brief period by Emperor Iturbide of Mexico. In March 1823, in the wake of the fall of Iturbide's empire, Costa Ricans adopted their first full constitution. A few months later, in May of that year, they adopted a third one, making Costa Rica part of the Federal Republic of Central America, at first a loose confederation, but in December 1824 in their fourth constitution it was transformed into a centralized federation. The next month, Costa Rica adopted a fifth constitution as required by the FRCA constitution, to be consistent with the latter and to supplement it for local purposes.

In the thirty years between 1841 and 1871, Costa Rica had seven constitutions. The country left the Federal Republic of Central America, became independent, and went from coup to coup. The 1871 constitution, however, which was adopted after the coup of Tomas Guardia, combined the best of the previous constitutions. It lasted until May 1948, although it was suspended a few times. In November 1949 Costa Rica's present constitution was adopted and it is now the oldest in Latin America. It was essentially a revision of the eleventh constitution (1869).

This is not to suggest that Costa Rica is a covenantal polity, only that it comes closer through its use of constitutionalism than other Latin American polities.

To sum up, the Iberian New World settlements in Latin America and the Caribbean continued the feudal pattern of being based on status rather than contract. Whatever covenantal expressions there may have been were integrated within the status framework that was sharpened by the caste division between a dominant white elite and a highly subordinated black underclass with at least two basic groups in between; the upper consisting of Creoles, that is to say whites born in the New World, and the lower the products of racially mixed unions. Whatever else happened within those societies, these status lines remained inviolable and have influenced all of Latin American and Caribbean history ever since those first generations when they were established.[9]

Nevertheless, the very fact of being new settlers introduced a certain fundamental or underlying equality that persisted and which may have had its impact at the time of the assertion of the independence of the colonies in question. Perhaps it was no more than local and regional interests that led Argentina, Brazil, Columbia, Mexico, Venezuela, and the Central American states to try to institute federal government as a major liberal dimension of their anticolonial revolutions, but in some cases it was also something else, surviving from the brief period when these were new societies.[10]

Despite the overall trend and the capture of the center by status-oriented hierarchs, pockets of settlers found their way to the peripheries where they developed freer societies, using the opportunities provided by the new territories to do so. The emptier the lands they chose, the greater the opportunity they had for doing so, mostly in Argentina, somewhat less in the Brazilian frontier regions, much less in heavily populated Mexico, except in the less populated desert areas, especially in the north, that offered these opportunities, least of all in Peru in the Andean viceroyalties. For example, Chile, long relatively unpopulated and open, initially experimented with federalism, but only briefly, since its hierarchical center around Santiago and in the north soon imposed its control over the rest of the country and eliminated any vestiges of it.

These peripheral regions also attracted such heretics and dissenters who found their way to Latin America, most especially Marranos, new Christians who secretly practiced Judaism and who fled to the New World in the hope that there would be less chance of their being discovered. In the sixteenth and seventeenth centuries there were major Marrano colonies throughout Iberian Latin America, as attested to by records of Inquisition crackdowns. They played a major role in the development of those colonies. The Spanish and Portuguese governments soon banned the emigration of new Christians to their Latin American lands because of the extent of the "problem." Great concentrations of Marranos were found in Mexico, Brazil, and Peru, but there was no part of Ibero-America into which Marranos did not penetrate, from New Mexico and north, whose Marrano roots are just now being rediscovered among their heirs, many of whom are still conscious of their Jewish connections, to Costa Rica and Brazil, both of which claim to have been heavily Marrano in their settlement, to southern Argentina and Chile. While the passage of time, the pressures of the Inquisition, and emigration to other lands where they could live openly as Jews drastically reduced the Marrano population after the mid-seventeenth century, for the first 150 years Marranos undoubtedly had a significant cultural influence on the Ibero-American colonies.[11]

In the end federalism, combined with a liberalism imported by the few intellectuals and cosmopolitans that well served the interests of the provincial landholders in their struggle with the center, was not enough. It survived in the larger countries along the east coast of Latin America because the balance of power between center and periphery made it necessary to constitutionally guarantee the inclusion of some measure of peripheral participation in the government, but it became very hierarchical.[12] Elsewhere in Latin America it either disappeared through consolidation or breakup or was never tried. There are even a few examples of efforts to establish covenanted communities, but they are so few and far between that their exceptionalism is their most notable feature.

In Central America the local planter oligarchies rather quickly beat down the impetus to federalism. Each of the new states went its own way under the kind of hierarchical rule for which Latin America is well known and which is coming back to haunt those countries and their patron, the United States of America.

Colombia, the only country to be at least nominally federal for at least fifteen years (half a generation) and then to voluntarily abandon federalism, went through decades of civil war until the issue was resolved operationally. In a sense, it has never been resolved ideologically. A federalist movement still exists in Colombia and occasionally gains strength and visibility. Perhaps significantly it is centered in Medellin, Colombia's second city, known as the home of the largest concentration of New Christians, many of whom continued to secretly practice Judaism for several hundred years, married endogamously to the extent possible, and almost unquestionably subliminally preserved aspects of Jewish political culture.

Mexico was one of the first of the Latin American countries to adopt federalism because of its highly diverse population and easily identifiable regions, which had some political as well as cultural identity in the colonial period. In 1920, at the very outset of the twentieth century, the country underwent a major revolution whose result was to establish single-party rule of the kind that vitiates federalism in reality. Still, the forms of federalism are considered very important in that country.[13] The drive for democracy in the Mexico of the 1990s is heavily predicated on the strengthening of Mexican federalism and intimately associates the two as in Canada and the United States, the other two North American countries that the Mexican establishment is trying so hard to emulate.

At the very end of the 1980s, Mexico began a modernization process that involved, inter alia, the invigoration of its economy and its polity through free enterprise market mechanisms and federal democracy respectively. Responding to the winds of change blowing throughout the world, the Mexican political establishment initiated a series of far-reaching measures on both fronts, chief among which was securing the North American Free Trade Agreement (NAFTA) as a means of economic union between the United States, Canada, and Mexico. The Mexican political leadership understood full well that this had consequences more far-reaching than merely better access to the U.S. and Canadian markets. It meant bringing Mexico under the watchful eyes of the United States in matters governmental as well, the price of being admitted to the North American "club."

The agreement went into effect on January 1, 1994. That same day, a guerilla movement initiated a predominantly Indian peasants revolt in the southern Mexican state of Chiapas. It was immediately subject to American public interest and scrutiny through CNN and other instruments of mass media, based upon the newfound Anglo interest in Mexico as a result of NAFTA.

The Mexican government responded accordingly. Instead of sending in the army for a brutal repression as it would have done in the past, it tried to restore order with a minimum of force and to begin negotiations at the highest levels for a peaceful and democratic resolution of the conflict. The Mexican leadership openly admitted that it was the NAFTA agreement which had led them to pursue this course of action as part of the price of admission to the "club." Mexican emphasis on federalism as a major dimension of democratization also shows how deeply rooted Mexican federalism is, even if it has often been honored only in the breech.

Argentina and Venezuela adopted federal systems after a generation of struggle between the elites in the capital and those in the provinces.[14] While the settlement that held each country together provided for federal structures of government, in each case the centralists have won against the federalists most of the time, although not to the extent as is true in Mexico. Both countries are also undergoing federalist revivals as part of the democratic reforms of the late 1980s and early 1990s. Venezuela introduced direct popular election of state governors and mayors and Argentina, following the end of military rule and its return to democracy in the wake of the defeat of its Falkland Islands adventure, has placed new emphasis on strengthening its provinces as well.[15]

Brazil was the last of the great countries on the Latin American continent to adopt federalism, doing so only after its elites rejected its imperial regime in the late nineteenth century for a republican one and then as a conservative reaction to liberal forces that were in the process of gaining control of the new republican institutions.[16] There, too, real regional divisions had existed since colonial times. Because of that, federalism has remained more real in Brazil than in any other Latin American country, in fact as well as in form.

A century and a half after the Spanish began settling the New World, the British and the Dutch either settled or conquered some of the Caribbean islands, precisely at the height of covenantal influences in their own home countries. To do so they used great trading companies in the style of the seventeenth century combined with military and naval forces sent to secure their imperial interests vis-à-vis the Spanish.[17]

Some of the covenantal influence of the home countries did cross the ocean to modify the existing plantocracies in ways which differed from island to island. Whatever the beginnings of Dutch and British colonization in the Caribbean, in the end Reformed Protestantism had little significant impact there. Rather, a white planter class emerged which imported African slaves and ultimately mixed with them to form a distinctive Caribbean population. They were joined by merchants, many of them Jews, who used the islands as jumping off points for the Latin American trade, which, while illegal under Spanish law, was encouraged by the British government.

The fourth element in this emergent Anglo-Caribbean civilization consisted of the pirates. Following the customs of the sea and reflecting the voluntary nature of piracy, they developed a contractual system of shares backed up by the exercise of naked force—a series of covenants with the devil, as it were.

In the Dutch colonies of Curacao, the Netherlands Antilles, and Surinam on the South American continent, much the same situation prevailed except that the merchant class was stronger, which meant more a society of contract rather than status.[18] In Surinam a moderately substantial body of Jewish settlers, mostly refugees from the abortive Dutch attempt to settle northeastern Brazil, established an autonomous ministate under overall Dutch jurisdiction known as Joden Savanne which organized itself as a Jewish community under Jewish law with all the covenantal dimensions involved therein. It continued to exist throughout the eighteenth century and only dissipated when the region's economy crumbled early in the nineteenth, leaving behind a remnant community to this day.[19]

Experiments in federation that went beyond this in the Caribbean have consistently failed because of the insular character of island life, whereby even the people on the smallest islands see themselves as self-sufficient or at least their island communities as self-contained.[20] Still, necessity has required the development and maintenance of confederal relations among these microstates as they became independent from the Netherlands after World War II and from Britain in the 1960s and 1970s, but in most cases they are the kind of arrangements which reflect necessity rather than a covenantal spirit. In the case of the Netherlands, which has a strong federal covenantal tradition of its own, the Netherlands Antilles achieved associated state status with the motherland. Subsequently Curacao became independent and Aruba became an associated state on its own, so that today the Kingdom of the Netherlands includes the twelve provinces of the Netherlands in Europe in a union with the Netherlands Antilles, and Aruba.

The former British islands developed a looser relationship detached from their former motherland. After the British failed to construct a West Indies Federation, each island or island group moved toward independence, pushed by a Britain no longer desirous of supporting them. Formally independent, the islands have had to unite in confederal arrangements out of necessity. They include a common market of sorts, a common currency and bank, a common university and a supreme court.[21]

Canada: Between Compact and Custom

A century after Spanish and Portuguese colonization of the southern half of the Western Hemisphere, just when the British were beginning to settle along the Atlantic coast, the French planted a colony on the shores of the St. Lawrence River which in due course became Quebec (1608). Needless to say, the seventeenth-century French did not found their colony on covenantal principles, but most who were attracted to it were Bretons who shared the underlying propensity toward covenantal directions of their fellow Celts. In Celtic society that propensity seemed to be one of commitment to a strong leader through a network of oaths.[22] Whatever its subliminal character, it found little expression in Quebec proper, where the influence of the established Catholic church and state was overwhelming. Instead it reached its apotheosis among the French Canadian voyageurs who went west from Montreal and Trois Rivieres to trap furs and to serve the great fur trading companies in the opening up of the Canadian and American northwest. Their freedom from the establishment came from going out to the far frontiers of Canada where they had to take charge of their own destiny.[23]

The French also settled in the western and northern parts of what are today the Maritime Provinces, particularly in New Brunswick. There they came into head-on conflict with the British, who were planting colonies in the same region to the east and south. Ultimately the British won control of that area after the first French and Indian Wars and many of the French were expelled—the Acadians of Louisiana are the descendants of those expellees—while others were brought under British rule relatively early on.[24]

At the same time, the British settled the far northern reaches of Canada, what they called Prince Rupert's Land, after the royalist cavalry leader of the English Civil War who headed the Hudson's Bay Company, chartered in England in 1668 after the Restoration to take over an area of some two million square miles—the whole of northern Canada—for the fur trade.[25] Ultimately the British conquered Quebec itself during the seventh French and Indian War and eliminated France from British North America (with the exception of two tiny fishing ports on the islands of St. Pierre and Miquelon in the mouth of the St. Lawrence River). With the exception of the Scots, who came out to trap and trade fur in Prince Rupert's Land, and the Scottish settlers in the Maritimes, especially Nova Scotia, the British governing class of Canada were all Tories.

In the 1789s, they were reinforced by the very Tory American loyalists who left or were expelled from the new United States of America at the time of the Revolutionary War. Indeed, Ontario, in time to become the dominant province of Canada, was settled by those Loyalists, who founded towns along the St. Lawrence River and Lake Ontario from Kingston to York (now Toronto) to Niagara Falls, today the developed heartland of the country. Quite naturally they brought their Tory ideas along with them, heavily reinforced as a result of their experiences in the American colonies.[26]

Overall, the Canadian experience is rooted in a tension between compact and custom, that is, is an effort to produce a synthesis of the covenantal and organic foundations of polity and society. This is most visibly reflected in the constitution of the Canadian confederation, which is an effort to combine federal and Westminster parliamentary forms and modes, but it is reflected throughout the Canadian experience from the time of the British conquest of Quebec in 1759 to the present. For 200 years after 1759, it found its primary expression topocratically; that is to say, through the organization of governments and societies along territorial lines, whereby the heads of the governments of those territories could speak more or less unchallenged in the name of their populations. Thus the French Canadians were protected, even while they were poor and uninfluential, because they were the overwhelming majority in the province of Quebec, while French Canadians who settled elsewhere in Canada were disadvantaged in many respects.

The very act of confederation was an effort to synthesize the covenantal and organic in the sense that it was designed to link two peoples, both of whom saw themselves as having their own organic roots, through a political compact providing for republican self-government through the combination of republican self-rule and in part through shared rule. This is the first and best definition of federalism. Both Canada's successes and its troubles have flowed from that basic tension and continue to do so.

With the exception of the Scots, who formed a majority only in the rather peripheral Maritime Provinces, an area that also benefited from intermigrational exchanges with New England, there was no covenant oriented migration to what is now Canada. Rather, the Canadian experience involved the necessity of building a modus vivendi between two ethno-religious groups, each with its own language and a long history of enmity between them going back to the Old World.[27]

At various points in Canadian history the effort to reconcile this tension led to the development of the idea of the Canadian Confederation, designed in 1862 and effectuated in 1867, as a political compact uniting these two groups through their territorial political institutions. Most of the time, however, organic evolution was the norm, and custom the basis of social and political development for both. In that sense there is only a weak direct covenantal tradition in Canada, but there is a mixed tradition of national and family compacts.[28]

If there is an area of Canada that has a truly covenantal base, it is probably to be found in the Maritimes, where Scottish and other Celtic settlers predominated from the first. The very first British colony was in Newfoundland, settled initially by small groups of fishermen who crossed the Atlantic to fish the Outer Banks and after a time began to set up supply stations and havens from storms on the Newfoundland coast without any overall royal backing or design. Of necessity these were at least contractual communities, since they were left to fend for themselves on a wild shore. The harsh terrain and climate has kept Newfoundland from ever becoming truly prosperous, and in Canada today, "Newfies" are a breed apart (at least partly because Newfoundland was a separate colony and then an independent dominion until it surrendered its independence in the Great Depression and finally joined Canada as the tenth province after World War II).[29]

Nova Scotia was settled by Scots, as its name indicates, with all the Scottish covenantal baggage transferred part and parcel. New Brunswick and Prince Edward Island were somewhat more mixed, but still with a strong Scottish component. All this was reinforced in the Maritimes by their close relationship with the New England colonies prior to the American Revolution and the cross-migrations that took place. Many New England families have branches in Nova Scotia, which became something of a deviant extension of New England in the colonial period because of their common covenantal foundations. An interesting question can be raised as to what impact the Loyalist emigration from New England to the Maritimes at the time of the revolution had in this context. On the one hand it may be fairly assumed that the Loyalists were among the least covenantal of the New Englanders. On the other, they were still Yankees.[30]

Loyalists were the founders of Ontario. Since they were not New Englanders, they were Loyalists with a vengeance. Their positive attitude toward Britain and its empire and negative attitude towards the United States continued to dominate Canadian policy overtly until the influx of non-Britons after World War II. Those attitudes are still powerful elements in Canadian public policy.

Moreover, since they were not New Englanders, they did not bring with them the same cultural base. They sought to establish a more elitist society in southwestern Ontario where they concentrated, but were successful only to a limited extent. The egalitarian characteristics of the frontier, especially when impacting on English-speaking people, had at least an equally powerful impact.

Nevertheless, because colonial rule persisted, the leading families of Toronto and environs were able to form a ruling oligarchy that cut across economic, social, and political spheres. It is of note that the interlocking relationships among the families came to be known as the Family Compact early in the nineteenth century. In time their influence was diminished, in part through the active opposition of their opponents, culminating in the short 1837 rebellion, and in part by the arrival of new settlers in the province, many of them Scots.

The settlement of Ontario by so many Scots brought, inter alia, the establishment of the United Church of Canada, a merger of Anglican, Congregationalist, and Presbyterian bodies into a single church community. With two-thirds of the merger coming out of the Reformed Protestant tradition and the other third coming out of the English establishment, something of a balance was developed between covenantal and Tory forms. The United Church became a powerful political and social influence in the nineteenth century, one that further reinforced a certain measure of covenantalism, albeit weak, in Ontario.[31]

Canada's rather placid history was punctuated by a few critical moments: the conquest of French Canada by the British in 1759, the settlement of Ontario by the Loyalists in 1784, the successful defense of the country against the Americans in both the Revolutionary War and the War of 1812, the abortive rebellions of 1837, and the establishment of the Confederation between 1862 and 1867. Canada's closest brush with revolution was in 1837, when there were brief uprisings in Upper Canada (Ontario) and Lower Canada (Quebec). William Lyon MacKenzie, the leader of the revolt in Ontario, was obviously of Scottish background while Louis Papineau, the leader of the revolt in Quebec, was of Breton stock.[32]

The Scots, indeed, became politically very prominent by the middle of the nineteenth century, with Sir John A. Macdonald being the foremost Canadian and the architect of confederation, but they for the most part made their peace with the oligarchic system that had developed in English Canada, more often becoming its leaders, like Macdonald, rather than its challengers, like MacKenzie. The 1837 revolt did succeed in breaking down the dominance of the Family Compact to the extent whereby a more egalitarian spirit could prevail. It jogged the British into a series of reform experiments that culminated in Confederation. At the same time it marked the Canadians' decisive abandonment of revolution as a strategy for political change.[33]

Unlike the United States, where the tensions surrounding the founding were between covenantal ideas of a religiously sanctified city upon a hill and the compactual ideas of Locke and the Enlightenment, the tensions surrounding the Canadian founding were between the English model of an organic polity, with its emphasis on elite rule through the Westminster system, and the necessity to reach some kind of compact between French and English Canadians. The first step was pure English. Lord Durham, sent out from Britain in the aftermath of the 1837 revolts to investigate their causes and recommend reforms that would prevent their recurrence, introduced both responsible government and the unification of Upper and Lower Canada into a single colony.

It soon became apparent that this approach was a failure and that some kind of federal system would be necessary. In 1862 and 1864 constitutional conventions were convened. The 1864 convention at Quebec City developed a plan of federal union for the now redivided Ontario and Quebec plus the three Maritime Provinces. Macdonald, the leading figure at the convention, was a reluctant federalist, but the demands of the French Canadians and the Maritime Provinces, who would only unite with their larger sisters through federation, led to the writing of a federal constitution. Three years later, it was enacted into law by the British Parliament as the British North America Act, which remained the heart of the Canadian constitution until its patriation over a century later.[34]

Witnessing the apparent disruption of the American union to the south, the Canadian founding fathers sought to write a constitution that would give maximum power to the general government (called the Confederation government in Canada in a reversal of the confederal-federal distinction developed in the United States nearly four score years earlier). Their effort to balance Westminster and federal principles was within a generation turned on its head, launching Canada on the road to a highly noncentralized federal system beginning in the 1880s. This change was accomplished through British Privy Council reinterpretation of the BNA Act in its capacity as the high court of appeal in matters constitutional, the rise to power of French Canadian leadership through the Liberal party, and the development of a compact theory of the Canadian polity, particularly by French Canadian theorists, to justify and deepen the change.[35]

The accession of British Columbia and Manitoba to the confederation after the Canadian purchase of Prince Rupert's Land from the Hudson's Bay Company in 1869 further encouraged this tendency, since it left only Ontario to support a more centralist interpretation of the constitution. Macdonald and his Conservative Party adapted to the new situation without much difficulty and the compact theory remained the regnant one until the Great Depression of the twentieth century brought with it new demands for activist government, particularly federal activism, and a new theory of cooperative federalism which, while not directly contradicting the compact theory, undercut its dualistic premises.

Following the British model of organic evolution through custom, the Canadians did not pay a great deal of attention to the BNA Act as a written constitution until the Quebec crisis erupted in the 1960s. True, the Privy Council in London had through its decisions endowed Canada with a body of constitutional law, but constitutionalism had not become the kind of living tradition that it was in the United States.[36]

Then the French Canadians in Quebec, once the weaker population on the Canadian scene, underwent modernization, prospered, and detached themselves from what had been their customary framework, Catholicism as embodied by the Church in Quebec, and developed an active nationalism in its place. For nearly a generation that nationalism, embodied in efforts to gain special political status for Quebec that at times became actively secessionist, made the question of the unity and integrity of Canada the most serious one confronting that country.[37]

The debate over the issue was conducted almost entirely in constitutional terms and in federal constitutional terms at that. As people of French stock, the Quebecois had an inclination toward centralized hierarchical government. Indeed, parallel to their efforts to change their status within Canada was a great growth and centralization of the provincial government of Quebec. Nevertheless it soon became apparent even to the most radical secessionists who still sought relief through the political process, that the debate would have to be couched in federalist terms.

There were essentially three positions in the debate: There were those—primarily non-French Canadians—who argued that Quebec and its people had to maintain the same relationship with the federal government and Canada as every other province, although they conceded that Canada had to do more to become binational and bilingual in practice as well as in theory. The more moderate advocates of Quebec nationalism sought a special status for their province within the existing federation, for example the right to take extraordinary measures to preserve the French language and a more direct role in Canada's foreign economic and cultural affairs.

The third position, that of the political extremists, proposed an arrangement that they labelled "sovereignty-association" that apparently involved something less than full confederation but something more than simply a league; perhaps closer in nature to the kind of associated statehood that has developed elsewhere as a new form of asymmetrical federalism where one large state and another smaller one are linked on a continuing basis, sharing some common features such as elements of a common market, currency, and banking system, but are otherwise independent. What is notable is that all three positions are federalist in orientation, and hence, reflect the covenantal tradition, albeit in its secularized and most instrumentalist manifestations.[38]

The Quebec crisis has been manifested through three concrete issues. One, the Language Act enacted by the Quebec National Assembly (for so they designate themselves) that replaced bilingualism in Quebec with the supremacy of French and that was ultimately declared unconstitutional in most of its provisions by the Canadian Supreme Court; two, the internal Quebec decision in regard to whether or not to proceed to negotiate for a basic change in the terms of the Canadian federation, which failed in a referendum in that province in 1980; and three, the issue of the terms of patriation of the Canadian constitution so that it would no longer be an act of the British Parliament with ultimate judicial review vested in the Privy Council but rather an all-Canadian document with ultimate power to change it either by amendment or by judicial review located in Canada.[39]

The festering constitutional crisis was brought to a head by federal Prime Minister Pierre Trudeau in 1982 after a series of premier's conferences and one final all-night session to which the premier of Quebec was not invited, at which ten of the eleven federal and provincial premiers, all except Quebec, agreed upon the terms of patriation of the Canadian constitution.

The terms of the premiers' agreement provided for reenactment of the BNA Act, as amended, by the Canadian Parliament as a constitutional act that only could be amended through special means and which vested certain provincial rights in the constitution so they could only be changed with provincial consent; the addition of a charter of human rights; and strengthening of the constitutional review powers of the Canadian Supreme Court. The agreement was accepted by the Canadian Parliament and nine of the ten Canadian provinces, over Quebec's objections. The constitution was patriated and the Canadian Supreme Court began to adjudicate the new Charter of Rights, responding more to the new constituencies based on nonterritorial interests such as women, aboriginals, and social deviants than to the traditional topocratic federal constituencies. Quebec continued its formal rejection of the agreement that gave rise to the patriation and its consequences but in essence accepted the results.

It was not until 1987 that another round of negotiations initiated by then federal Prime Minister Brian Mulroney, the Conservative successor to Liberal Trudeau, and including all ten provincial premiers, succeeded in securing Quebec's agreement and ratification. Under this, the 1987 Meech Lake Agreement, the provinces were given additional protections against possible federal encroachment. This agreement was presented to the country for ratification, which had to be secured from all the provinces separately. Eight of the ten provincial governments immediately signed on, including Quebec, the other two were wavering while new provincial elections were pending. The election of new governments in New Brunswick and Newfoundland derailed the process and set off the opposition of the new non-territorial interest groups. The Meech Lake Agreement finally was rejected, on the last day of the period in which it could be ratified, by the actions of an aboriginal (Indian) member of the Manitoba legislative assembly who was able to block a favorable vote on the subject and thus prevent unanimous ratification.

Yet another agreement was negotiated and, this time, put to a nation-wide referendum. It, too, was decisively defeated in October 1993. Canadians emerged from that campaign exhausted by the prolonged constitutional process so matters settled into a quieter status quo, leaving storm clouds on the horizon, particularly in the form of a closely decided 1995 referendum in Quebec as to whether or not Quebec sought sovereignty-association, or would remain in the Canadian confederation as it was. In an earlier such referendum, the Quebecois had voted by three to two for the status quo. This time, however, the secessionists came very close to victory. For the moment, the struggle over the essence and design of the constitution is in abeyance. The entire process has reflected the strong commitment to negotiated settlements characteristic of covenantal politics in general and law-abiding Canadians in particular.[40]

The second dimension of the Canadian effort to harmonize the organic and the covenantal is newer, although it has its roots in the compact between the Anglophone and Francophone peoples of 200 years ago. In Canadian parlance, it was originally referred to as multiethnicity but, by the 1990s, had become multiculturalism. Until World War II, Canada took the same position on immigration that other Anglophone frontier polities did. The doors were more or less open to people from outside the British Isles provided that they would, upon arrival, quickly learn to conform to the dominant culture. Since French rarely came to Canada, even to Quebec, this meant conforming to the English Canadian environment.

After World War II, Canada, seeing itself as underpopulated, opened its doors wide, first to Europeans of all backgrounds and then increasingly to Asians as well. As part of its efforts to define itself as against the United States, Canadian policy ceased to require the absolute assimilation of these new immigrants from different ethnic backgrounds to the dominant culture but rather encouraged them to preserve their own languages and cultures within the dominant culture.

For a while it seemed as if Canada might indeed become a new-style multiethnic state with Old World cultures retained to a sufficient degree without impinging upon the unity of Canadian culture. The children of Italians and Ukrainians learned to speak Italian and Ukrainian as well as English. Jews, once left a bit outside of the mainstream of Canadian society because of their Jewishness, were welcomed in, and every group was entitled to its own identity and government support for that identity. But the New World had its own impact and the children of the immigrants quickly became Canadian in a rather unhyphenated way, retaining little of their old cultures, certainly not in the public sphere, as they pursued opportunities as individuals within the Canadian economy and polity.

What they did retain was shifted from the rather separatist approach of multiethnicism to the new approach of multiculturalism. The basic premise of multiculturalism was sharing within the framework of a common civil society rather than separation along ethnic lines. Not only were the ethnic cultures welcome but so, too, were the aboriginal cultures of the native peoples who had inhabited the continent before the arrival of the French and the British, and such pseudo-"cultures" as women and social deviants who have common interests but are stretching matters a great deal when they think of themselves as cultures.

What is common to all of these groups is that they are not territorially based, but cut across the normal territorial divisions of Canada or any other country. Hence they address their most intensive lobbying pressures toward the federal government, looking for federal action, and have few, if any, territorial ties other than the national one. Moreover, since they are minorities (or at least functionally minorities, as in the case of women everywhere), they look to the courts for protection more than to the normal channels of democratic politics. Most of those who fit in this category have found each other and have entered into alliances with one another to advance their common aspirations and achieve their common goals in what may be becoming a new expression of covenantalism.

Canada, like the rest of the Western world, is involved in coming to grips with this new phenomenon. So far it has been trying to harness it to the older topocratic system, assisted in doing so by the strong resolve of the government and people of Quebec to hold on to their territorial rights and the dominance within their territory of those who express French Canadian national aspirations. On the other hand, perhaps the greatest barrier to the secession of Quebec today is the aboriginal peoples of northern Quebec, who do have a territorial dimension and insist that they will not allow their lands to remain in a Quebec any more independent of Canada than it is.

All in all, Canadians are another public that has never reified their state, although their intellectuals are more likely to speak of Canada as a "state" in European terms than are American intellectuals. Moreover, the Quebecois, rooted as they are in a continental European political tradition, do accept the idea of "the state" and their intellectuals see an independent Quebec as a state in the most European sense of the word. It is unclear as to whether the Quebecois population shares this view.

Notes

1. Walter Prescott Webb, *The Great Frontier* (Lincoln: University of Nebraska Press, 1986); Frederick Jackson Turner, *The Frontier in American History* (New York: Holt, Rinehart and Winston, 1962); Ray Allan Billington, *America's Frontier Heritage* (New York: Holt, Rinehart and Winston, 1966).
2. See *Covenant and Commonwealth*, "Iceland: An Oath-Bound Republic," in chapter 6 of the second volume of the Covenant Tradition in Politics series.
3. The only possible exceptions to this were the Galicians, like the Bretons of France of Celtic background, whose faces were also pointed westward but who were too few to be other than a leavening in the Iberian overseas colonizations. We know very little about the differences in approach between Castillians, Portuguese and Galicians, if any. It is another one of the elements in the history of covenant and politics that bears investigating.
4. D. W. Meinig, *The Shaping of America* (New Haven, CT: Yale University Press, 1986).
5. Alfred W. Crosby, *The Columbian Exchange: Biological and Cultural Consequences of 1492* (Westwood, CT: Greenwood Press, 1973).
6. Roger Bigelow Merriman, *The Rise of the Spanish Empire in the Old World and the New* (New York: Macmillan, 1925–1936), 4 vols.
7. John Huxtable Elliott, *Imperial Spain: 1469–1716* (Harmondsworth: Penguin Books, 1963).
8. Meinig, *The Shaping of America.*
9. Stephen Clissold, *Latin America: A Cultural Outline* (London: Hutchinson University Library, 1965); Bailey Wallace Diffie, *Latin American Civilization: Colonial Period* (Harrisburg, PA: Stackpile Sons, 1947).
10. Alicia Hernandez Chavez, *La Tradition Republicana del Buen Gobierno* (Mexico City: El Colegio de Mexico, 1993).
11. Cecil Roth, *A History of the Marranos* (Philadelphia, PA: The Jewish Publication Society of America, 1932); Seymour B. Liebman, *The Jews in New Spain* (Coral Gables, FL: University of Miami Press, 1970); idem., *New World Jewry, 1493–1825* (New York: Ktav Publishing House, 1982).
12. Daniel J. Elazar, *Exploring Federalism* (Tuscaloosa: University of Alabama Press, 1987).
13. Chavez, *La Tradition Republicana;* Donald C. Hodges, *Mexico, 1910–1982* (London: Zed Press, 1983); Marcello Carmagnani, *Federalismos Latinoamericanos: Mexico/Brasil/Argentina* (Mexico City: El Colegio de Mexico, 1993).

14. Juan E. Corradi, *The Fitful Republic* (Boulder, CO: Westview Press, 1985; Davide G. Erro, *Resolving the Argentine Paradox* (Boulder, CO: Lynne-Reinner, 1983).
15. Daniel C. Hellinger, *Venezuela: Tarnished Democracy* (Boulder, CO: Westview Press, 1991); *Venezuela in the Wake of Radical Reform,* ed. Joseph S. Tulchin (Boulder, CO: Lynne-Reinner Publishers, 1993).
16. Riordan Roett, *Brazil* (Westport, CT: Praeger, 1992); Ronald M. Schneider, *"Order and Progress": A Political History of Brazil* (Boulder, CO: Westview Press, 1991).
17. Amitai Ezioni, *Political Unification: A Comparative Study of Leaders and Forces* (New York: Holt, Rinehart and Winston, 1965), ch. 5; Bonham C. Richardson, *The Caribbean in the Wider World, 1492–1992* (Cambridge: Cambridge University Press, 1992); Franklin W. Knight, *The Caribbean: The Genesis of a Fragmented Nationalism* (New York: Oxford University Press, 1978).
18. Martin A. Cohen, *The Jewish Experience in Latin America* (Waltham, MA: American Jewish Historical Society, 1971); Zvi Loker, *Jews in the Caribbean* (Jerusalem: Misgav Yerushalayim, Institute for Research on the Sephardic and Oriental Jewish Heritage, 1991).
19. Robert Cohen, *Jews in Another Environment* (Leiden: E.J. Brill, 1991).
20. Amitai Etzioni, *Political Unification.*
21. Daniel J. Elazar, ed., *Federal Systems of the World,* 2nd ed., (Longmans, forthcoming).
22. F. Bosher, *The Canada Merchants, 1713–1763* (Oxford: Clarendon Press, 1987); Stanley B. Ryerson, *The Founding of Canada* (Toronto: Progressive Books, 1960).
23. Bosher, ibid; Ryerson, ibid.
24. W. Stewart MacNutt, *The Atlantic Provinces* (Toronto: McClelland and Stewart, 1965); Andrew Hill Clark, *Acadia* (Madison: University of Wisconson Press, 1968).
25. Donald G. Creighton, *Dominion of the North: A History of Canada* (Toronto: Macmillan, 1977).
26. Robert Bothwell, *A Short History of Ontario* (Edmonton: Hurting Publishers, 1986).
27. Arthur R. Lower, *Canadians in the Making* (Toronto: Longmans, Green, 1958); *idem, Colony to Nation* (Toronto: McClelland and Stuart, 1977).
28. Richard H. Leach, "Canadian Federalism Revisited," *Publius* vol. 14, no. 1 (Winter 1984); Filippo Sabetti and Harold M. Waller, "Introduction: Crisis and Continuity in Canadian Federalism," *Publius* vol. 14, no. 1 (Winter 1984).
29. Gerald Chadwick, *Newfoundland: Island Into Province* (Cambridge: University Press, 1967).
30. John B. Brebner, *The Neutral Yankees of Nova Scotia* (Toronto: McClelland and Stuart, 1969).
31. Bothwell, *A Short History of Ontario;* Joseph Shull, *Ontario Since 1867* (Toronto: McClelland and Stuart, 1978).
32. Samuel Delbert Clark, *Movements of Political Protest in Canada, 1620–1840* (Toronto: University of Toronto Press, 1978); Ramsey Cook, *Constitutionalism and Nationalism in Lower Canada* (Toronto: University of Toronto Press, 1969); Fernand Ouellet, *Lower Canada 1791–1840: Social Change and Nationalism* (Toronto: McClelland and Stuart, 1983).
33. Donald G. Creighton, *Canada's First Century 1867–1967* (Toronto: Macmillan of Canada, 1970).
34. Ibid.

35. Filippo Sabetti, *Covenant Language in Canada: Continuity and Change in Political Discourse* (Philadelphia: Working Paper of the Center for the Study of Federalism, 1980); Harold Waller, Filippo Sabetti, and Daniel J. Elazar, eds., *Canadian Federalism* (Lanham, MD: University Press of America and Center for the Study of Federalism, 1988).

36. "Crisis and Continuity in Canadian Federalism," *Publius*, vol. 14, no. 1 (Winter 1984).

37. Susan Trofimenkoff, *The Dream of Nation: A Social and Intellectual History of Quebec* (Toronto: Gage, 1983); Michael K. Oliver, *The Passionate Debate* (Montreal: Vehicule Press, 1991).

38. Daniel Latouche, "Problems of Constitutional Design in Canada: Quebec and the Issue of Bicommunalism," *Publius*, vol. 18, no. 2 (Spring 1988); Peter M. Leslie, "Bicommunalism and Canadian Constitutional Reform," *Publius*, ibid.); Pierre Fournier, *A Meech Lake Post-Mortem* (Montreal: McGill-Queen's University Press, 1991); Scott Reid, *Canada Remapped* (Vancouver: Pulp Press, 1992); Paul Painchaud, "Territorialization and Internationalism: The Case of Quebec," *Publius*, vol. 7, no. 4 (Fall 1977); Donald V. Smiley, "The Canadian Federation and the Challenge of Quebec Independence," *Publius*, vol. 8, no. 1 (Winter, 1978); David Close, Federal Provincial Politics and Constitutional Reform in Canada: A Study in Political Opposition," *Publius*, vol. 15, no. 1 (Winter 1985).

39. Edward McWhinney, *Canada and the Constitution: Patriation and the Charter of Rights* (Toronto: University of Toronto Press, 1982). Roger Gibbins, Rainer Knopff, and F.L. Morton, "Canadian Federalism, the Charter of Rights, and the 1984 Election," *Publius*, vol. 15, no. 3 (Summer 1985); Michael Howlett, "The Politics of Constitutional Change in a Federal System: Negotiating Section 92a of the Canadian Constitution Act (1984)," *Publius*, vol. 15, no. 1 (Winter 1985).

40. Thomas J. Courchene, *Meech Lake and Federalism: Accord or Discord?* (North York, Ontario: York University, 1987); Roger Gibbins, "Canadian Federalism: The Entanglement of Meech Lake and the Free Trade Agreement," *Publius*, vol. 19, no. 3 (Summer 1989).

9

The Southern Hemisphere
and the Asian Coast

Australia: From Convicts to Mates

In many respects Australia, among all the English-speaking new societies, is the hardest case for discovering the influence of a covenantal tradition.[1] First settled in the 1780s by convicts from Britain who were given the choice of being hanged or being deported to the very ends of the earth, Australia's beginnings were very inauspicious for any kind of civil society, not to speak of a covenantal one. Yet within two generations Australia became an attraction in and of itself for free people who came to seek their fortunes down under. Even the convicts should not be dismissed out of hand as bearers of nothing more than criminal records. The social conditions in late eighteenth- and early nineteenth-century Britain being what they were, often people with energy and talent who happened to be born into the wrong class were the ones who turned to what today would be considered petty crime but then were considered hanging offenses.[2]

Many of the later voluntary immigrants had a very special background in the covenantal tradition. They were Chartists. The Chartist movement flourished in England between 1838 and 1848 as a working class reform effort. The idea was pure covenant, albeit in secularized form. The movement was based on a "People's Charter" that pledged them to pursue a reform agenda designed to introduce universal manhood suffrage, equal political rights, and social improvements into British society.[3]

The charter effort was mounted to gain thousands of signatures of ordinary people and thus force the government to act. Chartist groups sprang up all over Britain, especially attracting Nonconformists, that is to say, those who belonged to churches other than the Church of England, most of which had their origins in the left wing of Puritanism. In other words, it was one of those periodic eruptions of the covenanting spirit characteristic of those within the covenant tradition, whose like had not been seen in Britain for two centuries.[4]

When Chartism failed in the mother country, disillusioned Chartists brought the movement's ideas to Australia. There, in a more egalitarian environment, they took root to become the basis of the political ideas of the Australian states in the mid-nineteenth century when responsible government was introduced.

Chartism had two aspects. One was its idea of a secularized covenant of liberal reform. Its impact was to establish that the political bedrock of Australia in Britain would be nineteenth-century British liberalism. The other was the importation of another lower-class element into Australian society, in this case respectable members of the working class but still lower class in the British scheme of things. The implications of both were far reaching. In the twentieth century, liberalism became the conservatism of Australia. This was reflected in partisan politics, where the country's two major parties from the time of federation in 1901 have been the Labor party to the left and Liberal party to the right. At the same time even Labor shared many of the underlying ideas of the old British liberalism. The socialists in Labor's ranks have constantly complained of this, suggesting that their party is not really socialist, but reformist in the Chartist spirit.

The second is reflected in the continuing working-class ambiance of Australia, from the country's common slang to its common accent to its common cuisine, not to speak of its politics. The culture of "mateship" is pronounced, with "mate"—a British working-class term—being the Australian covenantal equivalent of the American "pardner," both covenantal terms. Almost every commentator on the Australian scene has reflected on this phenomenon, on its influence on Australian attitudes toward work and leisure, toward what constitutes status, toward sport and recreation, toward government and its obligations to the citizenry, toward achievement and pleasure. Only with the arrival of substantial non-British immigration after World War II have any other elements been injected into the Australian scene.[5]

The particular Australian synthesis between Chartists and convicts, then, is unique among covenantal societies. It is far more secular than in any other covenantal society, although by the standards of other societies, religion still plays a significant role on the Australian scene, especially Protestant evangelical religion imported from the United States, where it was developed by people of strikingly similar backgrounds. Australian covenantalism is more protective than aggressive, less designed to achieve some vision of a more moral future than to implement the dream of a more pleasant one.

Another manifestation of this is the way the Australians, like other covenanted peoples, have never reified their state. In fact, as some scholars have suggested, Australians have even less of a political basis for their peoplehood than the Americans who rallied around their constitution and the laws and institutions flowing from it. Australians love their country and their mates and have developed their common identity through these geographic and social connections.[6]

But that is not quite the whole story. Australians also have an original tradition that their continent is the last best hope of mankind. This tradition goes back to the first discoverers of the Antipodes who, coming late to the region, saw in that distant island continent a very last chance for humanity to begin again, after the settlement of the Western hemisphere had shown that humans, no matter how noble their purposes, inevitably transplanted old evils into new climes. This "last best hope" syndrome is a common manifestation of covenantalism, religious and secular, which has a strong messianic streak. It is in order to achieve this last best hope that people often enter into morally based covenants that point out the direction in which they should go, the manner in which they should proceed and the institutions that they need in order to reach their goal. Thus messianism in this form tends to lead to covenantalism or covenantal expressions.

Despite its convict origins, this image of Australia as the last best hope continued to accompany the settlers of the land Down Under throughout the days of Australia's land frontier and continues as a point of reference down to the present.[7] Today, when Australians, like all other humans, know that whatever improvements have been engendered by settling the outlying territories of Europe's great frontier, the basic mix of human nature has not been altered, and the vision of Australia as a last best hope is more a measuring rod than an expectation. Thus even the Australian dream is judged by the standards of an Australian vision that by its very nature has a strong covenantal component.

South Africa: Between Covenant and Caste

The striking contrast between covenantal aspiration, the dark side of human reality, and the possibilities for redemption provided for from within the covenant tradition, is most manifest in the South African experience. Afrikaner culture and society is perhaps more grounded in covenant than any other of the new societies outside of Puritan New England. Yet the Afrikaners' encounter with the black population of Southern Africa led to their covenant emphasizing exclusivism on racial grounds to the point where those outside the covenant were denied all liberty wherever it was possible to do so, and equality under any circumstances. Thus the same covenant that created a proud, vigorous, and independent new people, transforming Dutch, Huguenot, and Scottish Calvinists into Afrikaners, became at the same time a covenant with the devil to oppress millions.[8]

Then, after this situation reached its apogee through the apartheid system, serious reform was begun from within the ruling group itself. In an amazing turnabout, the South African government led by the Afrikaner National party reversed itself, opened the doors to nonwhite participation, and proceded to negotiate a new constitutional settlement with the various parties and communities outside of Afrikanerdom by sitting around a table and working matters out. This extraordinary and unexpected step led to a new politics of reconciliation and the inauguration of a new constitution and a new democratic system for all South Africans early in 1994 in an extraordinary confirmation of the ability of that same covenantal tradition to lead from narrowness to enlightenment, from privilege for the few to democracy for the many.

The white settlement of South Africa was initiated in 1652 when the Dutch East India Company established an outpost, which later grew into the city of Cape Town, for resupplying their ships sailing to the Indies. Although the Dutch adventurers were not particularly religious, they carried their Calvinism and federal theology with them to Africa as well as to the Western Hemisphere during their great age of empire building. However, the structure of commercial colonization undertaken by the Dutch East India Company, the kinds of individuals who initially migrated during the seventeenth century, and the circumstances of settlement in some areas tended to mute and distort the republican features of the covenant idea as they had developed in the Netherlands proper. This was especially true in southern Africa.

In the years after 1652 the Dutch were joined by a few Germans and then in the 1680s by 200 French Huguenots, fellow Calvinists who were quickly assimilated into the Dutch community.[9] Over the next 150 years, these people developed their civilization under Dutch rule on the Cape peninsula and the western Cape province, virtually destroying the indigenous black population or mating with them in illicit liaisons to create the Cape Coloured who became a separate caste in its own right—today known as the Coloured.[10] As the Afrikaners, as they came to be known, spread along the coastal interior, they fought a series of frontier wars with the black tribes inhabiting the area, the largest of which, such as the Sotho, the Swazi, the Tswana, the Zulu and the Xhosa had migrated into the area from central Africa at about the time the whites were coming in from the sea.[11] In the eighteenth century these blacks were referred to as "kaffirs" or deniers of the true faith, an Arabic term picked up from Arab traders that much suited the Calvinist Afrikaners, and the wars with them were known as Kaffir Wars. In the process, the Afrikaners built a modest paradise for themselves and at the same time toughened their people for ordeals yet to come.

During the Napoleonic Wars, the British conquered Cape Colony twice and, after the second time, stayed. As part of the peace settlement the Dutch, who had been allied with Napoleon, had to forfeit their southern African colony to the British. In 1820 the British began their own colonization movement, in the process reorganizing both the polity and society of the Cape Colony. The result not only removed the Afrikaners from control, making them inferior to the new British ruling establishment, but also interfered with their religious and cultural patterns, engendering sharp tensions between the two groups.[12] At the same time, among the British migrants were Scottish Calvinists who brought about a religious revival among the Afrikaners, strengthening the Calvinist basis of a population already committed to the Reformed Church.[13]

Half a generation after the onset of the British effort, the Afrikaners had had enough. In 1835, they began their Great Trek out of the Cape Colony into the interior.[14] It was during this Trek that Afrikanerdom acquired its separate national character. Covenant came to the fore as an explicit political theme during the Great Trek of 1835–1843 when the Voortrekkers, moving in bands of families, organized themselves through the same kinds of compacts that Americans used to govern their wagon trains rolling westward.

That might have been enough but in addition, the Afrikaner myth was formed around the idea of covenant on the Trek. The story is simple and straightforward. One of the forward parties of Voortrekkers encountered Zulus, the most ferocious of the black African nations moving in from the north, on the banks of Blood River (in what is now KwaZulu/Natal) in 1838. The Voortrekkers made a covenant with God, promising faithful adherence to His will in return for victory. The subsequent victory opened the way for the Afrikaner advance into Zululand and the Blood River Covenant became the ideological basis for Afrikaner nationalism, including the Afrikaners' self-perception as a chosen people whom God had saved from the ferocious Zulus, who so greatly outnumbered them.[15]

December 16th, the day of the covenant and the battle, was memorialized as the Day of the Covenant, the Afrikaners' great national holiday. Subsequently, when Pretoria was built as the capital of Transvaal, a great monument was erected to the Voortrekkers on a hill overlooking the city and was sited so that precisely at noon on December 16th the sun would shine through it to form a beam of light that would focus on a sculptured representation of the Trekkers. Then and there a covenant renewal ceremony would take place each year.[16]

At the same time, inherent in that covenant was its dark side, its rejection of blacks as the enemy. For the Afrikaners, the blacks became the object of God's covenantal wrath. They were to be subjugated by the Afrikaners and made their "hewers of wood and drawers of water" in imitation of the Bible-reading Boers' (Boer is the Afrikaners' word for farmer; it became the accepted term for all Afrikaners) understanding of the cursed Canaanites' relationship to God's chosen, Israel.

The Bible does present the Canaanites as Hamites, cursed because their ancestor, Ham, had looked upon his father Noah's nakedness and therefore doomed to descend into barbarous idolatry and to have their land taken away from them by God and given to the Israelites. This understanding, only one of many dimensions of the biblical story, was reinterpreted by the Afrikaners to apply to their situation. They, a new Israel (every avowed covenanted people at some point or another sees itself as a new Israel), also needed a land that God would take from a corrupted race and give to them. In encountering the black Africans they found what for them was the model of that corrupted race of Hamites, cruel and idolatrous in their eyes just as the Canaanites were, and therefore deserving of God's punishment as part of God's order and justice.[17]

This unfortunate use of covenantalism by the Afrikaners in South Africa poses in its most extreme form the often difficult question of who shall be included as partners within a covenanted people. The Afrikaner covenant not only excluded nonwhites from partnership but did so in a way that denied them their basic human rights. Every community is by definition bounded and exclusive to some degree. This is not necessarily a moral or ethical problem so long as other communities are not injured in the process and there are equitable covenantal relations between communities. This was not the case in South Africa.

As a result of their trek, the Voortrekkers established two polities, the Orange Free State and Transvaal. So loosely organized were they that, for their first generation, it is hard to refer to them as states. Rather, the bands of Boers, each governed by a general meeting of all males able to bear arms, were loosely confederated with one another in each of these two concentrations, establishing for each a representative council in which each band was represented and that tried to institute some order within the territory under its nominal jurisdiction. The fiercely independent Boers were not about to surrender their independence, even to institutions of their own, beyond the bare minimum.[18]

Political consolidation came only in the 1870s even though the two republics had claimed their independence from 1854. The two states so closely followed the models of democratic republicanism for their white citizens that no less a person than James Bryce referred to them as model republics. In the meantime, the descendants of the Dutch, Huguenots, and Scots completed their melting into a new people, although it was interesting to note that those with Huguenot and Scottish names tended to dominate public life, whether in politics or religion. Both states were rigidly Calvinistic republics permeated by the religious spirit of Reformed Protestantism, with its federal theology and the covenantal relations among its people reinforced by that theology.

At the same time, the experience of isolation in the early days of settlement and then the strong feelings of fear and hostility toward the black Africans and the British gave the Afrikaners a tribalistic mentality. Like other historic covenants at Sinai and Philadelphia, the covenant at Blood River may be said to have formally created a people. However, the Afrikaners' ethno-religious base led them to bound their community by the organic notion of race, an anticovenantal concept. Whereas the Reformed tradition from which they derived their idea of covenant regards covenantal boundaries as being permeable in varying ways, with consent or a profession of faith being the main way of entry, for the Afrikaners race was an impenetrable boundary. There was no way to cross it. Hence the crucial element of choice was missing.

Not only was there no entrance but there was no exit, except by leaving the tribe and its land altogether. In effect the Afrikaners converted a consensual community of the faithful into a biological community of whites only, the new elect or chosen ones. This enabled them to later include the English, after a generation of warfare and another generation of political competition, but it prevented them from absorbing the Coloureds who were Calvinists like themselves, flesh of their flesh, at least partially, and eager to identify with the Afrikaners. Although the Coloureds shared much of the Afrikaner culture and outlook on the world, they were relegated to the position of an undercaste. In sum, the same covenant that gave the Afrikaners their nationhood and the moral foundation for their republics became an instrument for oppression on racial grounds.

At first, though, the Afrikaners had to deal with their British problem. The British were reluctant to see two independent Boer republics to the north of their colonies of Cape Province and Natal. The British were in the process of seizing as much of Africa for their own as possible and the Boer republics cut off their northward access. Thus they kept the two republics under constant pressure.

British desire to annex Boer territory grew even greater after the discovery of gold and diamonds in both republics in the 1870s and early 1880s. British subjects rushed north to found Johannesburg and other settlements along the Witwatersrand, the heart of the discovery area, threatening the Afrikaner social order even when they were not threatening it politically and militarily. In 1886 there was an abortive British effort to conquer the two republics that the Boers successfully repulsed.

Then, between 1899 and 1902, the British-initiated Anglo-Boer War led to an imperial victory and the loss of Afrikaner independence. During that war the Afrikaners, as the underdogs, had the sympathy of much of the world, including many Britons, as they fought their heroic but pathetic guerilla warfare against the imperial army. By the time the British secured their victory, it was clear that they would have to recognize legitimate Afrikaner rights to self-government.[19]

In 1910, a mere eight years after the war's end, a British initiative brought about the unification of South Africa as an independent, democratic (for whites) dominion within the British Commonwealth in which the more numerous Afrikaners controlled the politics while the wealthier British controlled the economy. This new Union of South Africa united the four provinces of Transvaal, Orange Free State, Cape Province, and Natal as a union, British style. The Afrikaners deliberately eschewed federation since they wanted to extend their control over the entire territory of South Africa. The provinces were given special status within the Union government and retained substantial local powers, but no more. The South African constitution in that sense was a compact between the two white nations in southern Africa that brought nearly two generations of peace.[20]

Not only did the Afrikaners take over the government of the new Union but from then until 1948 the prime ministers were former Boer generals. While they were relatively moderate on racial matters, they still believed in the exclusion of blacks and tried to foster a special status for Afrikaners even though their policy was based upon Afrikaner-British collaboration. Then in 1948 the Afrikaner National Party swept the parliamentary elections, giving the government over to extreme Afrikaner nationalists, some of whom had been Nazi sympathizers before World War II, who proceeded to introduce a new era of racial segregation and discrimination.[21]

In the wake of its massive victory, the new government imposed an extreme regime of racial separation to which it gave the name *apartheid*. The Afrikaner nationalists advertised apartheid as separate development for each of the races. In reality, it meant deepening the position of the whites as an upper caste, with Asians (who had come with the British in search for greater opportunity than was available on the Indian subcontinent) and Coloureds excluded but somewhere in the middle, and blacks as a lower caste.

For a generation their scheme worked. The Afrikaners prospered and broke the British grip on the economy. Segregation of facilities and their use became well-nigh total. Still, large numbers of nonwhites moved or were brought to the white areas as workers and there segregated in separate townships. Residents of nonwhite neighborhoods adjacent to white ones were forcibly evacuated to the townships.[22]

In an effort to carry matters to their logical extreme, the South African government established a number of black "homelands," four of which were given independence (unrecognized by any country other than South Africa itself) so that the black African tribes living in each or blacks descended from those tribes living in South Africa proper could be stripped of their South African citizenship on the grounds that they were citizens of these homelands.[23] In the face of British and Commonwealth opposition, South Africa left the Commonwealth and proclaimed itself a republic.

Laws were enacted not only to prevent whites and blacks from living in adjacent areas but from having personal relations of any intimacy with one another. Racial laws were enacted providing that even a tiny drop of "black blood" made a person nonwhite and thus excluded from any part of white society. As the apartheid regime became more extreme, it began to take on nondemocratic coloring even within the white community. Nothing typified this better than the decision of the government to change the name of the "Day of the Covenant" to the "Day of the Oath" in order to remove any dimensions of a civil society built on consent and in place to offer one in which whites took an oath to preserve ethnic purity.

In the end, however, the entire apartheid edifice came crashing down. The Afrikaners were fortunate in that they elected a government that took the lead in bringing apartheid down on its own initiative and thus avoided violent revolution. Initially these changes came step by step, in response not only to world pressure, which isolated South Africa, but to the internal pressures of whites dissatisfied with or at least made uneasy by the government's extreme measures.

The initial constitutional reforms took place at the end of the 1970s and represented an effort to introduce a kind of unequal consociationalism whereby Coloureds and Asians were recognized as having a stake in the governance of what was essentially to be a nonblack society. Each of these groups was given its own house in a three-chambered parliament (the largest chamber, of course, was reserved for the whites) and presumably the decisive say over matters of policy for their communities. In fact, the state president became even more powerful and the white legislative chamber continued to be dominant. Then petty apartheid, the kind of segregation of individuals that was so demeaning and offensive to its victims, was dissolved step by step. Finally, grand apartheid was dismantled by the government.[24]

After that, recognizing the handwriting that was on the wall, State President Frederick DeKlerk decisively took the lead by recognizing outlawed nonwhite political groups such as the African National Congress and the Pan-African Congress, and allowing blacks exiled from the country for subversive activities to return, in some cases after thirty years and more. Nelson Mandela, the ANC leader, was released from prison and a process was initiated to convene a constitutional conference involving all groups of all races, ethnic backgrounds, and tribes to develop a new democratic constitution for South Africa.[25]

Perhaps surprisingly, the effort succeeded. Perhaps because of a basic good will on the part of all South Africans, the groups were able to sit down together despite their fears and suspicions and, in due course and with judicious leadership on all sides, reach an agreement on an interim constitution and free elections. The interim constitution went into effect at the end of 1993 with the elections called for April 1994 held successfully, despite alarms from the Zulu opposition. The new multiracial government took force on May 14, 1994.[26]

In the negotiations, it was the ANC's turn to seek a unitary centralized state and the Afrikaners' turn to pursue solutions that would provide for constitutionalized power-sharing, preferably through federalism. In the end, the interim constitution entrenched a system of regional governments within a decentralized but not noncentralized South Africa, with the regions having certain constitutionally guaranteed institutions and powers and a share in the national government but not the usual powers of federal states. This intensified an already real crisis among black South Africans, with the Zulu-dominated Inkatha Freedom Party rejecting anything short of full federalism out of fear that the ANC, once in power, would quickly dispense with decentralization. In an effort to conciliate them, the interim constitution was amended in February 1994, to make it federal in essence, if not in name. These arrangements were ratified and in some ways strengthened in the permanent institution, adapted in 1996. In this way an original covenant, ostensibly with God but that had become a covenant with the devil, was modernized into a political compact which all significant groups in South Africa helped negotiate and to which they consented, in an exemplary demonstration of how the covenant tradition could serve noble ends, even after its original exemplars had gone bad.

It remains to be seen to what extent these covenantal influences will continue in the new South Africa but it is very likely that they will for two reasons. First of all, the Reformed Protestant covenantal heritage is very strongly embedded in the country, not only among the Afrikaners who had introduced it for their purposes, but in general among South

Africans of Christian background from all races and ethnic groups. For example, the Zulu, as earlier indicated, were a constituted nation rather than one that emerged organically, constituted by the use of extreme force by Chaka, their founder. When they became Christianized, they adopted much from the Reformed Protestantism of their Boer neighbors.

This was even more so in the case of the Coloured population who essentially saw themselves as Afrikaners of color and whose tragedy was that the Afrikaners would not recognize them as such, while the black Africans would not accept them as full Africans because of their mixed race. Even after so many generations of rejection, when the new South Africa was born they voted overwhelmingly for the National party which had been the party of the Afrikaners and apartheid, so much so in the Western Cape, where they hold the balance of power, that they secured victory for the National party in the provincial elections. Thus, in at least two of the three most important provinces in the country, KwaZulu-Natal and the Western Cape, there seems to be a solid basis for expecting covenantalism to continue to influence South African political life.

But the matter goes beyond the influence of Reformed Protestantism. Covenantalism also is reenforced by the second reason; in traditional African society there is a kind of mutualism that, while not itself covenantal, lends itself to covenantal expression. This was and is strongly associated with the consensual approach to political decision making found among African tribes and the accepted view that normally African tribal leaders are those who are able or whose task it is to facilitate this consensual decision making.

This was true even of those constituted African nations such as the Zulu, in which even Chaka's apparently undiluted dictatorship rested upon those older tribal ways and norms. There is even an African word for it, *ubuntu,* which all the southern African tribes recognize and which has many of the characteristics of the biblical *hesed* or the contemporary German *bundestreue*; that is to say, acting toward one's associates in a spirit of concern for protecting their needs as well as one's own. *Ubuntu* underlies the forms of conciliatory negotiation that are necessary for consensual decision making. What is significant is how important this conciliatory approach has been in the transition from all-white to democratic governance. Watching the negotiations, an outsider could clearly see all the parties listening to one another, apparently attentive to the need for working out appropriate responses to deeply perceived interests or needs. The result speaks for itself. They found an agreement that is far more reflective of that spirit of compromise and conciliation than of the original position of the ANC and the other African revolutionary parties or their original or historic demands in terms of the system of governance, while at the same time far from the historic demands of the National party with regard to the role of nonwhites in the civil society. The word *ubuntu* itself, once used exclusively within traditional African society, is beginning to surface as the word through which to express partnership and comity in the politics of the new South Africa. In the draft provincial constitution for KwaZulu-Natal it is explicitly introduced as the principle governing the constitution and constitutional negotiations.

The impact of the covenant idea and its political culture is felt in many subtle ways in every polity influenced by it. The intensification of those subtleties requires more comprehensive study than this series can provide. The South African experience, however, lends itself to the identification of some of these more subtle influences because of its particular complexity and the recent reversal of its application of the covenantal tradition from what was in essence a "covenant with the devil" to the beginnings of a more universalistic definition of covenant.

Those who examine the South African experience will soon note that while so much of its covenantal tradition was preempted by those whites, particularly Afrikaners, who sought to preserve a divided and segregated society, recognizing only those of European descent or origin as parties to the covenant, at the same time there were others coming from the same tradition who, in the spirit of that tradition, tried to do good works among the disenfranchised, whether black or Coloured, African or Asian. Only now is their impact able to be recognized for what it was and is.

In his autobiography, *Long Walk to Freedom*, Nelson Mandela describes his own early experiences moving from tribal life in the bush to the presidency of the new South Africa in part as a series of encounters of exemplars of that other side of the covenant tradition in white South Africa at decisive moments in his life, principally in schools established by churchmen from England and Scotland, many, if not most, of whom were of the Calvinist tradition, who gave him and other young African blacks who today occupy the leadership positions in the new South African government an opportunity to acquire a modern Western education and to develop their talents to the point where they could mount the peaceful revolution that they have mounted and take control of the reigns of governance sufficiently well-equipped to undertake the tasks demanded of them. For example, Mandela describes the only university open to blacks in South Africa prior to the demise of apartheid at Fort Hare as having been founded by Scottish Calvinist ministers and how their sense of fairness combined with a commitment to high standards of morality and integrity made a critical difference in his life and the lives of the other "country boys" (his term) like him as they struggled to enter a world beyond the tribal environment of their birth and how they not only learned Western ways there but learned that white authority could be challenged and did not simply have to be acknowledged and obeyed. The list of Mandela's fellow students reads like the leadership roll of the ANC in later years and now the leadership of the Republic of South Africa.

After the French Revolution, it was said the Jacobin revolutionaries were educated in the schools of the Jesuits, and while they broke with the beliefs of the Jesuits, those revolutionaries retained the political culture reenforced in those schools. The same can well be said in the case of South Africa. The ANC revolutionaries were educated in the schools of the Calvinists. Moreover, there is evidence that Afrikaners who joined the ANC before their recognition explicitly drew from their Calvinist-covenantal tradition to reconstruct their country. Those elements in their political culture that converged with the covenantal tradition were reenforced and given the opportunity to be adapted to new situations in both overt and subtle ways.

Israel: Covenant and Kinship

The last of the new societies of the modern epoch to be founded was modern Israel which, through the Zionist enterprise, represented both a rebirth of the ancient Jewish polity and a revolution against the traditional Judaism that emerged out of the wreckage of that polity.[27] One of the perennial debating topics among Israeli and other Jews is whether Zionism represents continuity or change in Jewish history. Of course, after an appropriate amount of discussion, at times ennervating and at times invigorating, most Jews come to the conclusion that it is something of both and that is the truth.[28]

What the Zionist movement did was to take traditional Jewish aspirations to return to the Land of Israel, combine it with the classic Jewish requirement that, for fulfillment, Judaism must be manifested through a political as well as religious framework, combine both with a revolutionary message opposing the condition of the Jews in their places of Old World exile and the extreme conservatism of what had become traditional Jewish practice in the hands of a highly conservative leadership, to mobilize the Jewish people for a massive effort at autoemancipation in keeping with the modern temper.

The fact that Zionism, to become more than rhetoric, had to be translated into organized effort, and organized effort necessarily took form under the modern principles of free association, would not in itself make the Zionist enterprise covenantal. Indeed, the Zionist theoreticians, who were in fact more polemicists and rhetoricians than serious thinkers, inadvertently did everything possible to keep the covenantal dimension of Zionism from being known. In the effort to mobilize the Jewish masses, they relied on the intellectual fashion of the time, which emphasized organic models and biologic analogies.[29]

Although there were proto-Zionist voices a generation and even two earlier, the Zionist movement emerged in the last generation of the nineteenth century at the height of the impact of Darwinism on social and political thought. Thus nationalism was justified on biological grounds— that every nation was an extended family defined by characteristics of kinship, language, and culture in which the role of individual consent was essentially nil. To the extent that will was involved, it was the will of the collective, the nation in its organic personality.

Under this theory of nationalism, so popular in the late nineteenth century, every nation had its own genius that had to be brought out for the human race to perfect itself. This genius could only be brought out through national self-determination, which almost invariably ended up meaning through an independent, politically sovereign state whose boundaries were coterminous with the ethno-cultural group in question. In the West this kind of thinking led to racism. In Central and Eastern Europe, the original heartland of the Zionist movement, it led to competing ethnic nationalisms among groups often intermixed in the same territory, engendering impossible situations. The Jews drew on their environment to develop a highly organic Zionist ideology, only they added the extra dimension of return to the land of their fathers, thereby trading local ethnic competition for what would prove to be a prolonged war with the Arabs who had occupied their former territory in the interim.

Only a handful of Zionist thinkers emancipated themselves from the fashions of the times. Some were the proto-Zionists like Moses Hess, much influenced by Spinoza, who wrote before the fashion had become so dominant.[30] Others were people like Martin Buber, much influenced by Althusius. One of the two or three commanding thinkers among the Zionists, he contributed much to the revival of covenantal thought in the twentieth-century world. There also were activists with ideas, like Louis Dembitz Brandeis, the American Zionist leader, who was much influenced by the covenantalism of the Puritan New England of the past and American Progressive thought of his time.[31] In retrospect these voices take on greater significance than they had at the time, now that biologic theories have been so discredited because of their propensity toward racism. Nevertheless, the real expression of the covenantal tradition was to be found in the practice of Zionism rather than its theory.

Both the necessities of building a new society under frontier conditions and the cultural predispositions of the founders and pioneers led in the direction of covenanting. In a sense, Theodor Herzl himself, the founder of the World Zionist Organization, followed such patterns, although in truth it is difficult to separate necessary organizational techniques from covenantal commitments. His idea of convening a representative body of world Jewry to fix a program for the transfer of all the world's Jews to a state of their own, authorized and recognized by a charter from the great powers, intertwines both elements.[32]

Herzl's strong commitment to the necessity of obtaining a charter, over which he had considerable conflict with those Zionists who believed that what was really needed was the far slower process of building new settlements, acquiring lands on a step-by-step basis (the "practical Zionists" as distinct from the "Herzlian political Zionists"), was a reflection of this. The charter Herzl sought can be characterized as a kind of covenant between the peoples of the world and the Jewish people, recognizing their nationhood and right of self-determination. At the same time it reeks of antiquarianism, whereby suzerain great powers would grant a kind of constitutional recognition to a subject people.

Meanwhile the practical Zionists were developing covenantal forms of their own. From the 1880s onward, the first Zionist settlements were established on a covenantal basis, at first in the most traditional sense, adapting traditional patterns of *kehilla* (Jewish community) organization to modern frontier conditions. This was as true of new urban neighborhoods founded even earlier as of rural settlements, all of which were founded as mutual aid or cooperative societies.[33]

This first federalist impulse was almost immediately countered by a strong centralist trend. The poverty of the first settlers and the difficult conditions under which they were forced to live and work, led them to seek the support of outside philanthropic sources, chief among which was the French Baron de Rothschild who in typical French fashion imposed a highly autocratic and centralized system of controls on them as the price of his aid. Having no choice, most of them paid it, introducing a struggle between federalism and centralism that continues in Israel to this day.[34]

After the turn of the century, when the vanguard of settlement passed into the hands of secular socialists, these covenants became compacts, secularized articles of association, promoted by socialist communitarians who sought to build small, harmonious communities in which all goods and resources were held in common to foster equality, harmony, and mutuality. In the 1920s the pattern became so routinized that model articles of association were made available by the pioneering movements and generally used.[35] Again, a very strong counterweight had appeared in the form of socialist collectivism, which had the same centralizing tendencies as the Baron de Rothschild's autocratic rule.

In the end, the pre-state Jewish *yishuv* (a traditional Jewish term used by the Zionists for describing on organized settled community) was based on a network of collectivist and semi-traditional covenants, compacts and articles of association, some of which were subsequently embodied in Orders in Council issued by the British Mandatory government, but only after consensus was reached among the Jews themselves. In this way a modern version of a traditional Jewish community emerged within a semi-secularized covenantal system with a strong collectivist dimension.[36]

The culmination of this pioneering effort was the establishment of the State of Israel in 1948. The Declaration of Independence establishing the state can be seen as its founding covenant, much like the American Declaration of Independence.[37] Indeed a comparison of the two documents shows their similar covenantal structure, while the substantial differences in their content reflects the different character of the two societies. Both combine universalism and particularism. The American Declaration addresses itself to the universal natural rights of men while the Israeli Declaration, reaffirming those rights, emphasizes the particularities of Jewish history. Both recognize the peoplehood of the population each Declaration is to serve; the American Declaration separates the American from the English people while the Israeli Declaration reaffirms the unity and common destiny of the ancient Jewish people wherever they might be. While the American Declaration clearly reflects the synthesis between the covenantal and political compact traditions ("nature and nature's God"), the Israeli Declaration clearly shows the tension and synthesis between covenant and kinship.

Because of the subsequent constitutional history of Israel, part of the Israeli Declaration actually was given constitutional status in 1958 by Israel's Supreme Court to serve as Israel's equivalent of a Bill of Rights, further enhancing its character as a founding covenant. In 1994, most of the rest of it was given similar status.[38]

In general, the history of the writing of a constitution for Israel, which is quite different from that of the United States, offers an example of a different manifestation of the covenantal tradition. Israel's first Knesset was elected to be a constituent assembly but the lack of consensus as to what a proper constitution should contain prevented its doing so. The religious parties wanted a state based upon Jewish religious tradition and the Marxist parties wanted a constitution similar to that of a people's republic.

Lack of consensus was the real reason, but David Ben-Gurion, who also did not want to be hampered by a constitution that might limit his forceful rule of the new state yet did not want to adopt a constitution that would not properly limit government in the future, gave the good reason that with a mass immigration pouring into the country, tripling its population within a decade, it was too soon to set its constitutional framework into stone. Ben-Gurion went on to state in a famous speech that there were really only two reasons why a new state had to adopt a written constitution in one fell swoop: one, to transform an autocratic tradition into a republican one, and the other, to regulate relations between the units of a federal system. Since, he then stated, that since Jewish tradition had always been republican rather than autocratic and since Israel was not a federal system, neither reason was valid in this case so Israel could move more slowly.[39]

The Knesset then decided to become a continuing constituent assembly and to empower its standing committee on constitutionalism to prepare Basic Laws as needed and as a consensus developed around them.

These would be enacted by a special majority and normally could only be changed by the same kind of majority so that, one by one, the articles of a final document would be adopted until the constitution was complete. Israel has faithfully adhered to this decision ever since, first enacting Basic Laws governing the organization of the institutions of the state and the electoral procedures for choosing them, then moving on to other topics of constitutional importance to Israel, so that by 1993, twelve Basic Laws had been adopted covering every subject except state-local relations and a comprehensive process for entrenching the constitution as a whole and amending it.[40]

In the meantime, in addition to the legislation designated Basic Laws, the Knesset has enacted other laws of recognized constitutional import, including a covenant (so-named) between the State of Israel and the World Zionist Organization institutionalizing relations between Israel and the diaspora Jewish communities in matters of common interest.[41] The Law of Return, providing that any Jew be automatically admitted to Israel under normal circumstances and is entitled to state citizenship, also has acquired constitutional status.[42] The Israel Supreme Court has asserted the right of judicial review under this constitution and has exercised that right increasingly and with ever more far-reaching effect, understandable in a polity animated by the covenantal tradition and the rule of law since earliest times. In 1992, the Court formally was granted those powers in a wide sphere of jurisdiction.[43]

The subsequent institutionalization of Israel's state structure strongly reduced the amount of covenanting and compacting in the old-new polity. Borrowing heavily from continental European models of the centralized bureaucratic state, Israel's leaders did not leave much room for the kind of individual initiative represented by the covenantal tradition. The result has been a continuing struggle between the federal political culture of the Jews and the state structure and institutions, the result of which has been that nothing is quite what it seems to be. Orders and directives issued from the putative center are not treated as such in the field and bargaining about everything is in fact the order of the day. Still, the clash between the two approaches is often dysfunctional and, if not paralyzing, certainly makes far greater effort necessary to accomplish even relatively simple tasks than should be the case. Whether or not there will be a constitutional reform in Israel that will adjust its institutions to its political culture remains to be seen.

If we take the fourfold model proposed in chapter 7 of the competition between individualism, corporatism, collectivism, and federalism in the United States and apply it to Israel, we find that the very first Zionist settlers fell squarely within the federalist orientation. They were succeeded by two generations of collectivists who were then swamped by the mass immigration of people who rapidly became individualists, at best with a strong sense of Jewish solidarity. In response to the transformed situation of statehood, the old collectivist institutions became corporatist in character as they became larger and more institutionalized so that today the state, with its extensive tie-ins with the Histadrut, Israel's labor-controlled economic empire, and the various banks, professional guilds, and associations of industries is highly corporatist. Collectivism has been pushed to the peripheries of Israeli society, dominant only in the most left-leaning kibbutzim, although expressed in subtle ways in other segments of Israeli society. Individualism is on the ascendancy in the private sector and in private life, while federalism is strongest in the religious community and is a continuing secondary influence in the society as a whole.[44]

Indeed, Israelis have had to come to grips with three political-cultural inheritances. One, from the Jewish political tradition and experience, is covenantal. A second, brought by the Zionist leadership, is statist, or organic, based on their experience with governance in Europe where the centralized, bureaucratized, reified state was the rule. The third was a subject political culture, very hierarchical, that reflected the experience of the Jews of Eastern Europe and the Afro-Asian countries in their relations with external authority, prior to modernization. In this respect they were no different than the non-Jewish subjects of those authorities.

Israel as a polity has been the locus of a struggle between these political cultures in its effort to develop a political culture of its own. Even among the collectivists there were subtle elements of traditional Jewish political culture that could not be avoided. Thus in imitation of the Russian *tovarich* (comrade), the Zionist socialists also adopted a salutation. The closest word they could find was *haver*, a classic term meaning a partner in the Jewish religious enterprise, usually Torah study, and which has taken on two additional modern meanings, "friend" and "member," none of which speak to the same sense of collectivist solidarity as "comrade."

New Zealand: A Nonideological New Society[45]

An even greater exception to the dominant pattern among new societies is to be found in the founding, settlement, and development of New
Zealand. In its settlement, New Zealand displayed all the characteristics
of a new society at first. But its settlers came there in search of peace and
prosperity, not to achieve any ideological expression. This is true of both
the Maoris from Polynesia who settled New Zealand in the tenth century,
and the British who came in the nineteenth and replaced the Maoris after
a struggle.

Being Polynesians, the Maoris ate the original inhabitants of the islands now New Zealand. The British were culturally constrained from
treating the Maoris in kind so they had to Christianize them. The wars
between the two groups were territorial wars, pure and simple, gilded
slightly with the idea of a British Christianizing presence.

The first white settlers to arrive in New Zealand were freethinkers,
Freemasons, Jews, and Quakers, the last three of whom had covenantal
roots and who organized themselves on at least a quasi-covenantal basis. While they were joined by others from the British Isles who were
less within the covenantal tradition, they were also followed by others
of their kind. As a result, New Zealand at the very least has a moralistic political culture and perhaps even more. This pattern was repeated
in settlements up and down both the North and South Islands, in some
places, Duneddin, for example, the leadership was in the hands of Scottish Presbyterians, some of whom were also Freemasons. While Jews
represented a small minority of the settlers, they were there from the
first and also can be considered part of this "covenantal coalition."
Since almost all played leadership roles in their local communities, this
was not insignificant.[46]

The New Zealanders were encouraged by the British to briefly experiment with a federal system but soon abandoned it before it could even
begin to take root. They were among the first in the world to enact progressive social legislation for their people, not for ideological reasons
but to secure their comfort in fairness. Motivated by decent instincts
spread wide in the society, New Zealanders developed into a nice, quiet,
and somewhat provincial people. In a sense they are still too new to have
lost all of the new society characteristics that animated them during their
land frontier era and too far away from the rest of the world to be much

influenced by the old societies from which they came. Whether or not that will continue, remains to be seen.

The Shift from Ideological to Territorial
Democracy in New Societies

In each new society, there quickly came a point when the great bulk of the population became more or less settled and developed ties to the land and the polity that were independent of those fostered by the original ideologies. This was particularly true among the young, whether native born or raised from early childhood in the country. To them, the country was "home," in a way that it could not be to their immigrant parents.

The initial ideology of the founders ceased to be all encompassing. In the United States, for example, Puritan New England underwent such a transformation, the paradigm of this process. The Pilgrims and Puritans who settled Massachusetts in the 1620s and 1630s were united by a great idea and their desire to transform that idea into concrete social realities. Puritanism, their religious ideology, was also the basis for their attempt to create a holy commonwealth in North America. To become a citizen of that commonwealth one had to accept the Puritan covenant, to join the congregations of the Puritans and to accept the doctrines for which those congregations stood.[47]

Leadership in that first generation of Puritan New England was vested in the hands of men who were considered to be the best representatives of the common religious ideology and, if they represented constituencies at all, that role was truly subordinate to their role as spokesmen for and interpreters of the Puritan idea. Moreover, they were accorded full legitimacy by their peers and constituents on that basis. Even those who disagreed with their interpretations did not dispute their right to lead but, rather, moved off to new territories to create congregations or sects (the religious equivalents of the ideological settlements and parties in Israel) of their own in which they could replicate the same political patterns to implement their conceptions of the holy commonwealth abuilding.[48]

By the second generation, however, the old ideology was no longer a sufficiently binding force to hold Massachusetts together. An increasing number of people who were sons and daughters of Massachusetts by virtue of their birth did not share in the ideological fervor of their parents. Even those who still stood well within the framework of Puritanism were not necessarily prepared to accept fully its dogmatics. Even more important, because they had been born within the Puritan framework rather than called to it, their relationship to its vision was necessarily different. Ultimately, they had to be accommodated within a political order that was not prepared to deny them citizenship but could not grant them full status as citizens without modifying its own ideologically based organization. To deal with this problem, the Puritans invented the half-way covenant that permitted those who shared the commitment to the community but were weak in ideology to acquire the rights of citizenship.[49]

This was much less a problem in Canada, Australia, and New Zealand. Since they were less pronouncedly covenantal in their founding, they had less of a wrenching transition. South Africa, on the other hand, also underwent a transition but only a century and a half after having formulated their ideology to the fullest were South Africans confronted with the necessity of moving from ideological to territorial democracy. They are presently in the process of doing so.

The evidence strongly suggests that Israel today is in a transitional situation similar to that which faced the Puritans of Massachusetts 300 years ago. The clear moral authority of the pioneers could not be transmitted to their successors (or even be fully retained by the active survivor) once the objective situation had changed. Moreover, as in the earlier case, the essence of the transformation lies in the movement from ideological to territorial democracy.

Here too, the biblical precedent is paradigmatic. According to the biblical account, the Israelite tribes relied exclusively upon the Mosaic covenant to unite them only until they reached Canaan. Then, as soon as possible, they very purposely grafted their ideologically rooted polity onto a territorial base which was endowed with a sacred character of its own through a recovenanting under Joshua.[50]

In the last analysis, democracy in the new societies must develop out of a synthesis between the ideological and territorial dimension. By their very nature, such societies require the maintenance of a national mystique (with its ideological overtones) as the basis for the consensus that holds them together while, at the same time, the sheer passage of time tends to promote the expression of certain aspects of that mystique through territorial units. Covenant and its derivatives are principal vehicles for doing so.

Notes

1. Douglas H. Pike, *Australia* (Cambridge: Cambridge University Press, 1966); Alan Lindsay Mcleod, *The Pattern of Australian Culture* (Ithaca, NY: Cornell University Press, 1963).
2. Reginald Thomas Appleyard, *British Emigration to Australia* (London: G. Weidenfeld and Nicolson, 1964); James J. Sydney, *Australia* (Sydney: Sydney University Press, 1991).
3. Donald Horne, *The Lucky Continent: Australia Today* (Baltimore, MD: Penguin Books, 1964).
4. Dorothy Thompson, *Outsiders* (London: Verso, 1993); Harold Underwood Faulkner, *Chartism and the Churches: A Study in Democracy* (New York: Columbia University Press, 1916); Robert G. Gammage, *History of the Chartist Movement 1837–1954* (London: F. Cass, 1969).
5. Horne, *The Lucky Continent.*
6. Mcleod, *The Pattern of Australian Culture;* Pike, *Australia.*
7. Mcleod, ibid; *Australian Cultural Studies*, John Frow and Meaghan Morris, eds. (Urbana: University of Illinois Press, 1993).
8. Leopold Marquard, *The Peoples and Policies of South Afirca* (London: University Press, 1969); Thomas Davenport, *South Africa: A Modern History* (Johannesburg: Macmillan South Africa, 1978).
9. Robert Lacour-Gayet, *A History of South Africa* (New York: Hastings House, 1978).
10. William Macmillan, *Bantu Boer and Briton* (Oxford: Clarendon Press, 1963).
11. Ibid.; Richard Elphick, *Kraal and Cattle* (New Haven, CT: Yale University Press, 1977).
12. Macmillan, ibid.; Heribert Adam, *The Rise and Crisis of Afrikaner Power* (Capetown: D. Philip, 1979).
13. Macmillan, ibid.; Leonard Thompson, *The Political Mythology of Apartheid* (New Haven: Yale University Press, 1985).
14. Ibid.; Manfred Nathan, *The Voortrekkers of South Africa* (London: Fordon and Gotch, 1937); Oliver Ransford, *The Great Trek* (London: J. Murray, 1972).
15. Ibid., all of the above, also Floris van Jaarsfeld, *The Afrikaner's Interpretation of South African History* (Cape Town: Simondrium, 1964).
16. Ibid.
17. Ibid.
18. Ibid.
19. Ibid.
20. Daniel W. Kruger, *The Making of a Nation* (Johannesburg: Macmillan, 1969).
21. Ibid; Margaret Ballinger, *From Union to Apartheid* (Cape Town: Juta, 1969).
22. Ballinger, ibid.; Thompson, ibid.; Edgar H. Brookes, *Apartheid* (London: Routledge and Kegan Paul, 1968).
23. Christopher Hill, *Bantustans: The Fragmentation of South Africa* (London: Oxford University Press, 1964).
24. John Bampallis, *Foundations of the New South Africa* (London: Zed Books, 1991).
25. Bertus de Villiers, ed., *Birth of a Constitution,* (Capetown: Juta and Co., 1994).
26. Daniel J. Elazar, "Form of State: Federal, Unitary, or..." in ibid.; Pierre Olivier, "Constitutionalism and the New South African Constitution," ibid.

27. In *The Jewish Polity*, "Government in Biblical Israel," *Tradition*, and elsewhere I have written extensively on the Bible as constitution and the emphasis on constitutionalism in scripture. Part of the evidence for that lies in the extensive and precise terminology used in the Bible to deal with constitutionalism and constitutional matters, especially the following key terms: (1) *Torah*, the comprehensive term for constitution—emphasizes constitution as teaching; (2) *hukkot*, almost invariably ritual commandments commanded by God for which no explanation is given; (3) *mishpatim*, civil and social laws, including corpuses of law such as *mishpat hakohanim* and *mishpat ha-melekh/melukhah*, (corpuses for priests and kings or civil rulers, respectively); (4) *hok ku'mishpat*, constitutional jurisprudence, consisting of *hukkot* on matters between man and God and *mishpatim* on matters between man and man, the latter of which include special legal codes or corpuses for at least two of the three *ketarim* (domains), all obligating *Adat Bnai Yisrael lishmoa* (to hearken) and observe *mitzvot*.

28. Shlomo Avineri, *The Making of Modern Zionism* (New York: Basic Books, 1981); David Vital, *The Origins of Zionism* (Oxford: Clarendon Press, 1975); Harry Sacher, *Zionism and the Jewish Future* (London: J. Murray, 1916).

29. Arthur Hertzberg, ed. *The Zionist Idea* (New York: Atheneum, 1970); Avineri, ibid.

30. Moses Hess, *Rome and Jerusalem* (New York: Philosophical Library, 1958).

31. Lewis J. Paper, *Brandeis* (Englewood Cliffs, NJ: Prentice-Hall, 1983).

32. Theodor Herzl, *The Jewish State* (New York: Herzl Press, 1970).

33. Avineri, *The Making of Modern Zionism;* Israel Margalith, *Le Baron Edmond de Rothschild et la Colonisation Juive en Palestine 1882–1899* (Paris: M. Riviere, 1957); Simon Schama, *Two Rothschilds and the Land of Israel* (London: Collins, 1978).

34. Margalith, ibid.; Schama, ibid.

35. Harry Viteles, *A History of the Cooperative Movement in Israel* (London: Vallentine, Mitchel, 1966).

36. Michael Wolffsohn, *Israel: Polity, Society, Economy, 1882–1986*, trans. Douglas Bokovsky (Atlantic Highlands, NJ: Humanities Press International, 1987).

37. Gary O. Jacobsohn, *Apple of Gold: Constitutionalism in Israel and the United States* (Princeton: Princeton University Press, 1993); Paul Eidelberg, *On the Silence of the Declaration of Independence* (Amherst: University of Massachusetts Press, 1976).

38. Daniel J. Elazar, ed., *Constitutionalism: The Israeli and American Experience* (Lanham, MD: Jerusalem Center for Public Affairs and University Press of America, 1990); Amnon Rubinstein, *HaMishpat HaConstituzioni Shel Medinat Yisrael* (Jerusalem: Schocken, 1991); *idem., Hok Yesod: HaKnesset* (Jerusalem: Hebrew University Press, 1993).

39. Elazar, ibid.

40. Elazar, *ibid; idem., The Constitution of the State of Israel* (Jerusalem: Jerusalem Center for Public Affairs,1987). Rubinstein, *HaMishpat HaConstituzioni.*

41. World Zionist Organization, *HaHuka Shel HaHistadrut Hazionit ha'Olamit* (Jerusalem: World Zionist Organization, 1982).

42. Meir Dennis Gouldman, *Israel Nationality Law* (Jerusalem: Hebrew University Press, 1970).

43. Elyakim Rubinstein, *LeReishito u'leDmuto shel Beit HaMishpat HaElyon* (Jerusalem: Schocken, 1980).

44. Manfred Gerstenfeld, *Israel's New Future: Interviews* (Jerusalem: Rubin Mass, 1994); Daniel J. Elazar, *Israel: Building a New Society* (Bloomington: Indiana University Press, 1986); Yakir Plessner, *The Political Economy of Israel: From Ideology to Stagnation* (Albany: State University of New York Press, 1994).
45. E.H. Oliver and B.R. Williams, eds., *The Oxford History of New Zealand* (Oxford: Clarendon Press, 1981).
46. Ibid.; D. Ian Pool, *The Maori Population of New Zealand 1769–1971* (Auckland: Oxford University Press, 1977).
47. James Truslow Adams, *The Founding of New England* (Boston: Atlantic Monthly Press, 1921); John Fiske, *The Beginnings of New England, or the Puritan Theocracy in its Relations to Civil and Religious Liberty* (Boston: Houghton Mifflin, 1898).
48. Ibid.
49. Ibid.
50. Daniel J. Elazar, *Covenant and Polity in Biblical Israel*, chs. 11–13.

10

Covenant as a Theo-Political Tradition: A Summary Statement

Great transformations rest on great ideas, great movements, and great actions, and occur when all three come together. Thus at the very beginning of the history of covenant there was the great idea of biblical covenantal monotheism whereby humans were envisaged as entering into a morally grounded and informal pact with God, out of which came the people Israel formed through the Exodus from Egypt and the Sinai experience. In the sixteenth century, through the Protestant Reformation, a new theology of covenant gave rise to Reformed Protestantism and the theo-political transformation that followed in countries such as Switzerland, the Netherlands, Scotland, and England.

Reformation covenantalism transformed into modernity made three major contributions to the world, each of which would have been transformatory by itself; the three together have been decisive. This book has traced the first of those contributions—federal democracy or federal democratic republicanism. It has mentioned the second, capitalism, without elaboration since R.H. Tawney and Max Weber and others have done a very good job in demonstrating that. The third great contribution is that of modern science, initially in its Baconian form but then in its Newtonian and finally its Einsteinian. Only its Darwinian form has pressed society in the opposite direction of organic models. Robert Merton has demonstrated this in *Social Theory and Social Structure* and *Sociology of Science*.[1]

What a combination of covenant theology, religious reformation, and local or national political transformation did for the sixteenth century, a revolution in political philosophy and a series of more or less radical movements culminating in the British Isles and British North America as whiggism, which led to the Glorious Revolution of 1688–89 and the formation of the American colonies as they were during that same period across the Atlantic, did the same for the seventeenth century. In the eighteenth century the great wave of ideas derived from the Enlightenment brought about the two great revolutions of the modern epoch, the American and the French, and the invention of Federalist and Jacobin democracy, modern constitutionalism, and the United States of America and modern democratic republicanism on both sides of the ocean.

At the same time, while political and social ideas and arrangements are most completely expressed when they are intertwined, they can also exist independently as well as causatively. That is to say, in causative situations ideas influence arrangements or arrangements influence ideas or there is interaction between the two. That is normally the case. It may ultimately become the case even in situations where the two initially exist independently. There are such situations in which people animated by one idea find congenial political and social arrangements that actually are associated with another one without adopting the other idea.[2]

We can identity eight major criteria for political societies based on covenant or compact. They are:

1. Widespread awareness of the idea.
2. A general political-social outlook that embraces the idea.
3. An institutional framework and network based on covenantal connections.
4. Behavior directed or influenced by the foregoing.
5. Central events that offer testimony to covenanting.
6. An appropriately covenantal political culture.
7. A common terminology that gives expression to the idea of covenant and its perspective.
8. A covenantal myth.

These are both real necessities and indicators for the political society and for those who observe it.

A major part of the newness of the modern epoch were the theo-political changes that took place both in theory and practice with regard to politics and society as a whole and covenant ideas and their implementaton in particular. In theory there was a shift of covenantal premises from the Divine to the human, that is to say, the critical aspect of covenanting now was not God's participation or witness but the fact that covenanting according to the most modern theories could be entirely the product of human reflection, choice, and action. The early moderns concealed this change in their discussions, although later modern historians of modern political thought have revealed it or claimed to.

In practice, the relationship between religion and politics changed from confrontation within the regime to confrontation outside of it. In other words, the Treaty of Westphalia in 1648 put an end to struggles over religion and politics within the European polities of the time by redefining religion as private. While it took 300 years to work that out in practice, at different rates, in different polities, the beginning of the modern epoch essentially witnessed the establishment of two separate spheres for religion and politics and placed politics outside the concerns of the religious sphere, unlike what had been the case up until that time in the ancient and medieval worlds and that remains the case in most of the Islamic world to this day where separation of the two into spheres is considered blasphemy.

Why Do Some Peoples Have a Covenantal Politics? —An Interim Explanation

At the beginning of this book the question was posed as to why some peoples have a covenantal politics. Recognizing that all political life is in some respects a combination of organic development (including accident), force or coercion, and pact based on reflection and choice, combined in one way or another, why is it that some peoples' political ideas, culture and behavior are built around the last, which informs and animates every aspect of their political life. Here, near the end of our exploration, what kind of at least tentative conclusions can we draw?

First of all, covenants and covenantal politics do seem to be associated with frontiers. The first recorded covenants originated in western Asia, the world's first "West," and have been a prominent feature of every subsequent frontier. This is partly because frontiers are new and involve migration and the settlement of new territories (or the equivalent) where there are no established patterns or populations, so new ones must be established by conscious design. It is also because frontiers are dynamic and fluid situations where customary patterns have difficulty meeting the new challenges and thereby maintaining their hold. To the extent that migration is involved and people are detached from familiar places and situations, both the possibility and the necessity for covenanting increase.

The formidable environmental influences in developing covenantal behavior and ultimately culture provided by the settlement of new lands is reflected in the confrontation between humans and the wilderness. When we speak of that encounter, the model that normally comes to mind is that of the United States and its advancing frontier of settlement as described by Frederick Jackson Turner and his students.[3] But the U.S. model is but one of at least four identifiable models for that encounter. The others are the Canadian model, the Scandinavian model, and the Israeli model.

The familiar American model is one which can be summarized as linear irreversible conquest. It is manifest in the inexorable westward advance of the frontier of settlement. Granted, there are some exceptions to that pattern even in the continental United States, but that is the overall thrust of the model and the way it has been portrayed for future generations.

The Canadian model follows the U.S. model in that it involves the linear conquest of a strip of territory approximately 100 miles wide between the U.S. border and the northern wilderness. This area was conquered and settled, leaving something close to an unchanging borderlands between the settled and the wilderness. While there is no single frontier line and settlement does advance and contract within that frontier region (and there are oasis settlements beyond, even far beyond it), Canada's settled area has passed through its original frontier stages while a more or less permanent unsettled wilderness exists to the north of it and will for an indefinite time.

The third model, that of Scandinavia, is one of permanent clearings in the wilderness, with settlement not being linear so much as a matter of establishing and enlarging clearings with the wilderness remaining around and beyond them.

The final model is the Israeli model of oases in the desert, often expanding or contracting, that is, a vast desert area punctuated with oases of settlement where conditions are favorable, e.g. where there is water. Those settlements are built around permanent cores with peripheries that expand and contract depending upon external conditions, where water is available or human endeavor can make conditions favorable for settlement, by providing irrigation.

All four of these models are legitimate examples of the contest with the wilderness characteristic of frontiers as dynamic environments. All produce the kind of cooperative relationships that more often than not give birth to covenantal societies. Where settlement comes in a rush or is imperceptable, the incentives for those kinds of cooperative partnerships are not present and covenantal societies are less likely.

If covenantal politics is most likely to develop in frontier regions and to serve frontier societies, it is next most likely to occur in borderlands where there are encounters between different peoples. There, too, customary patterns are unsettled by the encounter, which may lead to war, but which also may lead to some attempt at accomodation based upon deliberate choice and synthesis by design. Thus the great covenantal reservoir of Europe follows the Romano-Germanic borderland from the Alps to the North Sea and then the Celtic-Norse borderland northward to the Arctic. In both cases there was a fruitful meeting of peoples and cultures that led to a productive interaction and synthesis embodied in covenantal forms.

All of this works where there are either spatial or temporal frontiers or borderlands. So, for example, it has worked well in British North America and it has worked at the borders or intersections between epochs such as that which occurred in the seventeenth century at the time the modern epoch was born. With regard to the first, the British settlers most successful in North America were those who either brought with them or developed covenantal modes of political organization or governance. In the latter case, the political philosophies most successful in guiding the new epoch were those of covenant, compact, and contract, as reflected in the works of Hobbes, Spinoza, Locke, and Harrington.

It is not difficult to see the impact of spatial frontiers and borderlands, but investigation seems to indicate that whenever there has been a temporal frontier or borderland, covenant ideas and practices also have reasserted themselves, which is one of the reasons why they are doing so today at the border between the modern and postmodern epochs.

Covenantal forms have an even greater chance of flourishing when they are supported by both spatial and temporal forces. The American frontier is one of the best examples of this geo-historical convergence. Founded on an open continent at the very beginning of the modern epoch and advancing westward as the modern epoch unfolded, the American frontier was the quintessential combination of spatial and temporal factors supporting covenantal forms.

In a different way, the Swiss benefitted from a similarly appropriate geo-historical combination. Alpine geography encouraged the development of small agrarian republics and commercially oriented city states, while the general location of Switzerland made it both necessary and possible for the liberty-loving Swiss to combine to maintain their independence. That combination began to be successful with the confederation of the eight cantons in 1351 at the very beginning of a new epoch in the history of Europe, one that brought with it a revival of liberty on a variety of fronts, from the Hanseatic cities in the Holy Roman Empire to the city-republics of the Italian Renaissance. In other words, both the geographic location and the timing were right.

These are all useful explanations, but in and of themselves are not sufficient. For example, when the foregoing experiences are transient ones, the covenants are also transient. In other words, covenantal politics, like any other, needs to be reinforced by repeated appropriate experiences, at least until it is rooted in the political culture of the people in question, after which it seems to continue of its own accord on a latent, if not a manifest, basis.

Here the temporal dimension becomes important once again. Covenantal ideas seem to be particularly important at the time of epochal beginnings. Once a civil society has stabilized within a particular geo-historical framework, then its people turn to other explanatory principles, usually organic ones, to account for what to them seems an uninterrupted developmental flow. Among peoples with a covenantal political culture, covenantal ideas may be submerged, remain latent until the next epochal transformation when they will reemerge as needed to help redefine and master the new situation.

A good example of this is to be found in the history of the modern epoch in the United States. Covenantal thinking was at its height during the seventeenth-century founding of settlements in British North America. It was transformed into a secular political concept for the eighteenth-century founding of the United States. By the mid-nineteenth century, a stabilized if dynamic American people began to be influenced by organic theories of politics, polity and society drawn from German philosophy and Darwinian science. At least the intellectual elite slowly abandoned a covenantal understanding of the American experience. With the coming of the postmodern epoch after World War II, however, the newly unsettled American society, confronting a new world of decolonization abroad and civil rights and social revolution at home. Many Americans sought answers in a revived sense of covenant or its derivatives.

With all of this, there still seem to be certain peoples that are more predisposed to covenantal thinking and behavior than others. The question remains: why do people on some frontiers and on some borderland areas internalize the covenantal norms, ideas, and behavior patterns, while others do not? The French, for example, have passed through frontier experiences, but have not become covenantal and their borderland with the Germans led to separation and perpetual war rather than integration on the basis of mutuality (at least until they were exhausted and then turned to federal solutions in the form of the European Community to drastically change the situation). The Russians had a great Siberian frontier before them which in relatively marginal ways offered opportunities for greater freedom for subjects of the tsar and of the Soviets, but which, to the best of our knowledge, did not generate a covenantal dimension. On the other hand, the Jews, the Swiss, the Dutch, the Scots, and the Americans have had their covenantal spirit repeatedly rekindled.

Nor can this be explained as a result of marginality, an explanation that may work in the case of the Jews, where marginality replaced the territorial dimension of both frontier and borderlands in the years when the Jews had only a diaspora and did not live in their own country. Marginality, indeed, may explain why certain minorities are covenantal, but it does not explain why national majorities are.

Nor do any of the foregoing explain the moral-cum-religious dimension of covenant. Hobbes has demonstrated that the perception of the importance of this dimension need not be grounded in the traditional foundations of awe of Heaven, but can be attained through a highly materialistic concern with the senses. Be that as it may, what is characteristic of covenant-qua-covenant is that moral-cum-religious dimension. That is what distinguishes covenants from compacts which have a moral but not a religious dimension and both from contracts which require location in a common morality for them to be maintained but do not themselves have an especially moral dimension.

In the last analysis, the idea of covenant is a moral rather than a theopolitical one, in the sense that it is less concerned with the fine points of theology than with the strong points of morality and seeks to advance a particular moral order in the real, that is, political, world. It is that moral component that makes covenant more than contract or compact and so recurringly compelling generation after generation in every epoch, especially at those critical moments when epochal changes are taking place.

Beyond that, it is the moral basis of covenant that flows over into modern constitutionalism and makes the recognizedly strong constitutions hallowed and therefore maintained the constitutions of modernity as more than simply procedural documents. Only when a constitution has been invested with the moral force that comes from its covenantal origins has it been able to long survive. That investiture may come directly, as in the case of the United States constitution of 1787, or it may rest upon some prior covenant, as in the case of many American state constitutions that partake of the covenantal dimensions of the Declaration of Independence and are strengthened by it even beyond the awareness of their citizens.

Sometimes it is the act of covenanting or constitution-making in the covenantal mode that hallows the result. That is the case in Connecticut and Vermont or, for that matter, in Switzerland: in the first, the convention of the four towns, leading to the founding of Connecticut as a polity; in the second, the Vermont Declaration of Independence in 1777; and in the third, the Rutli Pact in 1291, which established the Helvetic Confederation that ultimately became Switzerland. While all three benefited from the theopolitical tradition of covenant, it was covenant's compelling moral dimension which led those acts to have the impact that they did.

It has been emphasized throughout this book that to some extent all humans are involved in oaths and pacts as they are in other forms of social organization. Nor are contracts and compacts uninfluential in political life. But covenant has that extra dimension that moves human affairs from the merely pragmatic and prudential to the pursuit of a loftier vision, to the search for the city upon a hill. That alone would draw humans to the covenant idea again and again. For to be fully human is to aspire to a higher vision even as one seeks to protect oneself and one's community in a difficult world.

The Covenant Idea as Political Theology

Without diminishing or denigrating the importance of secularized covenants, in the last analysis, the covenant idea remains within the ambit of political theology. This is so whether we are speaking of the origins of the idea, the perspectives of its principal advocates over the centuries, or the teleological dimension implicit in the covenantal approach to political and social life. In that respect, even the secular expressions of the covenant idea have something of political theology about them, designed as they are to perfect human life on earth.

For the most part, the political theological roots of the covenant idea are quite traditional, having their source in the will of God. At times the Divinity takes on a less personal dimension and becomes some transcendent power or source of power, or in its other extreme, the covenant idea has been used to express the idea of a divinity inherent in humans. This empirical statement is not meant to suggest that all three expressions of the divine are equal or even equal in covenantal thought. There seems to be little question that the full power of covenant grows out of a political theology emphasizing the first perspective, that of covenant as having its ultimate source in the will of God.

Nor has this understanding diminished in our very secular times. Among the American states, for example, there is hardly a single state constitution that does not acknowledge the ultimate sovereignty of God in its preamble and explicitly acknowledge God as the source of the power of the people of the state to establish their own government.[4] Nor are the American states alone in this. Most of the world's constitutions give similar acknowledgement to the Divine source of authority.[5]

Lest this be thought to be merely a mindless convention, one need only look at constitutional revision efforts in the American states after World War II. In some cases there were those who advocated elimination of the reference to God. In every case, whether or not there was a discussion, the reference was deliberately retained, while in the world as a whole, the number of such references seems to be increasing.[6]

But before we are carried away by metaphysics, we must understand that, even when a covenant unequivocally invoked the will of God, it emphasized the need for human action and responsibility. Covenant, after all is said and done, is a matter of partnership; in its highest political-theological form the greatest of all partnerships, that between God and man. Partnership, after all is said and done, requires equality or at least a sufficient measure of equality in regard to the task for which the partnership is formed. Thus covenant is a radically liberating force, one that frees humans to act but not at the price of denying the transcendent authority and power that sets the parameters within which they act and the terms under which their actions are legitimate and morally acceptable. Thus the covenantal bond links humanity with the universe and the transcendent power that governs it. Under covenant humans are free yet bound, or bound yet free; part of nature, yet separated from it. That is the essence of federal liberty in its theological sense.

Covenant theologians of a properly democratic persuasion would argue that neither human sovereignty nor Divine sovereignty is enough. Unrestricted human sovereignty is too much for humans to manage, even when sovereignty is vested in the people as a whole, a vast improvement over vesting it in any individual or group. The same corruptions associated with the mixed character of the human race will sooner or later come to the surface. The callow assumption that *vox populi* equals *vox dei* has long since been disproved in the eyes of sober-minded people. *Vox populi* may be better than *vox rex*, but to coin a phrase, we have seen how "Fifty million Frenchmen can be wrong."

Unlimited Divine sovereignty is also deficient, certainly under conditions where God does not appear clearly to exercise His sovereign powers on a daily and continuing basis. The Bible tells us that even when God did appear frequently, almost daily, the only way that He could enforce His sovereign powers was through the administration of drastic punishments, so drastic that they ceased to be sanctions. If God's only options in dealing with willful humankind are the death penalty or maiming or some other drastic punishment, it can only be invoked in cases of the gravest trespass, as Moses successfully argued with the Lord on numerous occasions. Otherwise God would have to go around creating and killing whole peoples, which would hardly accomplish His purposes. In the biblical history of ancient Israel, Moses and Joshua more or less kept things in balance, but once there was no *eved adonai*, that is to say, a prime minister who had direct and regular communication with heaven on a regular basis, only judges who did not have such regular contact, there was the recurrent problem of every man doing what was right in his eyes, something that happened at least once a generation and which led to moral, social and perhaps even political anarchy.

The solution was to combine both sovereignties through an association of partnership established by covenant. This is the model followed by covenanted peoples. In its classic formulation God retains sovereignty but limits Himself through covenant. He continues to intervene until His interventions are deemed to be too dangerous. This happened in ancient Israel until the Talmudic sages declared them to have no validity, that a decision by a majority of the members of the Sanhedrin outweighed heavenly voices.

The Americans tried a different tack. As moderns living at the time of the Enlightenment, they did not seek Divine rule, only Divine guidance and grace. They proclaimed the people politically sovereign on this earth under the authority of Heaven. God became the great governor of the universe instead of its king. Due intention was paid to His governorship, but stewardship was entrusted to the people. Under either system, in the polity God came to reign but not rule.

The Covenant Tradition as Political Culture

If the covenant idea is political theology, the covenant tradition is political culture. The covenant tradition may or may not be a theological political one. As has been shown in this volume, at various points in history, particularly in the modern epoch, the covenant tradition has been secularized and has continued to be powerful in more secular form. Still, it must be noted that where the covenant tradition persists, secularization has its limits. What distinguishes peoples and polities shaped by the covenant tradition in the modern and postmodern epochs, as distinct from those that have not been shaped by such strong covenantal influences, is that in the former at least a residue of religious commitment remains a powerful force and magnet shaping political culture and behavior.

The United States of America is perhaps the best example of this, where religion remains overtly powerful, even in a country that is known for its stand as a polity on behalf of strong church-state separation, but it is equally true in other covenanted polities as well. At the very least, covenanted peoples and polities are living off of the religious capital of the past. Contrast this with the situation in a country like France which also underwent a modern democratic revolution but without a covenantal heritage. There a truly secular society has developed.

The covenant tradition is a powerful shaper of political culture in other ways as well, influencing as it does the basic sense of equality among people, their striving for liberty, and their desire to come together in a political organization of free, consenting and equal citizens. It is no wonder that the covenant tradition is at the root of the matrix model of political organization and rejects both the pyramid and center-periphery models, opting for freedom and choice in constitutional design, rather than force or accident.

What has been noted in this volume is the interaction between institutions and culture, the culture shaping institutions but also institutions shaping culture. With all the thought that has been given to that interaction and all the illustrations of it that have been provided over the centuries and subsequently studied, it is still hard to go beyond the rather banal recognition of the interaction to explain it and how it influences human life. Perhaps it is of some use simply to identify which institutions and what cultures have had what kinds of influence as these volumes have tried to do.

Culture itself is problematic enough these days now that the term is again in vogue. Almost everything is described as "culture," making no distinction between culture—that which is more permanent and less amenable to change or amenable only after extraordinary experiences and/or the long passage of time—and style—that which is widely accepted as fashionable at any given time but is transient. There is also a difference between culture and deep culture. Covenantalism is part of American culture, as I hope this volume has demonstrated, but it still remains to be seen whether it is as deeply a part as it is in the case of the Jews and the Swiss, as demonstrated in volumes 1 and 2 of this series. For both peoples, covenantal culture is so deeply ingrained and has been for so long that when styles demand other forms of organization and behavior or impose other institutions, their covenantal culture and behavior patterns survive and resurface in some way, even in ways that are apparently dysfunctional because of the contrast with the institutional framework, but the culture is what survives.

Both the Jews and the Swiss also stand outside many of the rhythms of Western civilization as a whole because of their deep covenantal culture. By being the world pioneers, they achieved many of the characteristics of covenantal cultures sooner than anyone else. At the same time, perhaps because of their covenantal cultures they have been able to adapt successfully at the price of not having been recognized for having pioneered what later was in style, each following somewhat different patterns.

Not only that, but obscuring the differences between deep culture, culture, and style may also obscure the differences between real covenantalism and pseudocovenantalism for an observer who is not careful. If covenant is in style, everyone becomes covenantal. (The obverse is also true.) But that rarely leads noncovenantal peoples beyond the frosting and indeed at times even the frosting is pseudocovenantalism. These volumes have tried to identify real covenantalism, in part by emphasizing its longlasting character and in part by emphasizing its particular manifestations.

Beyond that, because covenant is based upon consent and the ability to establish bonds through pacts based on reflection and choice, covenantal cultures offer their adherants hope. Indeed, it is in covenantal cultures that messianism, the most extreme form of hope, has developed. But even without messianism it is in covenantal cultures that hope springs eternal. Even the mistakes of people informed by covenantal cultures often are the mistakes that flow from having hope, from being too optimistic, thereby making a vice out of that virtue.

Political Cultures, Modes, and Ideas

In some primordial way, humanity seems to be divided into four "mother" political cultures, expressed through four "mother" political modes, and animated by four "mother" political ideas. The four political cultures are the traditional, the traditionalistic, the individualistic, and the moralistic. The four political modes are tribal, subject, statist, and civic. The four political ideas are organic, hierarchic, marketplace, and commonwealth. Every political society and body politic represents some combination of these twelve categories, one from each of the groups, each modifying the others in the combination.

Premodern political societies were, perhaps with a rare exception, traditional societies; that is to say, their primary characteristic was being bound to the traditions they believed that they had inherited from their ancestors within a belief system derived from a Divine source. Thus, for example, in traditional political culture, law is not originally the product of human agency but of Divine revelation or of a Divinely-inspired lawgiver. The most that humans, or later generations of them, can do is to interpret the law. Even parliaments, such as there were before the end of the eighteenth century, saw their tasks as interpretation and judgment rather than lawmaking.

In modern times, most traditional cultures were shattered and underwent transformation, some into traditionalistic ones that preserved conservative and hierarchical elements of the old tradition within the framework of modernity and others that preserved the norms of the old tradition within modern frameworks.

The *traditionalistic political culture* is rooted in an ambivalent attitude toward the marketplace coupled with a paternalistic and elitist conception of the commonwealth. It reflects an older, precommercial attitude that accepts a substantially hierarchical society as part of the ordered nature of things, authorizing and expecting those at the top of the social structure to take a special and dominant role in government. Like its moralistic counterpart, the traditionalistic political culture accepts government as an actor with a positive role in the community, but in a very limited sphere—mainly that of securing the continued maintenance of the existing social order. To do so, it functions to confine real political power to a relatively small and self-perpetuating group drawn from an established elite who often inherit their "right" to govern through family ties or social position. Accordingly, social and family ties are paramount in a traditionalistic political culture; in fact, their importance is greater than that of personal ties in the individualistic political culture, where, after all is said and done, a person's first responsibility is to him- or herself. At the same time, those who do not have a definite role to play in politics are not expected to be even minimally active as citizens. In many cases, they are not even expected to vote. In return, they are guaranteed that, outside of the limited sphere of politics, family rights (usually labeled "individual rights") are paramount, not to be taken lightly or ignored. As in the individualistic political culture, those active in politics are expected to benefit personally from their activity, though not necessarily through direct pecuniary gain.

Where the transformation was most radical, the political cultures became individualistic. The *individualistic political culture* emphasizes the conception of the democratic order as a marketplace. It is rooted in the view that government is instituted for strictly utilitarian reasons, to handle those functions demanded by the people it serves. According to this view, government need not have any direct concern with questions of the "good society" (except insofar as the government may be used to advance some common conception of the good society formulated outside the political arena, just as it serves other functions). Emphasizing the centrality of private concerns, the individualistic political culture places a premium on limiting community intervention—whether governmental or nongovernmental—into private activities, to the minimum degree necessary to keep the marketplace in proper working order. In general, government action is to be restricted to those areas, primarily in the economic realm, that encourage private initiative and widespread access to the marketplace.

Where norms and ideas rather than modes were preserved, often moralistic political cultures emerged. The *moralistic political culture* emphasizes the commonwealth conception as the basis for democratic government. Politics, to this political culture, is considered one of the great human activities: the search for the good society. True, it is a struggle for power, but it is also an effort to exercise power for the betterment of the commonwealth. Accordingly, in the moralistic political culture, both the general public and the politicians conceive of politics as a public activity centered on some notion of the public good and properly devoted to the advancement of the public interest. Good government, then, is measured by the degree to which it promotes the public good and in terms of the honesty, selflessness, and commitment to the public welfare of those who govern.

Traditional political cultures initially and predominantly were tribal, and were shaped by organic political ideas. Traditionalistic cultures, on the other hand, tend to be hierarchical in their mode and subject in their structure; that is to say, the polity becomes the private preserve of its rulers and most of the population is left out of citizenship altogether. If they undergo republicanization, they often become statist.

Individualistic political cultures are normally in the market mode, hence they emphasize contract as the basis of political linkage. If they become statist, they tend to rely upon organic definitions of the polity to justify reifying the state. Where they are not statist or organic in conception, individualism becomes driven by a conception of the marketplace as the basis for political behavior in all spheres of life at least to some degree; that is to say, as long as the accepted rules of the game are universally shared, members of the body politic may behave as they please, pursuing happiness as each perceives it.

In the moralistic political culture, on the other hand, the goal of the body politic is to establish a commonwealth based on civic political ideas. All of its members are equal citizens, or potentially that. The polity pursues some shared conception of the good life and it is the responsibility of government to play a leading role by dominating a statist polity but by supporting and to a certain extent guiding body politic toward the implementation of the norms of the commonwealth. Such a political society is civic in character in that all are not only citizens or potentially citizens but are expected to play an appropriate role in the public life of the commonwealth and to do good and abjure evil.

It hardly needs to be said that the ideal covenanted commonwealth is moralistic and civic, although in fact there also have been traditional covenanted commonwealths organized along tribal lines as in the case of the classic biblical commonwealth. There have been subtle mixtures of kinship and consent; that is to say, organic and civic or covenantal elements in which a tribal basis continues to exist within a set of covenantal ideas and a covenantal political culture.

In modern times the moralistic synthesis usually has not been with organic or tribal modes but with the individualistic and marketplace political culture and mode. This, indeed, has introduced salutary modifications into the puritan rigidities that always are inherent in a moralistic political culture, but it has not been able to provide the same kind of continuity as the organic or tribal bases because of the orientation of the market toward promoting change, which means discontinuity. Many of the problems of American society have to do with the discontinuities brought about by that synthesis in the United States whose political culture is a combination of marketplace and commonwealth.

It is historically true that polities that have attempted to be strictly moralistic have become oppressively so. They do not have that leaven of freedom and humor needed for humans to survive in the world as it is. That freedom and humor can be supplied by the market or at least allowed to emerge through market processes that are inevitably more individualistic than not, but if allowed to be carried to their logical conclusion, they become deadly in their way. Modern Israel, on the other hand, may find that many of its problems are rooted in its particular combination of commonwealth and tribal or organic society, whereby the organic leads some Jews to extreme rejection of other.

On those rare occasions when statist political ideas are coupled with moralistic political culture to foster hierarchical organization with moralistic norms, polities can actually slide over into totalitarianism. Both Nazi Germany and Soviet Russia reflected this particular distortion, one through the most particularistic principles of a "master race" and the other through the most universalistic ones of "scientific socialism." Both were humanly disastrous.

It is difficult if not impossible to pinpoint the connection between political culture and the covenant tradition, but the fact of connection seems to be more strongly borne out, at least by the circumstancial evidence. Societies and peoples shaped by covenant also seem to be those rooted in the moralistic political culture who fancy themselves as pursuing commonwealth ends of government in a civic manner. They are antihierarchical and totally reject subject status for themselves (although occasionally they are prepared for others to be subjects for cultural or ideological reasons, as in the case of the Afrikaners vis-a-vis nonwhite peoples of South Africa until recently). They are equally antistatist for reasons clearly associated with the covenantal outlook, about how polities are formed, and how individual souls constitute them and fit within them.

This convergence became particularly telling in modern times when the idea of covenant in its manifest form receded and was replaced by constitutionalism, in many respects a practical secular variant of the covenant idea. If this correct, then it is no accident that constitutionalism in its fullest form developed in covenanted commonwealths with strongly moralistic civic cultures, just as it seems to be no accident that the most statist modern polities were also those with the most hierarchical political cultures (in some cases these were modified by very individualistic cultures outside the political realm, as in France). By the same token, the market mode of political and social organization promotes the individualistic political culture but is at its best when that mode is connected to an individualistic political culture from the first.

Covenantal Manifestations of Political Behavior

Political behavior is shaped by the intersection of political thought and political culture. The political behavior of covenanted peoples and individuals in covenanted societies is thus shaped by both the covenant idea and the covenantal tradition. Put too simply, the covenant idea shapes their conception of justice, while the covenant tradition shapes their management of power. Covenanted government meets on four major elements of political thought and action:

1. Constitutionalism—the idea of limited government and limitations on the governors;
2. Republicanism—the idea that human rulers are temporary custodians of power responsible to the ruled;
3. Federalism—the idea that different political entities can be united into a common whole without losing their own integrity, by covenant;
4. Balancing of Powers—the idea that government is best controlled when no person, group of people, or institution has a monopoly of political power.

Where both the covenant idea and covenantal tradition are present, the behavioral result is a covenanted people. In some cases, one dimension is present without the other, which leads to various deviations from the norm. Thus there are peoples that have adopted covenant ideas without being able to develop a covenantal tradition to translate those ideas into behavior. There are peoples in which a covenantal tradition or some degree of a covenantal tradition persists but who are no longer moved by covenant ideas.

To some extent every modern democratic polity operating under a constitution adopted by the people or their representatives pays tribute to the covenant idea without necessarily having a covenant tradition to give that constitution meaning in a covenantal sense. Conversely, in Britain, many of the descendents of the very same segments of the population that were at the forefront of sixteenth- and seventeenth-century covenantalism became the primary exponents of liberal reform and Fabian socialism in the nineteenth and twentieth centuries, through pacts and charters developed with the framework of British politics, willy-nilly replacing covenantal ideas of justice with collectivist ones, to be implemented, in the eyes of some, through centralized and hierarchical structures rather than federal ones.

It is not unfair to conclude that in the modern epoch federalism became a permanent operational embodiment of the covenant idea. Federalism only worked fully where it was grounded in covenantal thinking. To "think federal" is to introduce the principles of partnership and morally grounded obligation into political life. While there are political systems that call themselves federal but ignore these aspects of federalism, they are universally recognized as deficient in their federalism. Often they are federal in name only, even if many of them pay lip service to those principles of federaism that have been identified as covenantal.

One way to clarify the various possibilities in the combination of idea, tradition, and behavior is by viewing the constitution of a polity in Aristotelian terms that both distinguish and combine three dimensions - the frame of government, the socioeconomic distribution of power, and the moral basis of the regime. The covenant idea provides the moral basis of the regime, the covenant tradition that flows from it shapes the socioeconomic distribution of power, and together they determine the frame of government in a completely covenanted polity. On the other hand, in certain modern polities, the covenant idea is present in the frame of government but is lacking in the moral basis of the regime. Hence the socioeconomic distribution of power is shaped by some other set of ideas or tradition. In others, the socioeconomic distribution of power is derived from a covenantal tradition but the moral basis of the regime is grounded in some other set of ideas. The frame of government is consequently torn between two contradictory influences. In still others, it is the form of government that is not covenantal, generating a different set of dysfunctional ties.

The Covenantal Bond

To be truly bound by covenant means having a sense of common vocation, acceptance of individual responsibility in the pursuit of that vocation, and commitment to a struggle with the evils of the world through a moral equivalent of war.

The character and content of the covenantal bond can be summarized in four main points: (1) that God's sovereignty and justice are at the foundations of the moral order; (2) humans are bound by that moral order, yet free to act within it; (3) as such, humans enjoy federal liberty, that is to say, liberty defined by covenant which combines freedom and responsibility; (4) that the highest concrete expressions of federal liberty are to be found in constitutionalism and the rule of law, whereby people design and order their own lives through covenant and constitution within the framework of God's sovereignty and justice. Certain peoples do so more completely and comprehensively than others. They see themselves or can be seen as the world's covenanted peoples who more often than not are at the cutting edge of human striving for self-improvement—for the reformation of the world.

Covenanted peoples are comfortable with their existence only when they are pursuing the vocation which they adopted as one of the terms of the covenants through which they came into being. For the United States, for example, the political dimension of this vocation is anchored on what Abraham Lincoln termed the "regular marriage" of the states of a great continental republican union. For Israel it depends upon the marriage of a people and its land. For Switzerland it depends on the marriage of communities. For the Scots and the Dutch, it depended on the marriage of a people and its "kirk" or "kierk" (church in the sense of both doctrine and polity).

What flows from the combination of these four principles in political life is a constitutional order based upon federal liberty, the rule of law, power sharing, and partnership. Politically, the covenant idea and the covenantal tradition promise an appropriate combination of self-rule and shared rule, both between humans and God and between humans. In this respect, the placing of ultimate sovereignty in the hands of God prevents it from being placed in a reified state. God, the ultimate sovereign, becomes the source of political sovereignty in the world which, over time, covenanted peoples have found it appropriate to vest in themselves, that is to say, in the people, so that all governments merely have delegated powers.

This combination of self-rule and shared rule is to be found in every arena of political organization from the largest to the smallest. The essence of political science in the broadest sense is to make the combination possible, including within it both the pursuit of justice and the organization of power. Man is both political and egoistic by nature. In that respect both Plato and Hobbes are right in their starting points regarding the nature of individuals, societies, and states. Maimonides points out this paradox. It is the way of humans that every individual seeks to be part of a political society, to enjoy the protection and benefits thereof, and to cooperate with others in partnership, pooling talents for a common good and mutual benefit. At the same time, it is equally part of the way of humans to be egoistic, to seek to maximize their power as individuals, to pursue selfish ends, to avoid external restraints. This is something of a paradox, but is simply one of many of the fundamental paradoxes that underlie human existence. It becomes the task of politics to reconcile the manifestations of that paradox operationally, since the paradox itself is built in and cannot be changed.

What constitutes federal liberty, whether in an absolute sense, or in a contingent one for particular communities, peoples and polities, remains a cardinal question of political science as well as political theology. We may or may not ever find the final answer, but even contingent ones have helped covenanted peoples walk the narrow line between hierarchy and oppression on one side and anarchy and license on the other, and to reach an appropriate synthesis between freedom and responsibility.

Openness and Exclusivity

There are three kinds of human community: *organic community* that grows out of the common life of family, tribe, and village and is bound by kinship; *civil community*, a limited association that grows out of the necessity of people who choose to do so to live together and is bound by *compact* defining their common purposes, the terms of their association, and the rules by which they live; and *holy community (kahal kadosh)*, an unlimited conjuration that grows out of the aspirations of likeminded people to achieve the worthy life together and is bound by *covenant* or the promise of mutuality necessary to achieve that end.

One of the major problems with covenanted peoples pursuing a combination of self-rule and shared rule in a constitutional manner under a rule of law based upon the principals of federal liberty is the problem of how to balance openness and exclusivity. There are aspects of covenantal political theology and political culture that carry them in both directions. On one hand, to be covenanted is in a sense to be exclusive. Only *b'nai brit*, the children of the covenant, are members of the covenanted community, since only they have accepted the federal bonds as defined by that community. Only they are called to live under the constitution and laws of the community and, by assuming their responsibilities, are entitled to the liberties and benefits which that entails. In many covenanted communities, the exclusivity thereby established sharpens the parochial tendencies present in all humans and even misanthropic ones to the extent that the members see themselves as specially chosen and therefore set apart from all others.

On the other hand, communities established by covenant are often more open to new members because the criterion for membership are no more than accepting the terms of the covenant. In this respect they are open communities, not closed off by such factors as race, caste, tribe, or family. As such, the covenantal community transcends the parochialism that often accompanies organic societies where kinship is of the essence for belonging.

In the political realm, the Afrikaners and their covenant were perhaps the worst post-World War II example of the former situation, while the Americans and their covenant are perhaps the best example of the latter. The combination is such that it leads to constant tension within the covenanted community between exclusiveness and universalism, between a desire to preserve the community by keeping it pure and to extend its influence by bringing in new parties to the covenant. It also leads to tensions between the covenanted community and those outside it who see the former as exclusivist (a charge frequently levelled at the Jews) or aggressively imperialist (a complaint frequently made against the Mormons) or both.

Among religions, the Mormons are an excellent example of a community that maintains an exclusivist way of life but is aggressive in pursuit of new members, seeking at the same time to build a separate brotherhood, but one that will ultimately encompass all mankind. One can think of no equivalent political example in our times, though it can be argued that certain imperial powers in the past may have had those characteristics, the difference being that as they sought to extend their reach, they did so by adding what the Romans referred to as *foederatii*, the Latin equivalent of the Hebrew *ba'alei brit* (masters of covenant) and only much later tried to transform them into *b'nai brit*. That, indeed, seems to be the province of religion. The most that the Romans could do was to add local gods to the Roman pantheon, usually by finding their Roman equivalents.

The British Empire, which may be another example of an ecumenical polity that at times considered a federal approach, ultimately developed something of a three-circle arrangement. To use the Biblical terminology, Christian settlement and settlers could be *b'nai brit*, within the first circle. The connection between Britain and the Islamic world served as a means of becoming *ba'alei brit*, the second circle. Beyond that, monotheistic Britain with its strong Puritan and Scottish covenantal emphases was prepared to extend its rule over non-Christian and indeed nonmonotheistic countries and peoples and to allow them to pursue their own customs and ceremonies as long as they were not utterly repugnant to Christian morality (for example, the Hindus had to abandon sutee, the burning of the widow along with the deceased husband's body). When the issue arose as to whether the Empire would be transformed into an imperial federation, the first and only successful steps in that direction were taken in connection with the Christian dominions, those new lands settled by British pioneers and predominantly British in character, which thereby shared the British Christian tradition.

One of the failures of British imperialism was its inability to overcome social distinctions based upon race and class, so that even those "natives" who became Christian ultimately were unable to gain acceptance in the British world. Many of them became the leaders of the anticolonialist struggle as a result. A less intensive alliance was pursued for a while with the Muslim world, but the antiimperialist, anticolonialist movements of the twentieth century along with Britain's own reservations about true imperial federation brought down the whole experiment, so that even the British dominions became independent, establishing their own covenants, as it were.

In sum, all forms of society have open and closed dimensions, but covenant offers a mechanism for combining openness and closure. The mechanism involves the use of covenants to establish open, closed, and mixed partnerships whereby the parties to the covenant can establish the degree to which they wish to become covenanted communities (*b'nai brit*) or confine themselves to alliances (*ba'alei brit*). Closed partnerships can only be the former. In mixed partnerships there is usually a covenanted community with exclusivist categories of membership, plus a secondary group recognized as being in alliance with the covenanted community because of a shared moral commitment but not admitted to full partnership.

It seems that a strong measure of isolation, either environmental or self-constructed, is necessary for covenantal peoples and polities to develop, especially at the beginning. Once again, the Bible's presentation of God's admonitions to the Israelites requiring them to reject the ways of the Egyptians from amongst whom they came and the Canaanites, occupants of the land that they were to inherit, was a very strong one. It has already been suggested that to be covenantal was to break with the simply natural, good as well as bad, and to set a standard normally too high for most human beings to even want to pursue, much less attain.

It has also been demonstrated that there have been moments in human history when the possibilities exist for covenantal movements to emerge and capture whole populations, in the process transforming them, even if ultimately failing to achieve the covenantal vision put forward. A big part of that transformation is isolation, at least during the formative period. Thus the stress on isolation in the Bible and the laying by the prophets of the failure to achieve the covenantal vision on the Israelites' perversions or neglect of that isolation. So, too, were the Swiss, the Icelanders, and the New Englanders isolated in their formative periods, with about the same positive consequences.

What we learn from all four cases is that when the isolation broke down, so did the overall faithfulness to the covenantal vision, though in each case the breakdown came first from within, that is to say, their own people aspired to seek connections with their foreign neighbors more than the other way around. Granted, in no case was isolation ever total but it was sufficient isolation to allow what was in effect designed way of life to be fostered and flourish as against simply following natural human inclinations.

One of the reasons that covenantal societies are so closely connected with frontiers is that the frontier offers that kind of isolation, at least at the beginning. Covenantal societies also tend to use ruralism as a means of maintaining isolation. Cities and the urban life tend toward the cosmopolitan, toward seeking outside connections, while the rural life tends to be inward-turning. The rural life then both encourages isolation and leads to its own self-destruction as people, no longer able to bear the isolation of rural life, seek connections beyond the rural, usually in cities.

The Dutch may be the one covenantal people to stand almost entirely outside of this model, the exception that proves the rule. Their isolation came very early when they first settled the peripheries of the lowlands and reclaimed the peripheries of those peripheries from the sea. By the time their covenantalism was ready to flower, they were already urbanized and in contact with the world around them. Therefore, the fathers of Dutch covenantalism had to build artificial means for self-isolation through Reformed Protestant religion and its institutions. That they did so at all is impressive and contains within it lessons for others. That they did so even more incompletely than other covenantal peoples is not surprising given the situation with which they had to deal.

Covenant and Constitutionalism

Covenantal systems are legally grounded in oaths, pacts, and/or constitutions. Each of the three can be a sufficient grounding in and of itself, or they can be used in combination. As we have seen, covenants invariably conclude with an oath and may be embodied in a constitution. On the other hand, the oath may be a sufficient grounding for the relationship, the covenant may take the form of a mutual compact, and the constitution may be in the form of a charter. The distinction is not between written and unwritten constitutions but between constitutions-as-law and constitutions-as-convention or custom. The U.S. constitution is an example of the former; the British (English) constitution of the latter.

The political institutions of covenantal societies are all built upon the premises of constitutional legitimacy which flow from the basic covenantal consensus that forms the polity. The formal aspects (the frame of government) of the polity's overall constitutional structure give the polity legitimacy while the sociological and ethical contents give it form.

Every polity develops, over time, a constitution that encompasses an outline of its formal political structure and the fundamental allocation of authority power, responsibility, and influence within it. Generally speaking, this constitution consists of a frame of government, modifying non-statutory documents, and modifying customs and traditions for the whole and each constituent government (and quasi-government). Identification of this constitution is fundamental to, and a key to the understanding of the process of government in any polity. Furthermore, certain issues—particularly those relating to governmental structure and the scope of formal jurisdiction, and the alteration of the internal equilibrium of the policy—are constitutional issues and, as such, arouse a greater degree of conflict among the politically empowered in the civil society.[7]

Constitutional choice is the greatest political power and constitutional design the noblest political act. We have already noted that a constitution normally is the extension of a covenant, its practical translation into a political order embracing a rule of law and rules of the game. While constitutions normally follow covenants, those covenants may be included within them, either anew or as restated. The classic Biblical model is the book of Deuteronomy that restates the ancient constitution of Israel in systematic form, as adapted for a settled and landed rather than a nomadic population.[8] It begins with restatement of the covenant and ends with a public recovenanting.

The Massachusetts Constitution of 1780 does much the same, beginning with the covenant establishing Massachusetts as a civil society and then ordering the rules of that civil society. On the other hand, for the United States as a whole, the Declaration of Independence stands separately as the American founding covenant, while the Articles of Confederation and the federal Constitution of 1787 build upon the Declaration rather than repeating it. Figure 10.1 suggests the variety of constitutional parts in theory and practice.

All constitutions are a tribute to covenantalism in that they are an attempt to give every nation or people an opportunity to design their own political order through covenant, but a constitution does not a covenanted people make, which is why so many constitutions remain dead letters or at most, ornaments. Yet it may be that, given enough time, even noncovenanted peoples who live under constitutional regimes with constitutions of their own design will acquire a covenantal dimension and at

FIGURE 10.1
Examples of Constitutional Pacts

	Formal Pact	Oath	Tacit Agreement
Individuals	Hobbesian Covenant Rousseau's Social Contract Massachusetts Constitution	Icelandic Cheyenne Soldier Societies	Burke's Intergenerational compact
Institutions/ Polities	U.S. Declaration of Independence Maastricht Treaty	Swiss Coniuratio of 1291	Canadian constitution under BNAA
Tribes/ Primordial Groups	Sinai Covenant	Bedouin confederations Hungarian Pact	Indian Tribal Confederations

least add a covenantal overlay to their historical experience with organic or hierarchical models.

So it may be with France. A state founded by conquest, its founders and their heirs used every power available in a hierarchical system to force those living within their territory to acknowledge that they were French no matter what their actual national or ethnic background. In the course of 600 years, they more or less succeeded in doing so, to the point where Frenchmen knew intellectually that France was the product of conquest, but thought of themselves as an organic people. In the eighteenth century, through a revolution influenced by the American revolution of a few years earlier, the French sought to refound their polity on covenantal principles. The immediate result of the revolution was terror. Its proximate result was even more hierarchy instituted by Napoleon in the name of popular government and retained by all French successor regimes, even those that most opposed the Bonapartist legacy. Hence through constitution after constitution, or more accurately revolution and constitution after revolution and constitution, France was unable to reforge a national consensus; no matter who ruled, from a quarter to a half of the people rejected the legitimacy of the regime.

One hundred years after the revolution, the founding of the Third Republic moved France a step closer to constitutional democracy, but that founding required the exacerbation of other tensions which brought the Third Republic down after two generations. It was not until the 1950s when Charles de Gaulle was able to build a wall-to-wall consensus around the founding of the Fifth Republic that constitutionalism finally seems to have succeeded in adding another quasi-covenantal dimension to French society without in any respect making the French a covenanted people or replacing France's penchant for centralized hierarchies with a federal matrix of equals. Apparently the age of modern constitutionalism has been as yet too short to provide an answer to that question, but there are signs of a direction. For example, in the wake of the constitution of the Fifth Republic, France began a modest decentralization through regional economic development and a modest dismantling of the hierarchical administrative system to vest greater powers in elected local authorities. While the movement in these directions has been slow, it is nonetheless movement.

Once we have accounted for the cultural predisposition of certain groups for covenantal systems of order and the circumstantial pressures that lead groups toward covenantal arrangements, we are left with the fact of periodic ideological-cum-practical explosions of covenantal phenomena such as in biblical Israel in the thirteenth through eleventh centuries before the Common Era or the more recent and better documented case of the Protestant Reformation in the sixteenth century and its spinoffs in the seventeenth and eighteenth. Any one of these phenomenon or two in combination would have their impact. For example, the descendants of the Celts in Brittany hve retained certain oath-oriented forms of social expression, even though they were not located in the Latin-Germanic borderlands and were influenced ideologically and practically by being part of hierarchical, centralized France.

Belgium had its origins in Belgic oath societies. Their cultural legacy, in turn, was reinforced by its position on the borderlands between Catholic and Protestant Europe. Hence Belgians have tended toward preserving local liberties through pacts, even as they remain Catholic and monarchic.

The fullest expression of the covenantal way is to be found where all three factors coalesce. Thus, the Swiss, with Helvetic (Celtic) and

Alemannic origins, went through two experiences in succession: one preserving local liberties in the mountains against imperial designs, and the second location in the Rennish borderlands between Roman and Germanic Europe—were particularly susceptible to and, more important, generative of the covenantal ideology of the Reformation and its practical application in government and politics, so that their cantons became the incubators of a full-fledged covenantal system. So, too, the Celtic Scots with their own borderlands between Roman England and tribal Scotland were early recruits to the covenantal religion of the Reformation, which they applied creatively to their own political situation.

In a variant on the theme, the Norse who sailed to Iceland came from an oath-pact civilization and in Iceland encountered a new frontier, reinforcing the necessity for a society based on oaths and pacts, but did not pass through a theo-political experience of Reformed Protestantism, so never acquired a covenantal ideology to give form and meaning to their covenantal ways. In the seventeenth century, Protestant Europeans were to encounter a great frontier at a time when covenantal theology and its politics were reaching their fullest development in Europe. This new frontier was able to take the resulting ideology and refine it out of necessity through practice into modern constitutionalism.

Notes

1. Robert Merton, *Social Theory and Social Structure* (New York: Free Press, 1968); and *Sociology of Science* (Chicago: University of Chicago Press, 1973).
2. Obviously if one goes back far enough or deep enough one can find some idea attached even to those arrangements, but for our purposes it is enough to make the point that the utter lack of awareness even on the part of the intellectuals of a particular polity or society that there is an idea behind the arrangements animating their polity or society goes unrecognized.
3. Frederick Jackson Turner, *The Frontier in American History* (New York: Henry Holt and Co., 1953).
4. James Macgregor Burns and Jack W. Peltason, *Government By the People* (Englewood Cliffs, NJ: Prentice-Hall, 1986).
5. A.P. Blaustein and G.H. Flanz, eds., *Constitutions of the Countries of the World* (Dobbs Ferry, NY: Oceana Publications, 1971).
6. See John Markoff and Daniel Regan, "Religion, the State and Political Legitimacy in the World's Constitutions," in Thomas Robbins and Roland Robertson, eds., *Church-State Relations: Tensions and Transitions* (New Brunswick, NJ: Transaction Books, 1987).
7. For discussion of the role of the idea and practice of civil society and the overthrow of twentieth century totalitarian states and the introduction of democracy into other countries, see the *Kettering Review* (Winter 1990). This entire issue is

devoted to exploring these phenomena. For the origins of the idea of civil society, see Wade Davies, "A Glance at the Roots of Civil Society," *Kettering Review* (Winter 1990):57–63. Davies traces the roots of the term back to Aristotle's use of *koinonia politike*. *Koinonia* is also the closest equivalent to the Greek term for a political society erected on the basis of a political pact or compact, in other words, a federal society, thus indicating that the close connection between the idea of political compact and civil society extends back to the very beginning of systematic political thought, whether in the Bible or among the Greeks. For an exposition of the role of voluntary associations or public non-governmental institutions in the United States, see the *Kettering Review* (Fall 1984), which, *inter alia*, reprints the classics of De Tocqueville, Adlai Stevenson, and Theodore Roosevelt on the subject.
8. Daniel J. Elazar, "Deuteronomy as Israel's Constitution," *Jewish Political Studies Review,* vol. 4, no. 1 (Spring 1992).

Index

Commentary, 186

Common Era, 269

Commonwealth(s), 22, 24, 40, 70, 79, 94, 96, 111, 138, 153, 160, 179–180, 238, 255, 257–258; American, 109, 160; biblical, 258; (British), 225–226; covenantal, covenanted, 6, 25, 94, 147, 257, 259; Puritan, 6, 9, 26, 140, 149, 178

Communist, Communism, 162, 172

Communitarian(s), communitarianism, 27, 48, 137, 156; republican, 169

Community, communities, 194; civil, 42, 162, 263; cooperative, 177; covenantal, covenanted, 53, 148–149, 156–157, 161, 163, 194, 200, 263, 265; holy, 263; organic, 262; political, 102, 111

Compact(s), 5, 7–8, 18, 20, 30–31, 37–39, 47, 50–51, 55, 61–63, 65, 69, 75, 84, 86, 88, 90, 92, 96, 107, 111, 113–114, 123–142, 159, 169, 194–195, 204–206, 208–209, 212, 221, 225, 233, 247, 249–250, 263, 266; constitutional, 20; covenantal, 103; Family (Canada), 207–208; Hobbesian, 49–50; Lockean, 50; Mayflower 19, 24, 39, 47; political, 2, 6, 12, 88, 90, 93, 96, 114, 124, 126, 128, 134, 158, 194, 198, 206, 227, 234; political social, 160; social, 19, 75, 168, 194

Compact theory, Calhoun, 129; southern, 124

Compacting (political), 112–113

Compactual (base), 7, 19, 30, 48, 78, 107, 112–113, 169, 208

Condolence ceremony (Iroquois), 13

Confederacy, confederation, 27, 81, 83, 89–90, 93, 198, 205, 208210, 248; Articles of, 76, 82–84, 87, 89, 91, 93; Helvetic, 250; intercolonial, 76; New England, 28; of the United States, 89; (southern), 124, 129; Swiss, 82

Confederacies of communities, 28–29, 42

Confederacies, tribal, 12–13; Creek, 13; Illinois, 13; Iroquois, 13

Confederal, confederated, 77, 114, 179, 203–204, 209, 223

Congregational, Congregationalism, 77, 132

Congregationalist(s) (church), 52, 68, 77, 207

Congress (American), (of the) United States, 48, 54–55, 65–66, 68, 87–90, 93, 107–111, 123, 134; Act of, 179; continental, 67; General, 53, 65

Congressional, 86, 180; elections, 171

Congressional Government, 134

Connecticut, 24, 26, 28, 52, 76, 91, 108, 250

Connecticut Yankee in Ring Arthur's Court, A, 157–158

Consensual, 228

Consent, and democracy, 62

Conservatism, 119, 218

Conservative party (Canada), 109, 211

Consociationalism 226

Constituencies, federal, 211

Constitution (American), 26, 80, 86–87, 95, 124, 127–128, 136; United States, 17, 51, 76–77, 91, 94–95, 103, 105, 123, 137, 169, 180–181, 250, 266

Constitution, British (English), 266; Canadian, 209, 211; Massachusetts, 8, 39, 75, 267; of the Five Nations, 13; South African, 225

Constitution- charter , 3

Constitution(s), 2–3, 8, 10–12, 22, 25–26, 32–33, 37, 39–40, 47, 50–51, 60, 63, 70, 75–96, 107–108, 110–113, 117, 123, 131, 209, 212, 219, 250, 260, 266–268; democratic, 227; federal, 87, 92–94, 103, 105, 135, 180, 195, 209, 267; political, 30; state, 92–95, 105, 113

Constitution-makers, making (American), 102, 105, 112, 250

Constitution, traditional, 3

Constitution, written, 3

Constitutionalism, 7, 10, 19, 38–43, 50, 79, 82–83, 87, 90–92, 95, 105, 107–108, 110, 112–113, 117, 136, 169, 173, 179–180, 182, 208–212, 220, 226–227, 229, 234–235, 253, 261, 266–267

Constitutional Convention, 77–78, 83

Constitutional tradition, American, 18, 38